VOCABULARY POWER 3

PRACTICING ESSENTIAL WORDS

Kate Dingle

PEARSON
Longman

Vocabulary Power 3: Practicing Essential Words

Pearson Education, 10 Bank Street, White Plains, NY 10606

Staff credits: The people who made up the *Vocabulary Power 3* team,
representing editorial, production, design, and manufacturing, are Rhea
Banker, Christine Edmonds, Stacey Hunter, Laura Le Dréan, Francoise
Leffler, Christopher Leonowicz, Amy McCormick, Linda Moser, Edith Pullman,
and Barbara Sabella.
Cover and text design: Barbara Sabella
Cover photos: (wave) © P. Wilson/zefa/Corbis; (car) © Schlegelmilch/Corbis;
(windmills) © Firefly Productions/Corbis; (bulb) © Chris Rogers/Corbis;
(train) © Tim Bird/Corbis; (volcano) © Jim Sugar/Corbis;
(type) © Don Bishop/Getty Images; (shuttle) © Stock Trek/Getty Images
Text composition: Laserwords, Inc.
Text font: 11/12.5 New Aster Medium

Library of Congress Cataloging-in-Publication Data
Dingle, Kate.
    Vocabulary power 3 practicing essential words / Kate Dingle.
       p. cm.
    ISBN 978-0-13-243178-1 (student bk. : alk. paper)—ISBN 978-0-13-243179-8
(answer key : alk. paper)
    1. Vocabulary. 2. Vocabulary—Problems, exercises, etc.
I. Title. II. Title: Vocabulary power three.
PE1449.D557 2007
428.1—dc22   2007006164

LONGMAN ON THE **WEB**

Longman.com offers online resources for
teachers and students. Access our Companion
Websites, our online catalog, and our local
offices around the world.

Visit us at **longman.com.**

Printed in the United States of America
1 2 3 4 5 6 7 8 9 10 —VHG —11 10 09 08 07

CONTENTS

Giving your students an excellent vocabulary doesn't have to be difficult. *Vocabulary Power* simplifies the process to make vocabulary acquisition effective and interesting.

THE LATEST RESEARCH

The Most Important Words

Research shows that it is possible but not probable for the human mind to learn 1,000 new words a year (Nation 2001). In light of this, it is no surprise that English language learners are often frustrated by their limited vocabulary. Even if they manage to learn 1,000 words a year, the words they acquire may not be those that they need for academic and professional success. *Vocabulary Power* solves this problem by teaching the words that are most worthy of their time and attention.

Of the 100,000+ words in the English language, only the 2,000 most frequent words (compiled in the General Service List) are necessary for students to understand at least 80% of daily conversation and writing (Nation 2002). If students know the 2,000 most frequent words in English, in conjunction with 570 high frequency academic words found on the Academic Word List (AWL), they may understand close to 90% of academic text (Nation 2001, Coxhead 2000). The combined knowledge of the General Service List (GSL) and the Academic Word List (AWL) will strengthen your students' ability to understand a textbook, follow an academic lecture, or read a newspaper with ease.

- **Vocabulary Power 1** teaches Low Intermediate students words from the GSL.
- **Vocabulary Power 2** teaches Intermediate students more challenging words from the GSL and words from the AWL.
- **Vocabulary Power 3** teaches Advanced students more challenging words from the AWL.

Effective Methodology

Vocabulary Power is different from most vocabulary books because it is based on research on memory. Memorizing a word often requires that it be encountered seven or more times. It is important that words are not simply seen on each occasion, but encountered in new contexts, retrieved, and used (Nation 2001).

Vocabulary Power exposes students to each word in at least eight different contexts. This not only fixes new words in the memory, it offers learners a rich understanding of words. The eight different exposures follow a process approach, guiding the learner through the cognitive stages of noticing, retrieval, and generation. This approach teaches learners not only to recognize and understand a word, but also produce it.

HIGH INTEREST CONTENT

Vocabulary Power is unique because it makes vocabulary learning enjoyable. Examples are modern and realistic. The readings are adapted from articles in current newspapers, magazines, or online news sources on a variety of up-to-date topics. Students are encouraged to apply new words to their own lives, making vocabulary more relevant and useful.

CLASSROOM FRIENDLY FORMAT

Each chapter is organized as follows:

- **Words in Context:** understanding new words from context
- **Words and Definitions:** matching the words with their definition (or adapted definition) from the *Longman Dictionary of American English*
- **Comprehension Check:** checking comprehension of the words
- **Word Families:** expanding knowledge of the words with word families
- **Same Word, Different Meaning:** expanding knowledge of the words with multiple meanings
- **Words in Sentences:** using the words to complete sentences
- **Words in Collocations and Expressions:** understanding collocations and expressions featuring the words to improve memory and activate production
- **Words in a Reading:** using the words to complete a reading adapted from a current news article
- **Words in Discussion:** applying the words to real life with lively discussion questions
- **Words in Writing:** using the words in writing about a relevant topic

In addition:

- Ten Quizzes throughout the book make it easy for teachers and students to check the students' progress.
- The Word Builder exercises and charts in the Appendix also provide an opportunity to focus on the meaning and use of word parts.
- A complete Answer Key (for all exercises and quizzes) is provided in a separate booklet.

Vocabulary Power can be used as a supplement to reading, writing, grammar, or speaking classes. It can be used in class or assigned as homework. It can also be used as a self-study text. This flexibility makes the book an easy way to strengthen the academic curriculum of a class.

REFERENCES

Coxhead, A. 2000. A new academic word list. TESOL Quarterly, 34(2000), 213-239.

Nation, P. 2001. Learning Vocabulary in Another Language. Cambridge University Press: Cambridge.

Nation, P. 2002. Managing Vocabulary Learning. SEAMEO Regional Language Centre: Singapore.

ACKNOWLEDGMENTS

I am grateful to the wonderful editorial team at Longman for their contributions to this series. In particular, I would like to thank Stacey Hunter, Amy McCormick, Christopher Leonowicz, and Jennifer Lebedev. I also thank Longman for allowing me to use definitions, the pronunciation table, and transcriptions from the Longman Dictionary of American English. This book could not have been developed without the insights of students, so I would like to thank my students at Northeastern University who piloted these materials and gave me great feedback.

TO THE STUDENT

Do you want to improve your vocabulary, but don't know which words are most important to learn? Is studying vocabulary sometimes boring for you? Do you want to remember words easily, and know how to use them when speaking and writing? Do you need a better vocabulary to be ready for studies at the university level? If you can answer "yes" to any of these questions, this is the book for you.

Which words are important to learn?

The English language has over 100,000 words, but you only need to know the 2,000 most common words (the General Service List) to understand 80% of daily conversation and reading. After this, learning a group of 570 special academic words (the Academic Word List) will increase your comprehension to almost 90% of academic speaking and reading. This book only teaches words from the General Service List and the Academic Word List. Whether you are preparing for academic work or simply wish to better your vocabulary, studying these words is an excellent use of your time.

How can I remember new words easily?

To remember a word, you need to see it used several times, in different ways. Every new word in this book is taught through eight different exercises. By the end of a chapter, every word will be a part of your memory.

How can I enjoy learning vocabulary?

Learning vocabulary should be interesting! This book can help you enjoy learning new words in four ways:

1. The examples of the words are modern and realistic. (You don't have to worry that you will sound old-fashioned or strange when you use a new word.)

2. The readings in the book come from newspapers, magazines, and online sources (such as *The New York Times* and *National Geographic*) and cover up-to-date topics like technology, music, and sports.

3. Special exercises show you common collocations (word combinations) and expressions to help you use the words in conversation and academic writing.

4. Engaging discussion questions about your opinions and your life give you the opportunity to use the words in interesting conversation.

Now that you understand how you can get a better vocabulary, you are ready to start *Vocabulary Power.*

ABOUT THE AUTHOR

Kate Dingle has taught English in Poland, Italy, and the United States. Her interest in vocabulary acquisition developed at the Institute of Education, University of London, where she completed her Masters in TESOL. She now lives in Boston and is an instructor in the English Language Center at Northeastern University.

Key Words

ambiguous	deduce	link	objective	react
cooperate	deny	mature	pursue	vary

WORDS IN CONTEXT

*Use the sentences to guess what each key word means. Choose the meaning that is closest to that of the key word in **bold**.*

1. ambiguous
/æmˈbɪgyuəs/
-*adjective*

- When the presidential candidate was asked how he planned to help the environment, he gave an **ambiguous** answer, so no one knows his plans.
- Sam was **ambiguous** when we asked him if he'd come to the party; my husband and I couldn't understand if he would come or not.

Ambiguous means . . .
    a. easy to understand   b. interesting   ⓒ not clear

2. cooperate
/kouˈɑpəˌreɪt/
-*verb*

- Is it easy for you to **cooperate** with other people, working together toward a common goal?
- Both governments are **cooperating** to build a bridge that will connect the two countries.

Cooperate means . . .
  a. to work with someone else to achieve something that you both want
  b. to create problems for other people
  c. to do something even though you don't want to

3. deduce
/dɪˈdus/
-*verb*

- Hallie told me the age of her two brothers, so I was able to **deduce** that she is twenty-five.
- By listening to Chloe's accent, we **deduced** that she was from France.

Deduce means . . .
  a. to be told a fact
  b. to make a judgment based on the information you have
  c. not to understand something important

4. deny
/dɪˈnaɪ/
-*verb*

- The actor **denied** rumors that he used drugs, insisting that he led a clean life.
- An honest person will admit that he or she made a mistake rather than **denying** it.

Deny means . . .
  a. to say that something is true
  b. to agree
  c. to say that something is not true

5. link
/lɪŋk/
-*verb*

- The programmer **linked** his music web site with the web site for his favorite radio station.
- Zara can **link** her interest in English to her goals for the future.

Link means . . .
  a. to make a connection
  b. to separate
  c. to find

6. mature
/mə'tʃʊr/
-*adjective*

- Americans usually believe that a teenager is **mature** enough to leave home at age eighteen.
- Wesley is not very **mature**. He's twenty-six, but he acts as if he were sixteen.

Mature means . . .
    a. behaving in a reasonable way
    b. irresponsible and silly
    c. acting like a child

7. objective
/əb'dʒɛktɪv/
-*noun*

- One of my **objectives** this year is to be accepted by a good university.
- What **objectives** do you hope to achieve in the next six months?

Objective means . . .
    a. something unimportant
    b. something you work hard to achieve
    c. idea

8. pursue
/pɚ'su/
-*verb*

- Whenever Terrance has a goal, he **pursues** it until he is successful.
- Marie is **pursuing** a career as a video editor, so she is moving to New York, where there is a lot of video editing work.

Pursue means . . .
    a. to choose
    b. to try to achieve
    c. to wish for

9. react
/ri'ækt/
-*verb*

- When the fire started, Matt **reacted** quickly and threw water on the flames.
- How would you **react** if your neighbor played loud music at 2:00 A.M.?

React means . . .
    a. to behave in a certain way when someone says or does something
    b. to agree with something someone says or does
    c. to do nothing when someone says or does something

10. vary
/'væri/
-*verb*

- Instead of eating the same thing every night for dinner, it is healthier to **vary** the foods you eat.
- My sister's moods **vary** according to the weather.

Vary means . . .
    a. to change or differ
    b. to be the same
    c. to continue

▌ WORDS AND DEFINITIONS

Read each definition and write the word it defines on the line.

1. _____*link*_____ to make a connection between two things

2. _____ to say that something is not true

3. _____ to behave in a particular way because of what someone has done or said to you

4. _____ to differ, or to change often

5. _____ something that you are working hard to achieve

6. _____ not clear because it could have more than one meaning

7. _____ to make a judgment based on the information you have

8. _____ to work with someone else to achieve something you both want

9. _____ to continue trying to achieve something over a long time

10. _____ behaving in a reasonable way like an adult

COMPREHENSION CHECK

Choose the best answer.

1. In which of the following quotes is someone **denying** something?
   a. "It's true that I lost your keys."
   b. "No comment."
   c. "I didn't do it!"

2. Which of the following things would a **mature** teenager NOT do?
   a. drink a lot of beer and drive a car
   b. come home at a reasonable time at night
   c. help clean the house

3. An **objective** is
   a. a problem.
   b. a fact.
   c. a goal.

4. A person who **cooperates** easily
   a. could work well with a team.
   b. had better work alone.
   c. creates problems in an office.

5. If your life in the United States **varies** from your life in your home country, it is
   a. the same as your life in your home country.
   b. different from your life in your home country.
   c. more interesting than your life in your home country.

6. Which of the following things is NOT possible to **pursue**?
   a. a dream
   b. a medical degree
   c. a headache

7. If you saw a friend who had wet hair and was carrying a gym bag and goggles, what would you **deduce**?
   a. that she had just been taking a math test
   b. that she had just been walking her dog
   c. that she had just been swimming in the pool

8. If a girl asks her boyfriend where he was last night and he gives an **ambiguous** answer, she might say,
   a. "Why are you being so unclear?"
   b. "I love you, too."
   c. "I understand."

9. Which country was once **linked** with Alaska?
   a. Mexico
   b. Thailand
   c. Russia

10. How would a student probably **react** on being accepted by Harvard University?
   a. take a nap
   b. shout with happiness
   c. cry angry tears

WORD FAMILIES

Now that you have studied the ten key words and their basic definitions, you are ready to learn words that belong to the same family as some of the key words. A word family includes words that look alike but have different functions (noun, verb, adjective, or adverb). Their meanings are related but different.

A. *Look at each model phrase and decide whether the word in **bold** is used as a noun, verb, adjective, or adverb. Put a check (✓) in the correct column.*

	NOUN	VERB	ADJECTIVE	ADVERB
1. cooperate				
• happily **cooperate** with		✓		
• full **cooperation**	✓			
• a **cooperative** coworker			✓	
2. deny				
• totally **deny** it				
• quick **denial**				
3. link				
• **linked** the ideas				
• an interesting **link**				
4. mature				
• a **mature** child				
• **immature** friends				
• surprising **maturity**				
5. react				
• **react** quickly				
• an unusual **reaction**				
• a **reactive** person				
6. vary				
• often **varies**				
• a lot of **variety**				

B. *Read the first half of each sentence and match it with the appropriate ending on page 6.*

__e__ 1. Ismael likes to read a(n)

____ 2. When Ava yelled at her coworker for his mistake, I realized that she is a(n)

____ 3. You'll appreciate having Mike Perez in your group; he's very

____ 4. In kindergarten, kids learn about

____ 5. Thirty-year-old Arturo tells childish jokes; he's really

____ 6. Weren't you surprised by her emotional

____ 7. It's important that every camp counselor has a certain level of

____ 8. Do you think there is a

____ 9. You and I had discussed it, so I was surprised by your

a. **immature**.

b. **reaction** to the news?

c. **denial** of the problem.

d. **reactive** person.

e. **variety** of books.

f. **cooperation** and respect.

g. **maturity**.

h. **link** between junk food and obesity?

i. **cooperative**.

SAME WORD, DIFFERENT MEANING

Most words have more than one meaning. Study the additional meanings of **cooperate**, **objective**, *and* **pursue**. *Then read each sentence and decide which meaning is used.*

a.	**cooperate** *v.*	to work with someone else to achieve what you both want
b.	**cooperate** *v.*	to do what someone asks you to do
c.	**objective** *n.*	a goal that you are working to achieve
d.	**objective** *adj.*	not influenced by your own feelings, beliefs, or ideas
e.	**pursue** *v.*	to continue trying to achieve something over a long time
f.	**pursue** *v.*	to chase or follow someone or something in order to catch him, her, or it

___f___ 1. The police **pursued** the bank robbers down the highway.

_____ 2. Let's set our **objectives** for this meeting before we begin.

_____ 3. Should a judge make **objective** decisions or decisions based on his personal feelings?

_____ 4. When Sam was arrested by the police, he told them that he would **cooperate** fully and not give them any problems.

_____ 5. I am **pursuing** a career in nursing.

_____ 6. The Vietnamese and French offices will **cooperate** on effective management training.

WORDS IN SENTENCES

Complete each sentence with one of the words from the box.

ambiguous	deduce	immature	objective	reaction
cooperative	~~deny~~	link	pursuing	vary

1. R. J. didn't _____deny_____ that he was bad dancer when his brother laughed at him in the nightclub. In fact, R. J. laughed, too.

2. A jury must be _____ when considering the facts in a court case.

3. There is a _____ between smoking and lung cancer.

4. I'm interested in hearing about your _____ to what happened.

5. A good detective can always _____ who is guilty.

6. Young children usually can't do one thing for a very long time, so it's important to
_____ their activities throughout the day.

7. Sara's relationship with Leo is _____ to me; I don't know if they are dating or just friends.

8. On TV, we can often see detectives _____ a criminal down a busy city street.

9. Even though Hannah is eighteen, she is really _____, so I don't trust her to babysit my two-year-old.

10. My cousin Joe isn't _____; he argues a lot and doesn't work well in a team.

WORDS IN COLLOCATIONS AND EXPRESSIONS

Following are common collocations and expressions with some of the key words. Read the definitions and then complete the conversations with the collocations and expressions. You may have to change word forms for correct grammar.

1. **ambiguous**	
• **ambiguous answer**	an answer that is confusing or unclear because it could be understood in more than one way
2. **cooperate**	
• **refuse to cooperate**	refuse to work with someone or do what someone asks you to do
3. **mature**	
• **mature for his/her age**	said of a child who acts more grown up than most children his or her age
4. **objective**	
• **main objective**	the most important goal that you are trying to achieve
5. **pursue**	
• **pursue the (matter, question, argument)**	to continue trying to ask about, find out about, or persuade someone about a particular subject
6. **vary**	
• **vary from place to place**	to be different in different places

1. EMPLOYER: Why do you want to pursue a career in medicine?

   JOB APPLICANT: My father was a doctor, and I became interested in his work when I was a child. For as long as I can remember, my ____*main objective*____ has been to become a doctor, too.

2. DETECTIVE: You killed Mary Jones.

   DEFENDANT: No! I deny it.

   DETECTIVE: Then why did you react by running when I entered your office?

DEFENDANT:	I won't tell you anything!
DETECTIVE:	If you _____, things will be much harder for you. I'm going to _____ matter until I find the truth.
3. MOTHER 1:	Wow, kids really _____. My twelve-year-old niece in San Diego needs a babysitter, but her twelve-year-old cousin in Boston is really _____; she babysits other kids. Maybe kids in Boston grow up faster!
MOTHER 2:	That's an interesting idea, but I don't agree with you. I think maturity depends on the kid, not the city.
4. HISTORY TEACHER:	Jason, why didn't you do your homework?
JASON:	How did you know I didn't do my homework?
HISTORY TEACHER:	First, you stared at your feet when I asked for volunteers to answer the questions. Then, when I called on you, you gave such a(n) _____, I deduced that you hadn't done the assignment.
JASON:	It's true. Sorry!

▌WORDS IN A READING

Read this article about alternative fuel for cars. Complete it with words from the boxes.

ambiguous	~~deducing~~	objective	variety

CAN VEGETABLE-OIL CARS SAVE THE WORLD?

Gas is expensive. Old vegetable cooking oil from restaurants is free. A car can actually run on either. So why aren't more people ___*deducing*___ that they should give up petroleum and use
                                              1
peanut power instead?

"Making the switch couldn't be simpler," said Patrick Kuhn, who converted one of four trucks at his company, Charlotte Moving Truck Rentals, to run on vegetable oil earlier this year. He said his customers love it and constantly choose the veggie-powered vehicle over his others.

But while Kuhn's truck may be popular, for many people life with a veggie car might not be so easy. And although this alternative fuel may be cheap and clean, its potential widespread effect on the environment seems _____ because there simply isn't enough of it to make a big dent in
                         2
our gas consumption.

Kuhn said it cost $3,500 to convert the truck to veggie power, which can be done to any diesel engine. For convenience, he buys used restaurant cooking oil from a dealer about an hour away—the same guy, actually, who installed Kuhn's veggie fuel system. Kuhn pays the supplier—who collects, filters, and delivers the oil—about $1.50 a gallon. Compare that with the $3 a gallon he said he'd pay for diesel.

Kuhn is part of what Lee Briante, a spokesman for Greasecar, the largest purveyor* of veggie fuel conversion kits, says is a growing market. In the first few years, people drove vegetable oil cars as a way to help the environment. These days, the more common _____ is saving money.
                                                                                              3

Indeed, the economics of veggie oil are even better for a car than they are for a truck. A _____ of car conversion kits are available online. These kits cost about $800. You can
              4
install the system yourself, or it can be installed at one of two dozen Greasecar-certified mechanics nationwide for another $600.

| cooperates | denying | linked | pursue | react |

But Briante said that the government regulations _____ to vegetable oil fuel make it
                                                                  5
hard for most people to keep their veggie-cars fueled. Many people have to fuel up by forming a relationship with a local restaurant, which leaves its old cooking oil out back in five-gallon jugs for the user to collect. (Restaurants usually have to pay to get rid of this oil, so proprietors are often happy to do so.)

Another downside: Many drivers _____ negatively to the news that they have to
                                                    6
strain the oil to clean out the old French fries before they pour it into the tank.

And since there just isn't that much vegetable oil available to power cars, it's unlikely that there will ever be a large push for these cars. Briante said there are about 100 million gallons of waste restaurant oil generated annually. That would replace only about 0.07 percent of the 140 billion gallons of gas Americans use each year, and that's assuming that everyone _____, switching from
                                                                                          7
gasoline to diesel engines. Using new vegetable oil—not the used stuff from restaurants—raises similar scarcity questions.

One environmental group, which declined to be identified, pays little attention to the prospect of veggie oil reducing oil dependency or clearing up the air, _____ that these cars are a real
                                                                              8
environmental issue.

But that doesn't mean more people won't _____ veggie cars. "With $3 diesel, I don't
                                                          9
think it will take long before someone realizes, 'Hey, there's money to be made in this,'" said Kuhn.

*Purveyor: *someone who provides goods or services to people as a business*

(Adapted from "Can Vegetable Oil Cars Save the World?" CNNmoney.com, July 24, 2006.)

Apply the key words to your own life. Read and discuss each question in small groups. Try to use the key words.

1. **objective**

   An objective I have this year: _____ *to improve my English* _____

   Someone I know who can't make objective decisions: _____ *my emotional aunt* _____

2. **react**

   How I would react if I won $1 million: _____

   How I would react if you spilled coffee on my shirt: _____

3. **pursue**

   Something I want to pursue this month: _____

   Something I once pursued that was a mistake: _____

4. **mature**

   How much of the time I am mature: _____ percent of the time

   Someone I know who is really silly and immature: _____

5. **ambiguous**

   Something that seems ambiguous to me but that I want to understand:

   _____

   Something that is not at all ambiguous to me: _____

6. **vary**

   How frequently I vary the kinds of foods I eat: _____

   How much my life now varies from my life a year ago: _____

7. **link**

   What memories I link with chocolate: _____

   The person with whom I have the strongest link: _____

8. **cooperate**

   A person I have a difficult time cooperating with: _____

   A situation in which it's really important to cooperate: _____

9. **deny**

   Something I'd deny if my grandmother asked me about it: _____

   The last time I denied something: _____

10. **deduce**

    What people can deduce about me from looking at me: _____

    What people can deduce about me from how I lead my life: _____

❚ WORDS IN WRITING

Choose two topics and write a paragraph on each. Try to use the key words.

1. In your home country, does culture **vary** from city to city? Describe the **variety** in culture that can be found throughout your country.

2. What career are you **pursuing**? Explain why you chose this career, and what your main **objective** is this year in working toward this job.

3. Do you think a child's **maturity** is **linked** with how his parents raised him or her does it depend more on personality? Explain with examples from your life.

4. Do you believe that there is any situation when it is okay for a person to refuse to **cooperate** with the police? If so, when? If not, why do you believe that total **cooperation** with the police is necessary?

5. How would you **react** if your best friend borrowed $50 from you and never returned it? Do you think that it would be better to have a strong **reaction** or to forget about it?

▌WORDS IN CONTEXT

*Use the sentences to guess what each key word means. Choose the meaning that is closest to that of the key word in **bold**.*

1. accompany
/əˌkʌmpəni/
-verb

- The artist's neighbor will **accompany** her to the gallery.
- Who would you like to **accompany** you on your next vacation?

Accompany means . . .
    a. to be separate from
    b. to compete with
    c. to go with or happen together

2. contradict
/ˌkɑntrəˈdɪkt/
-verb

- The police questioned two men about a bank robbery. The second man's story **contradicted** the first man's story. The police knew that one of them was lying.
- This report **contradicts** the other report about life on Mars, so one of the reports must be wrong.

Contradict means . . .
    a. to agree with what someone or something said
    b. to support a story with details
    c. for one story to be so different from another that both cannot be true

3. crucial
/ˈkruʃəl/
-adjective

- The marketing team spent the entire weekend working because they had to prepare for a **crucial** meeting with the Tokyo office.
- Walter believed that choosing the right university was a **crucial** decision, so he researched his choices carefully.

Crucial means . . .
    a. very important
    b. somewhat important
    c. not important

4. dynamic
/daɪˈnæmɪk/
-adjective

- Because Professor Adams is a **dynamic** speaker, there is always a waiting list of students who want to take his class.
- If you want to have an entertaining dinner party, invite **dynamic** guests.

Dynamic means . . .
    a. tired and boring
    b. unpleasant
    c. lively

5. generate
/ˈdʒɛnəˌreɪt/
-verb

- Your body **generates** heat when you exercise.
- The new advertising director has to be someone who can **generate** creative ideas.

Generate means . . .
    a. to slow or stop something
    b. to talk about
    c. to produce or make something

6. **initial**
/ɪ'nɪʃəl/
-adjective

- At their **initial** meeting, Margaret was impressed by Helen's skill, so she invited her to come for a second interview.
- During the **initial** days of class, the teacher encouraged students to get to know one another.

Initial means . . .   a. first   b. middle   c. last

7. **interpret**
/ɪn'tɚprɪt/
-verb

- Maria will **interpret** what we say for her parents, who speak only Spanish.
- Eli **interpreted** his son's silence as anger.

Interpret means . . .   a. to translate or explain the meaning of something   b. to change the meaning of something   c. to tell

8. **perceive**
/pɚ'siv/
-verb

- When Daniel **perceived** the tension in the room, he quickly explained that he had not meant to offend anyone with his joke.
- Do you **perceive** a glass as half empty or half full?

Perceive means . . .   a. to discuss   b. to understand   c. to show

9. **precise**
/prɪ'saɪs/
-adjective

- The **precise** amount of money that Xavier spent in Barcelona is 4,926 Euros.
- New technology allows surgeons to be more **precise** in their work.

Precise means . . .   a. approximate   b. exact   c. incorrect

10. **sustain**
/sə'steɪn/
-verb

- Jim is working seventy hours per week, but I doubt he can **sustain** that for long.
- Though it wasn't very exciting, my mother's cooking **sustained** my growth when I was a child.

Sustain means . . .   a. to make something continue   b. to fail or stop something from happening   c. to change quickly

▌WORDS AND DEFINITIONS

Read each definition and write the word it defines on the line.

1. _____ extremely important

2. _____ to go with or happen together

3. _____ to translate or explain the meaning of something

4. _____ exact or correct in every detail

5. _____ to produce or make something

6. _____ to understand, sense, or notice

7. _____ interesting, lively, and full of energy

8. _____ first; happening at the beginning

9. _____ to make something continue to exist or happen over a period of time

10. _____ for one statement, story, etc. to be so different from another that both cannot be true

▌COMPREHENSION CHECK

Choose the best answer.

1. If an athlete **sustains** his pace when running, he
   a. stays at the same speed.
   b. speeds up.
   c. slows down.

2. Which statement **contradicts** Vince's story that he stayed home last night because he was sick?
   a. "I didn't see Vince last night."
   b. "I talked to Vince last night on the phone. He sounded terrible."
   c. "Vince and I had a great time dancing in a nightclub last night."

3. What is NOT possible to **interpret**?
   a. one language into another
   b. the lyrics of a song
   c. a snowstorm

4. What is a **precise** answer?
   a. 4.2
   b. I have no clue.
   c. maybe 10

5. What **generates** energy?
   a. the wheels of a car
   b. a boring speaker
   c. the sun

6. What does a typical person do during the **initial** days of his or her life? He or she
   a. says good-bye to his or her family and friends.
   b. sleeps a lot in his or her mother's arms.
   c. works long hours at the office.

7. What CANNOT be **crucial**?
   a. gossip
   b. a meeting
   c. a decision

8. Which statement describes a **dynamic** person?
   a. Ling is always tired.
   b. Lucy has a charming and interesting personality.
   c. Carl bores everyone he meets.

9. Which word is NOT a synonym of **perceive**?
   a. notice
   b. sense
   c. miss

10. If Hank asks Miriam to **accompany** him on a walk, he wants her to
    a. walk with him.
    b. carry his umbrella and bag.
    c. follow him.

WORD FAMILIES

Now that you have studied the ten key words and their basic definitions, you are ready to learn words that belong to the same family as some of the key words. A word family includes words that look alike but have different functions (noun, verb, adjective, or adverb). Their meanings are related but different.

A. *Look at each model phrase and decide whether the word in **bold** is used as a noun, verb, adjective, or adverb. Put a check (✓) in the correct column.*

	NOUN	VERB	ADJECTIVE	ADVERB
1. **contradict**				
• **contradict** each other				
• a surprising **contradiction**				
2. **crucial**				
• a **crucial** event				
• **crucially** needs				
3. **initial**				
• our **initial** idea				
• **initially**, we believed that				
4. **interpret**				
• **interpret** a conversation				
• your **interpretation** of what happened				
5. **perceive**				
• **perceive** a change				
• an interesting **perception**				
• a **perceptive** person				
6. **precise**				
• the **precise** day				
• use **precision**				
• recall **precisely** what happened				

B. *Detective Brown is talking with the Chief of Police about an investigation. Complete their conversation with words from the box.*

contradiction	initially	perception	precisely
crucial	interpretation	perceptive	precision

CHIEF: Detective Brown, it's _____ that we get your help with this. Can you give us your _____ of these clues?
₁
₂

BROWN: Tell me _____ why you want my opinion.
₃

CHIEF: I want your opinion because you are so _____.
₄

BROWN: Okay, here it is. _____, I thought this footprint suggested that an intruder broke into the house. Now, however, I see a(n) _____ in
₅
₆

that: the footstep is at the wrong angle. This means that it was put there deliberately to mislead us, meaning that the husband may be the killer.

CHIEF: Yet again we are amazed by your extraordinary _____ and
_____, Detective Brown. Thank you.
7
8

SAME WORD, DIFFERENT MEANING

*Most words have more than one meaning. Study the additional meanings of **contradict**, **dynamic**, and **initial**. Then read each sentence and decide which meaning is used.*

a. **contradict** *v.*	for one statement, story, etc. to be so different from another that both cannot be true
b. **contradict** *v.*	to say that what someone else has just said is wrong or not true
c. **dynamic** *adj.*	interesting, exciting, and full of energy
d. **dynamics** *n.*	the way in which systems or people behave, react, and affect each other
e. **initial** *adj.*	first
f. **initial** *n.*	the first letter of a name

_____ 1. Annie told the kids that they could watch TV, but then her husband **contradicted** her, saying that the children needed to do their homework.

_____ 2. Emily Bronte's **initials** are E.B.

_____ 3. The conference will begin with a lecture by a **dynamic** speaker.

_____ 4. Professor Blaine's research results **contradict** Professor Timm's research results.

_____ 5. Psychologists who study family **dynamics** are interested in how family members behave when they are together.

_____ 6. Wan's **initial** plan was to be a doctor, but later he decided to become an actor.

WORDS IN SENTENCES

Complete each sentence with two of the words from the box.

| accompany | crucial | generate | interpret | precisely |
| contradict | dynamics | initial | perceive | sustain |

1. Mr. Andrews invited Joe to _____ him to a business lunch, during which he asked Joe to _____ some new ideas for the marketing project.

2. Because the meeting between the presidents of France and Turkey was _____, the world's top French-Turkish translator was hired to _____ their discussion.

3. Alessandro is very sensitive, so I'm sure that he will _____ any tension in the group _____.

4. "Don't try to _____ me," Julie told Fred. "You can't deny that I told you _____ what happened."

5. Eleanor was very successful in her _____ semester of college, but after that she could not _____ her good grades, so she dropped out and became a waitress.

WORDS IN COLLOCATIONS AND EXPRESSIONS

Following are common collocations and expressions with some of the key words. Read the definitions and then complete the conversation with the collocations and expressions. You may have to change word forms for correct grammar.

1. **contradict**
   - **contradict yourself**   to say something that is the opposite of what you have said before
   - **a contradiction between**   a difference between two stories, facts, etc. that means they cannot both be true

2. **dynamic**
   - **dynamic personality**   an interesting, exciting, and energetic personality

3. **generate**
   - **generate an idea**   to create an idea

4. **perceive**
   - **perceive a change in (sth)**   to notice a change in (something)

5. **precise**
   - **to be precise**   used when you add exact details about something

ADVISOR: I asked you to meet with me, Jeff, because I have _____ 1 your work recently.

JEFF: Thank you, Professor! I know I've gotten a few bad grades, but I've improved a lot, haven't I?

ADVISOR: Jeff, you just _____ 2. How can you be improving if you're getting bad grades? Let's face it, your work has not been good; you're having problems.

JEFF: I just started my Ph.D.! You can't expect me to be perfect yet.

ADVISOR: No, not perfect, but you do need to be serious about your work. Take your last experiment.

JEFF: What do you mean, exactly?

ADVISOR: Well, _____ 3 there was a glaring _____ 4 your results and well-known research in the field, but you didn't explain it. And you still haven't proposed a research topic of your own. What's going on?

JEFF: I'm having a hard time balancing classes and assisting in the lab. It's a challenge to do all that. And now I need to _____ a great _____ for my research!⁵

ADVISOR: I know it's hard to sustain your energy, but you've got to figure it out. It's crucial. Go back and examine your faulty research. Hand in your proposed research topic by next week. If you have questions, you can call or e-mail me.

JEFF: OK. Thanks.

ADVISOR: I think you could be an excellent professor one day, Jeff. You're intelligent and you have a _____⁶. No one ever said this would be easy.

JEFF: You're right. I'll do my best.

▌WORDS IN A READING

Read the article about face reading. Complete it with words from the boxes.

contradict	dynamic	initially	interpret	precise

A FACE CAN TELL A THOUSAND STORIES

Over time, most law enforcement investigators who regularly interview suspects or victims develop their own personal techniques to _____₁ the various facial expressions of the person they are questioning. The way a person's face or eyes move can often give away more information than the person being interviewed intends to show.

Glenna Trout, a former Bellevue, Washington, police and training officer, has taken that idea one step further by using "face reading" to understand an individual's strengths and beliefs, as well as to find information they may not willingly share. The retired patrol lieutenant and field training officer has studied face reading for more than twenty years, and she now devotes her time and energy to conducting _____₂ courses on the subject for law enforcement officials around the world.

According to Trout, the face carries the majority of the information a person transmits. By using the "tools" she has developed, Trout shows students in her introductory workshops how to recognize and "read" _____₃ aspects of a person's face—the exact traits include personality styles, life experiences, underlying beliefs, attitudes, and health issues.

Much of what Trout teaches in her courses has little to do with genetic traits, such as eye color, but a lot to do with interpreting an individual's experiences, attitudes, and belief systems. By using face reading techniques, Trout says it is possible to learn to recognize the masks people wear that may _____₄ their true feelings. It can help us understand why the individual thinks, feels, and acts as he or she does. Such training can expand an officer's interview abilities, she says, adding that studies have shown that emotions are expressed on the face the same way cross-culturally.

One face reading method Trout uses is called "face mapping." A face, or photo of a face, can give an overview of the subject as a person—the person's life pattern and where the person is going in life. The face is then divided into nine sections, which makes it possible to gain a deeper understanding of a person's life experience.

"The information contained on a face is hugely complex," she comments. "This is why a nine-segment division of the face is utilized. Each section contains at least six different kinds of information and that makes a total of fifty-four components of the face that we have to study. These nine sections and six types of information still make the face far more comprehensible than taking it on as an organic whole, at least _____."
5

accompanied	crucial	generated	perceived	sustained

Taken individually, each of the nine sections represents a personality aspect. For example, the right side of the mouth illustrates a person's social impact system, or how they get what they want from people. The left side of the mouth shows social orientation, what a person expects from or feels about other people. Taken together, the full mouth demonstrates social interface, how someone is seen by others—their persona or style.

As a police officer herself, Trout was skeptical when she was first introduced to the concept of face reading at a college class in the mid-1980s, but she says she quickly became fascinated by the subject. "By the end of the evening I had hundreds of questions and was inspired by all the applications I _____ would be possible with this knowledge," she remembers.
6

Her interest was _____ through thorough research on the topic. Trout studied both
7
psychology and other related fields to broaden her knowledge of the human anatomy.

After retiring from her job as a police officer in 1993, she married John Bishop, then a British police officer, and moved to the east coast of England. There her ability to identify potential troublemakers on the videotapes of local soccer crowds _____ interest on behalf of the
8
Ipswich (England) Police Department, and her international speaking and training career took off.

Since then, Trout has traveled extensively, conducting training seminars and conference workshops throughout the United States, Canada, Britain, and Europe for law enforcement personnel and arson* investigators and in the private sector.

Trout is working on a book that explains both how and why to use face reading. She hopes to explain that face reading is a valuable tool but one that must be _____ by compassion.
9
She does not want it to be used to hurt or ridicule anyone.

"When reading a person's face, it is _____ that you approach the task in an empathic
10
and caring manner," she concludes. "This is a human being with a life history, feelings, personality, and

destiny who requires a caring understanding. The key to the approach is to respect the integrity and needs of the person and of the situation for which you are doing the reading."

*arson: *the crime of deliberately making something burn, especially a building*

(Adapted from "A Face Can Tell a Thousand Stories," officer.com, November 2005.)

▌WORDS IN DISCUSSION

Read the questions and choose the best answers. Then discuss your answers in small groups.

1. If a friend who had a terrible cold wanted to **accompany** you to a movie, what would you do?
   a. I'd be happy to have my friend join me. I'm not afraid of germs.
   b. I'd tell my friend, "Sorry, but you can't come with me until you're well."
   c. I'd pretend that I had canceled my plans and then secretly go to the movie alone.

2. In your opinion, which will be the most **crucial** decision in your life?
   a. which career I choose
   b. whom I marry
   c. what values I choose to live by

3. If someone asked you to **interpret** one of Shakespeare's poems, explaining what it meant, how would your interpretation be?
   a. Excellent. I love poetry and understand it well.
   b. OK. I'm not an expert at Shakespearean poetry, but I'm an intelligent person.
   c. Extremely bad. I don't have a clue about poetry.

4. Which could you give a **precise** description of?
   a. a mathematical equation
   b. the face of a person I love
   c. directions to my home

5. Where would you like to see your **initials**?
   a. on a suitcase
   b. on a bathrobe
   c. on a piece of money

6. How easy is it for you to **perceive** the smell of perfume in a room?
   a. It's extremely easy. I can smell everything, like a dog.
   b. It's not really easy, but I can smell the perfume if it is strong.
   c. It's difficult. I rarely smell anything.

7. Are you a **dynamic** public speaker?
   a. Yes. I am a lively speaker, and people find my talks interesting.
   b. Sometimes. If the group isn't too large, and the topic is very familiar, then I can speak well.
   c. No way. I am really nervous and disorganized when I speak in public.

8. What could you most easily **generate**?
   a. money
   b. creative ideas
   c. scientific solutions

9. If you are speaking to someone who states a fact that is wrong, will you **contradict** him?
   a. Of course. I will point out his mistake.
   b. I will correct him only if he is a friend.
   d. No. I will not contradict him.

10. Which of these activities could you **sustain**?
    a. swimming for forty minutes
    b. walking for three hours
    c. running for an hour

▌WORDS IN WRITING

Choose two topics and write a paragraph on each. Try to use the key words.

1. Describe a **crucial** moment in your life. Give **precise** details to explain why it was so important.

2. When, if ever, do you feel that children should **contradict** their parents? Why do you feel that such **contradictions** are justified?

3. Describe a person whom you feel is **perceptive**, that is, a person who **perceives** a lot.

4. What do you wish you could **interpret**? Explain.

5. Imagine that you have to **generate** a plan for an exciting new restaurant. What **dynamic** people (people you know or celebrities) would you hire to help you?

Key Words

attain	evolve	fundamental	imply	random
coherent	flexible	illustrate	portion	sufficient

WORDS IN CONTEXT

*Use the sentences to guess what each key word means. Choose the meaning that is closest to that of the key word in **bold**.*

1. attain
/əˈteɪn/
-verb

- After years of study, Emmanuel **attained** his doctoral degree in computer systems.
- Today, more women **attain** high positions in business and politics than they did forty years ago.

Attain means . . .　a. to achieve　　b. to think about　　c. to fail

2. coherent
/ˌkoʊˈhɪrənt/
-adjective

- Julie got the highest grade on the history exam because she wrote the most **coherent** essays.
- Maya is **coherent** when she speaks Spanish, but it's difficult for her to speak clearly and logically in English.

Coherent means . . .　a. confusing　　b. clear　　c. very difficult

3. evolve
/ɪˈvɑlv/
-verb

- Our idea of opening a coffee shop **evolved**; in the end, we decided to open a small restaurant.
- Charles Darwin was the first person to believe that humans **evolved** from apes.

Evolve means . . .　a. to develop gradually　b. to remain the same　c. to be separate

4. flexible
/ˈflɛksəbəl/
-adjective

- Chris doesn't like to follow a strict schedule, so he wants a job with **flexible** hours.
- Do you need to eat at the same time every day, or are you **flexible** about your mealtimes?

Flexible means . . .　a. lazy　　b. unable to change　c. able to change

5. fundamental
/ˌfʌndəˈmɛntəl/
-adjective

- Clean air and water are **fundamental** needs for children.
- Peter didn't want to buy the house because it needed some **fundamental** changes, such as new heating and plumbing systems.

Fundamental means . . .　a. extra and unnecessary　b. necessary　　c. expensive

6. illustrate
/ˈɪləˌstreɪt/
-verb

- Children's books are often **illustrated** with colorful pictures.
- A talented artist will **illustrate** the book of fairy tales.

Illustrate means . . .   a. to write or discuss   b. to publish   c. to make pictures

7. imply
/ɪmˈplaɪ/
-verb

- William didn't say that he disliked Joe, but he **implied** it by avoiding him at the party.
- Would you tell your dinner guests that you were ready for them to leave or only **imply** it by yawning?

Imply means . . .   a. to say directly   b. to suggest indirectly   c. to announce

8. portion
/ˈpɔrʃən/
-noun

- Lucy heard only a **portion** of the news report, so she wasn't clear about the details.
- My grandmother suggested that I put a **portion** of my salary into a savings account every month.

Portion means . . .   a. something entire   b. a part of something larger   c. something important

9. random
/ˈrændəm/
-adjective

- Lotteries use a **random** selection of winning numbers.
- Have you ever had a **random** meeting with an old friend in a completely unexpected place?

Random means . . .   a. careful   b. deliberate   c. unplanned

10. sufficient
/səˈfɪʃənt/
-adjective

- When we have **sufficient** information, we can write the report.
- Most people need eight hours of sleep, but for some people three or four hours are **sufficient**.

Sufficient means . . .   a. not enough   b. enough   c. more than enough

▌ WORDS AND DEFINITIONS

Read each definition and write the word it defines on the line.

1. _____ enough; as much as you need for a particular purpose

2. _____ to suggest that something is true without saying or showing it directly

3. _____ part of something larger

4. _____ to develop and change gradually over a long period of time

5. _____ to achieve something after trying for a long time

6. _____ necessary, basic, and important

7. _____ able to change easily

8. _____ happening without a plan, pattern, or reason

9. _____ to draw, paint, etc. pictures for a book

10. _____ clear and easy to understand

COMPREHENSION CHECK

Choose the best answer.

1. It is 67° F on a beautiful spring afternoon. What is **sufficient** clothing?

   a. a winter coat

   b. a bathing suit

   c. a T-shirt

2. Which is impossible to **attain**?

   a. a stable relationship

   b. a new car

   c. a problem

3. Who is **implying** something?

   a. Jack says, "I hate spinach."

   b. Kelly looks at the clock several times when the meeting runs late.

   c. Ben watches his favorite movie on Friday night.

4. Which is an example of a **portion**?

   a. Everyone saw the concert on New Year's Eve.

   b. No one ate the pizza.

   c. We gave some of our money to the poor children.

5. Who is **coherent**?

   a. Hugh writes clearly and logically.

   b. Ana, completely unprepared for her presentation, confuses everyone.

   c. Oliver, who has studied Spanish for two days, tries to have a long conversation in Spanish.

6. Which is a **random** event?

   a. The poetry club scheduled a meeting for Tuesday afternoon.

   b. Isabelle carefully selected her new puppy.

   c. A meteor unexpectedly crashed into the woods behind our house.

7. Who is **flexible**?

   a. Boris goes to bed at 9:00 P.M. 365 nights a year.

   b. Alan refuses to cooperate; he must do everything his way.

   c. Nadia is open-minded about changing her plans.

8. If a project **evolves**, what happens to it?

   a. It gets worse.

   b. It slowly develops.

   c. It suddenly improves.

9. What CANNOT be used to **illustrate** a book?

   a. paragraphs

   b. drawings

   c. graphs

10. What is **fundamental** to human life?

    a. air

    b. television

    c. chocolate

▌WORD FAMILIES

Now that you have studied the ten key words and their basic definitions, you are ready to learn words that belong to the same family as some of the key words. A word family includes words that look alike but have different functions (noun, verb, adjective, or adverb). Their meanings are related but different.

A. *Look at each model phrase and decide whether the word in **bold** is used as a noun, verb, adjective, or adverb. Put a check (✓) in the correct column.*

	NOUN	VERB	ADJECTIVE	ADVERB
1. **attain**				
• **attain** a good position				
• an **attainable** dream				
2. **coherent**				
• a **coherent** idea				
• no **coherence**				
• **coherently** explained				
• my **incoherent** neighbor				
3. **evolve**				
• **evolve** slowly				
• human **evolution**				
4. **illustrate**				
• **illustrate** a book				
• a beautiful **illustration**				
• a talented **illustrator**				
5. **imply**				
• What are you **implying**?				
• a serious **implication**				
6. **random**				
• the **random** occurrence				
• **randomly** started singing				
7. **sufficient**				
• **sufficient** supplies				
• **insufficient** funds				
• answer the question **sufficiently**				

B. *Read the first part of each sentence and match it with the appropriate ending. The exercise continues on page 26.*

_____ 1. The students were upset because they had

_____ 2. Your speech wasn't clear. You need to work on

_____ 3. I'm interested in hearing about the

_____ 4. The lottery winners were chosen

a. **coherently**.

b. **evolution** of your idea.

c. **illustrator**.

d. **sufficiently**.

e. **coherence**.

_____ 5. The pictures were drawn by a talented

_____ 6. His French is so bad that when he speaks he is

_____ 7. I was offended by your

_____ 8. You'll do well in college English 1 because you write fluently and

_____ 9. The vivid colors in this

_____ 10. If she wants to pass her driver's test, she needs to prepare

_____ 11. Claudia's goals are realistic and

f. **insufficient** time to finish the exam.

g. **implication** about my relationship with Doug.

h. **attainable**.

i. **illustration** remind me of summer in Spain.

j. **randomly**.

k. **incoherent**.

SAME WORD, DIFFERENT MEANING

Most words have more than one meaning. Study the additional meanings of **flexible**, **illustrate**, and **portion**. Then read each sentence and decide which meaning is used.

a. **flexible** _adj._	able to change easily
b. **flexible** _adj._	easy to bend
c. **illustrate** _v._	to draw, paint, etc. pictures for a book
d. **illustrate** _v._	to explain or make something clear by giving examples
e. **portion** _n._	a part of something larger
f. **portion** _n._	an amount of food for one person, especially when served in a restaurant

_____ 1. Rubber is used to make diving suits because the material is **flexible**.

_____ 2. I read only a **portion** of the article.

_____ 3. Children like books which are **illustrated**.

_____ 4. When we ate breakfast in the diner, we were surprised by the huge **portions**.

_____ 5. My schedule is **flexible**, so I can help you whenever you like.

_____ 6. The professor offered three examples to **illustrate** his point.

WORDS IN SENTENCES

Complete each sentence with one of the words from the box.

attain	**evolve**	**fundamental**	**imply**	**random**
coherently	**flexible**	**illustrates**	**portions**	**insufficient**

1. American restaurants serve giant _____.
2. This study _____ that colors can affect our moods.
3. Why did you wink at me, Steve? What are you trying to _____?
4. You need to call me; in this case, e-mail is _____.
5. If you work hard, you can _____ a nice house.
6. Gymnasts can move their bodies in positions that most other people can't. They are incredibly _____.
7. Freedom of religion is a(n) _____ right in many countries.
8. Callie, please don't ask _____ questions that aren't relevant to this class.
9. The lawyer won the case because he presented the facts _____.
10. Good, simple business ideas can often _____ into something more.

WORDS IN COLLOCATIONS AND EXPRESSIONS

Following are common collocations and expressions with some of the key words. Read the definitions and then complete the conversations with the collocations and expressions. You may have to change word forms for correct grammar.

1. **coherent**		
	• **a coherent answer**	a clear answer that is easy to understand
2. **flexible**		
	• **flexible hours**	hours that can change easily
3. **fundamental**		
	• **the fundamentals of (sth)**	the most important ideas, rules, etc. that something is based on
4. **illustrate**		
	• **illustrate this point**	to explain a point using an example
5. **imply**		
	• **imply that**	to suggest indirectly that
6. **random**		
	• **randomly selected**	selected without any plan

1. MARK: I can't get to work until ten every morning. Is that going to be a problem?

   BOSS: Not at all. You can work _____ here, as long as you work eight hours a day.

2. TEACHER: I've explained what gravity is. Now, to _____, I'd like to ask you to hold out your arms for two minutes. Ready, go!

   STUDENT: My arms feel heavy!

3. KIM: I wanted to take a night class, but I didn't know which one to take, so I _____ a pottery class. What a mistake! It's such a waste of time.

   TESSA: You should take a class in _____ cooking. Let's face it; you need to learn the basics.

4. MS. KLINE: Have you thought about retiring, Bob?

   BOB: Of course not. Are you _____ I'm not a good bus driver because I am eighty years old? I refuse to stop working!

5. ADVISOR: Your essay really confused me, Wen. You were supposed to write about why the Chinese language evolved the way it did. I don't understand why you wrote two paragraphs about basketball.

   WEN: Sorry, Professor. I'll start again and try to write a more _____ .

▌ WORDS IN A READING

Read this article about global issues. Complete it with words from the boxes.

coherent	fundamental	illustrating	portion	sufficient

AMAZON TRIBES: ISOLATED BY CHOICE?

No one knows exactly how many people live in isolation from the industrial-technological world. Although they make up a small _____ of the humans on Earth, these groups are
                                    1
significant. Many of these people, perhaps thousands, are believed to thrive in the remote areas of the Amazon River Basin of South America. Anthropologists and indigenous rights groups say that _____ evidence for the existence of these remote tribes can be found in stories of contact
   2
with other indigenous groups, deduced from abandoned dwellings, and observations of developers planning to take resources from the forests.

The rights groups believe that land is a _____ right for isolated people. These groups
                                        3
call for setting aside lands where the isolated people are believed to live, to protect them from the intrusion of developers in the Amazon. It is difficult to know the exact number of isolated people there are, as the only way to find out for sure is to go and find them, which can cause problems.

Brazil is believed to have the largest populations of indigenous people living in isolation from the outside world. The government-established National Indian Foundation (FUNAI) estimates there are more than fifty such groups and has established several reserves to protect their isolation. Evidence exists for other populations in Peru, Colombia, and Ecuador. Some of these groups are truly uncontacted and have no direct knowledge of the outside world. Other groups' isolation is a choice; these groups know about the outside world but are actively choosing to live in isolation.

In an interview for *National Geographic Today,* Gil Inoach, president of the Interethnic Association for Development of the Peruvian Jungle (AIDESEP), offered a(n) _____ explanation of
4
the tribal life, _____ how these people have everything they need to survive without help
5
from the outside world.

attain	evolving	flexible	implies that

"They have the ability to fish, hunt, and detect danger. They have the knowledge to develop their own health care systems through the discovery of medicinal plants in order to adapt to any illnesses in their surroundings. They have their own birthing techniques."

Anthropologist Janet Lloyd said that most of these people are not lost in otherwise uninhabited lands, but rather are surrounded by other indigenous groups and under constant pressure from loggers and other developers. This _____ the people know about modern life but actively choose
6
not to be a part of it.

Disease and death have plagued indigenous communities in South America since they first came into contact with outsiders from Europe in the 1500s. The indigenous populations had no immune protection against smallpox, measles, and flu, which wiped out thousands of communities.

Then, in 1836, Charles Goodyear, an inventor from Philadelphia, Pennsylvania, refined a process that kept rubber from melting in warm weather and cracking in cold weather. At first rubber was needed for bicycle tires; later this _____ material was needed for automobiles. During
7
the late nineteenth and early twentieth centuries, entrepreneurs came to the Amazon to harvest sap from the rubber trees. They enslaved the indigenous people who lived in the forests, forcing them to work at rubber harvesting.

To secure their own survival, indigenous communities that escaped enslavement by the rubber tappers retreated deeper into the forests and today actively avoid contact with the outside,
_____ world.
8
Today, indigenous rights groups are at the forefront of a movement to set aside lands where the isolated peoples are believed to exist, protecting them from the intrusion of developers looking to
_____ riches from the natural resources of the Amazon. The rights groups hope to
9
prevent a repeat of the tragedy that killed so many of the indigenous peoples' ancestors.

(Adapted from "Amazon Tribes: Isolated by Choice?" National Geographic News, March 10, 2003.)

WORDS IN DISCUSSION

Apply the key words to your own life. Read and discuss each question in small groups. Try to use the key words.

1. **illustrate**

   How talented I am at illustrating: _____

   The types of illustrated books I like: _____

2. **portion**

   How often I eat large portions of food: _____

   The portion of my home that needs to be cleaned: _____

3. **attain**

   Something I would like to attain: _____

   A degree (bachelor's, master's, doctoral) I hope to attain: _____

4. **sufficient**

   The amount of money that is sufficient for me to live comfortably for one month:

   _____

   The number of vacation days that are sufficient for me in one year:

   _____

5. **coherent**

   How coherent I am when I am giving a presentation in English: _____

   Someone I know who is rarely coherent: _____

6. **fundamental**

   A right which I believe is fundamental for all people: _____

   A fundamental question I have about life: _____

7. **evolve**

   How strongly I believe that life on Earth is evolving in a positive way:

   _____

   How long I think it will take my English to evolve to a level of excellence:

   _____

8. **flexible**

   How flexible my body is: _____

   How flexible I am when making plans with my friends: _____

9. **imply**

   What I imply by the way I dress: _____

   How I imply that I am bored: _____

10. **random**

    A person I met in a random way: _____

    A random idea that entered my mind in the last few minutes: _____

WORDS IN WRITING

Choose two topics and write a paragraph on each. Try to use the key words.

1. Describe a **fundamental** problem in your native country.

2. When, if ever, do you believe that peace on Earth will be **attainable**? Explain how you think a peaceful Earth might **evolve**.

3. Do you believe in the theory of human **evolution**, which states that humans **evolved** from apes? Explain why or why not.

4. Do people in your country eat reasonable **portions** of food, or are portions out of control? **Illustrate** your explanation with examples.

5. Do you feel you are more or less **flexible** than you were when you were younger? Explain why.

QUIZ 1

PART A

Choose the word that best completes each item and write it in the space provided.

1. Water is a(n) _____ need of all living creatures.
   - a. flexible
   - b. ambiguous
   - c. fundamental
   - d. random

2. This example _____ the problem.
   - a. attains
   - b. illustrates
   - c. cooperates
   - d. perceives

3. The essay was so disorganized and confusing, the professor wrote, "This is _____,"
   on it.
   - a. dynamic
   - b. coherent
   - c. incoherent
   - d. sufficient

4. When Janet's assistant told the employees to do something different from what Janet had
   instructed, Janet told her, "Don't _____ me."
   - a. deduce
   - b. interpret
   - c. contradict
   - d. react

5. Having seen the evidence, I can _____ what happened here.
   - a. sustain
   - b. generate
   - c. cooperate
   - d. deduce

6. My dad gave me advice about how I could _____ my goal.
   - a. attain
   - b. imply
   - c. accompany
   - d. illustrate

7. As the three marathon runners approached the finish line, one slowed down, one
   _____ her speed, and one managed to run faster.
   - a. sustained
   - b. perceived
   - c. implied
   - d. linked

8. In the concert tonight, a pianist will be _____ the violinist.
   - a. interpreting
   - b. denying
   - c. generating
   - d. accompanying

9. The biologist explained that our understanding of DNA has _____.
   - a. pursued
   - b. reacted
   - c. evolved
   - d. denied

10. Jorge asked his coworkers how they _____ their boss's silence after his
    presentation. Had their boss been impressed or bored?
    - a. interpreted
    - b. cooperated
    - c. varied
    - d. evolved

PART B

*Read each statement and write **T** for* true *and **F** for* false *in the space provided.*

_____ 1. A large **portion** of Mexico's population speaks Chinese.

_____ 2. A **dynamic** person is quite boring.

_____ 3. An **objective** judge has a strong personal opinion about a case.

_____ 4. George Washington's **initials** are G.W.

_____ 5. A clear answer is **ambiguous**.

_____ 6. A new president is **randomly** selected.

_____ 7. A successful business **generates** profits.

_____ 8. A **crucial** discussion is often silly and entertaining.

_____ 9. If you have **sufficient** information, you don't need any more information.

_____10. Criminals often **pursue** the police.

PART C

Match each sentence with the letter it describes.

_____ 1. This person **reacts** quickly when you call his station.

_____ 2. A person who is in **denial** says this.

_____ 3. When Laura **implies** that it is time for her guests to leave, she says this.

_____ 4. This person must be **precise**.

_____ 5. If Kara often **varies** her activities, she likes this.

_____ 6. A **perceptive** person might say this.

_____ 7. This person does not always **cooperate** with his or her parents.

_____ 8. If Josh discovers a **link** between two ideas, he finds this.

_____ 9. A **mature** student will not do this during class.

_____10. A **flexible** person can do this with her body.

a. a heart surgeon

b. "I notice everything."

c. tell jokes

d. a two-year-old child

e. touch her fingers to her toes

f. a firefighter

g. "It's getting late, isn't it?"

h. change

i. "No, I didn't!"

j. a connection

CHAPTER 4

Key Words

assess	contemporary	neutral	retain	target
cease	highlight	ratio	source	theory

▌ WORDS IN CONTEXT

*Use the sentences to guess what each key word means. Choose the meaning that is closest to that of the key word in **bold**.*

1. **assess**
   /əˈsɛs/
   -verb

   - During the driving test, an examiner will **assess** your skills on the road.
   - Do you know enough about sports to **assess** the ability of professional athletes?

   Assess means . . .   a. to follow   b. to make a judgment about   c. to teach someone how to do something

2. **cease**
   /sis/
   -verb

   - The news report said that fighting had **ceased** and negotiations had started again.
   - By morning, the strong winds had **ceased**, but heavy rain continued throughout the day.

   Cease means . . .   a. to stop   b. to continue   c. to start

3. **contemporary**
   /kənˈtɛmpəˌrɛri/
   -adjective

   - Because Megan prefers to read about **contemporary** issues, she never reads history books.
   - Not all of our **contemporary** art will be remembered one hundred years from now.

   Contemporary means . . .   a. happening in the past   b. happening in the future   c. belonging to the present time

4. **highlight**
   /ˈhaɪlaɪt/
   -verb

   - Eva **highlighted** an important equation in her math book with a yellow pen.
   - When we were giving the presentation, we **highlighted** the key ideas by writing them on the board.

   Highlight means . . .   a. to treat everything the same   b. to make something easy to notice   c. to ignore

5. **neutral**
   /ˈnutrəl/
   -adjective

   - Because I liked both basketball teams, I felt **neutral** about the outcome.
   - Hank didn't want to take sides in the argument, so he remained **neutral**.

   Neutral means . . .   a. supporting one side of an argument strongly   b. supporting one side of a war slightly   c. not supporting either side in an argument, competition, or war

6. ratio
/ˈreɪʃiˌoʊ/
-noun

- There are six men and three women in my Spanish class; the **ratio** of men to women is 2:1.
- In some university lecture classes, the student-teacher **ratio** is 50:1.

Ratio means . . .
a. two numbers that are equal
b. two numbers that are divided
c. a relationship between two amounts

7. retain
/rɪˈteɪn/
-verb

- If the company wants to **retain** its employees, it had better offer better benefits, or they may leave to work for its competitor.
- Is it easy for you to **retain** new vocabulary, or do you forget it easily?

Retain means . . .
a. to lose
b. to try to get
c. to keep something

8. source
/sɔrs/
-noun

- The sun is the **source** of the Earth's light and heat.
- When you write a research paper, list the **sources** in which you found your information.

Source means . . .
a. the thing, place, or person you get something from
b. something you work with
c. something you finish

9. target
/ˈtɑrgɪt/
-noun

- At the sales meeting, the car dealers set their monthly **target**; they hoped to sell fifty more cars than they had in the previous month.
- We plan to open the restaurant on May 1; we need to work hard to meet that **target**.

Target means . . .
a. a date
b. an aim
c. salary

10. theory
/ˈθiəri, ˈθɪri/
-noun

- I have my own **theory** about why Jim was late, but I have to ask him to make sure I'm right.
- Were you taught Darwin's **theory** of evolution in school?

Theory means . . .
a. an idea
b. a question
c. an answer

WORDS AND DEFINITIONS

Read each definition and write the word it defines on the line.

1. _____ to stop doing something or to make an activity stop happening

2. _____ an idea that explains something, especially one that has not yet been proven to be true

3. _____ to keep something; to keep facts in your memory

4. _____ to make a problem, subject, etc. easy to notice so that people will pay attention to it

5. _____ not supporting either side in an argument, competition, or war

6. _____ belonging to the present time; modern

7. _____ a relationship between two amounts, represented by two numbers that show how much bigger one amount is than the other

8. _____ an aim or a result that you try to achieve

9. _____ the thing, place, or person that you get something from

10. _____ to make a judgment about a person or situation after thinking carefully about it

▌COMPREHENSION CHECK

Choose the best answer.

1. A **neutral** person
   a. strongly supports one person.
   b. can be a fair judge.
   c. causes problems.

2. Which of the following is an example of a **ratio**?
   a. 5 + 5 = 10
   b. 8
   c. 4:1

3. Where are we most likely to find a person who enjoys **contemporary** art?
   a. at the Prehistoric Museum in Shanghai
   b. at the Tate Modern Art Collection in London, England
   c. at Santa Maria della Salute, a Renaissance church in Venice, Italy

4. What is probably the **source** of Bob's terrible headache?
   a. He will take some aspirin.
   b. He slept well last night.
   c. He listened to loud rock music for four hours.

5. Alice plans to run twenty-six miles in the Boston marathon next month. What is the **target**?
   a. next month
   b. to run 26 miles
   c. Boston, Massachusetts

6. At a concert, when the music **ceases**, people usually
   a. sit down.
   b. listen.
   c. clap their hands.

7. If your company wants to **retain** customers, you
   a. tell them to go away.
   b. invest money in advertising to attract new customers.
   c. keep the customers you already have happy.

8. A **theory**
   a. has not yet been proven.
   b. has not yet been tested.
   c. is always scientific.

9. During lectures, professors usually try to **highlight**
   a. little details.
   b. the most important ideas.
   c. everything.

10. What is probably the best way to **assess** the value of a used car?
    a. Look at a picture of it.
    b. Ask a mechanic to examine it.
    c. Buy it.

WORD FAMILIES

Now that you have studied the ten key words and their basic definitions, you are ready to learn words that belong to the same family as some of the key words. A word family includes words that look alike but have different functions (noun, verb, adjective, or adverb). Their meanings are related but different.

A. *Look at each model phrase and decide whether the word in **bold** is used as a noun, verb, adjective, or adverb. Put a check (✓) in the correct column.*

	NOUN	VERB	ADJECTIVE	ADVERB
1. **assess**				
• **assess** a situation				
• my **assessment**				
2. **contemporary**				
• a **contemporary** film				
• Marie Curie's **contemporary**				
3. **neutral**				
• a **neutral** position				
• **neutralize** the effect				
4. **retain**				
• **retain** our workers				
• vocabulary **retention**				
5. **theory**				
• only a **theory**				
• **theoretical** problem				
• **theorize** about life				
6. **target**				
• our **target**				
• **target** a new group				

B. *Read the first half of each sentence and match it with the appropriate ending.*

_____ 1. The advertisement for baby food

_____ 2. A person living in the same period of time as someone else is his or her

_____ 3. Rick asked for the real estate agent's

_____ 4. Using DNA to clone humans has not happened yet; it is only a

_____ 5. The school board of the inner-city high school wants to improve teacher

_____ 6. The increase in my salary

_____ 7. In the lecture, the scientist

a. **assessment** of the property.

b. **retention**; members are discussing how to keep the teachers at the school.

c. **contemporary**. For example, Shakespeare and John Webster both lived in the early seventeenth century, so they were contemporaries.

d. **theorized** about the beginning of the universe.

e. **targeted** new mothers.

f. **neutralized** the effect of my high heating bill.

g. **theoretical** possibility.

SAME WORD, DIFFERENT MEANING

*Most words have more than one meaning. Study the additional meanings of **highlight**, **source**, and **target**. Then read each sentence and decide which meaning is used.*

a. **highlight** *v.*	to call attention to a problem, subject, etc.
b. **highlight** *n.*	the most important or exciting part of a movie, sports event, etc.
c. **source** *n.*	the thing, place, or person you get something from
d. **source** *n.*	the cause of a problem, or the place where a problem starts
e. **target** *n.*	an aim or a result that you try to achieve
f. **target** *n.*	a person, place, or thing that is chosen to be reached or attacked

_____ 1. The **source** of this bottled water is Poland Springs, Maine.

_____ 2. Christopher tried to throw a paper ball into the trash can, but he missed his **target** and hit his geometry teacher.

_____ 3. A **highlight** of Ray's visit to Hawaii was surfing at Sunset Beach.

_____ 4. Our **target** is a profit of $50,000.

_____ 5. My biochemistry class is the **source** of a lot of stress for me.

_____ 6. The conference will **highlight** strategies for peaceful co-existence.

WORDS IN SENTENCES

Complete each sentence with one of the words from the box.

| assess | contemporaries | neutral | retain | target |
| ceases | highlighted | ratio | sources | theory |

1. At the end of the essay, you list the _____ from which you found your information.

2. An inspector came to _____ the damage to the house caused by the hurricane.

3. I like soup and I like salad, so I don't care which we eat; I'm _____.

4. The _____ of animals to humans on the farm is 10:1.

5. Both Louis Armstrong and Ella Fitzgerald were famous jazz vocalists. Because they both performed between the 1930s and 1960s, they were _____.

6. To _____ new vocabulary, Jeff tries to use two or three new words every day.

7. Carrie _____ an important formula in her math book with a pink marker.

8. When there _____ to be any oil left on Earth, people may need to use solar energy.

9. The news report revealed that cigarette companies wanted to _____ young teenagers with their advertising.

10. Explorers in the fifteenth century disproved the popular _____ that the world was flat.

WORDS IN COLLOCATIONS AND EXPRESSIONS

Following are common collocations and expressions with some of the key words. Read the definitions and then complete the conversations with the collocations and expressions. You may have to change word forms for correct grammar.

1. **assess**
   - **assess what (verb)** — to judge carefully

2. **neutral**
   - **a neutral color** — a color such as brown or gray that is not strong or bright

3. **ratio**
   - **ratio of (sth) to (sth)** — the relationship of the amount of one thing to another

4. **source**
   - **source of (sth)** — the place where a problem starts

5. **theory**
   - **in theory** — said about something that should be true, but may not actually be true
   - **theoretically speaking** — speaking about a situation that could exist but does not exist

1. PET STORE OWNER: _____, there should be an equal number of cats and dogs in this town, but we sell a lot more dog food than cat food. Did your survey of our customers explain anything?

   MARKETING RESEARCHER: Yes. My findings correspond to your sales. According to my survey of pet owners, the _____ dogs _____ cats is 2:1 in this town.

2. SISTER 1: Why don't you ever wear pink or red?

   SISTER 2: I prefer _____. They look better on me.

3. BASKETBALL PLAYER: I can't believe we lost the game!

   COACH: There's no need to yell. Let's talk about this rationally and _____ went wrong.

4. WIFE: Are you sure you want to destroy our credit cards?

   HUSBAND: Yes. They are the _____ all our financial problems.

5. LINGUISTICS PROFESSOR: Esperanto is a simple language that linguists created to improve global communication.

   STUDENT: Why don't more people speak Esperanto?

   LINGUISTICS PROFESSOR: _____, Esperanto is a good idea. However, most people don't have the patience to learn a language that has no native speakers.

Read this article about American history. Complete it with words from the boxes.

cease	contemporary	ratio	source	theory

EVIDENCE OF SIXTEENTH-CENTURY SPANISH FORT IN NORTH CAROLINA?

A long-standing theory says that more than four centuries ago Spanish explorers arrived in the foothills of what is now North Carolina. They stayed long enough to possibly change the course of European settlement in the New World, then disappeared into the fog of time.

Until recently, historians regarded a sixteenth-century Spanish presence this far north as more _____ than fact. But archaeologists working in a farm field near the tiny community of
1
Worry Crossroads might change that perception.

Combining detective work with old-fashioned digging, the team may have unearthed evidence that Spanish soldiers did indeed explore the Appalachian Mountains. The researchers think they've found the site of Fort San Juan, where Spanish explorers reportedly stayed from 1566 to 1568. The outpost was near the American Indian village of Joara, about fifty miles (eighty kilometers) east of the _____ town of Asheville.
2

Although the Spaniards' stay in western North Carolina would have been brief—about eighteen months—it would have been long enough to be the _____ of dramatic influence on
3
American history. Scholars think the Spanish may have brought diseases to the area, such as smallpox, which killed many Native Americans.

The great decline of Indian populations created a lower _____ of Native Americans
4
to British settlers. Combined with the Spaniards' decision to _____ living at Fort San
5
Juan and several other settlements, this may have helped England's later colonization efforts.

assessed	highlighted	retain	target

English settlers tried and failed to establish a colony in 1587 on Roanoke Island on the coast of North Carolina. They were later able to _____ their first permanent settlement in
6
Jamestown, Virginia, in 1607.

A team of researchers has spent decades looking for clues about sixteenth-century Spanish trips into North America and has _____ how those expeditions may have affected Native
7
Americans. They knew that the Spanish liked to build forts near Indian villages, where they could obtain food. The team thought there were several Indian villages that might have attracted the explorers.

Then they discovered an account by Juan de la Vandera, a writer on the Pardo expedition who told the story of Pardo's attempt in 1566 to find a route from the Spanish port of Santa Elena (now Parris Island, South Carolina) to the Spanish gold mines in Mexico.

The scholars compared de la Vandera's account with what they already knew about sixteenth-century Native Americans in the area and created a theory about where the Spaniards went and where Indian villages may have been. Still, it was only a theory.

Then in the early 1980s Robin Beck, a student, showed some artifacts he'd found near Worry Crossroads to the scholars. Charles Hudson, who wrote a book about Pardo's expedition, wondered if Beck had found the location of the Indian village of Joara. If he had, a Spanish fort might have been nearby. This area became the _____ of their research.
8

The theory became more believable when archaeologists discovered the remains of four buildings in the nearby field that were likely to have been part of Fort San Juan. They also found artifacts that the Spaniards would have been unlikely to trade, such as bullets, nails, and small brass clothing items.

Hudson said that the evidence of the Spanish presence is "not very spectacular stuff," but he doesn't think there's any other way these artifacts could have been found in the North Carolina foothills. Hudson said he and his colleagues have "advanced the first sustained argument" for the existence of Fort San Juan.

The finds also _____ the need for future research in the area. This past summer of
9
2004 was the fourth season for the excavation at Worry Crossroads. The National Geographic Society funded the latest dig, during which evidence of a fifth building from the old fort was apparently discovered. The archaeologists were to resume their work the next summer.

(Adapted from "Evidence of 16th-Century Spanish Fort in Appalachia"? National Geographic News, November 22, 2004.)

▌WORDS IN DISCUSSION

Apply the key words to your own life. Read and discuss each question in small groups. Try to use the key words.

1. **neutral**

   A neutral color I sometimes wear: _____

   A subject about which I have neutral feelings: _____

2. **highlight**

   How often I highlight information in books: _____

   The highlight of my life in the past year: _____

3. **source**

   The source of my interest in the English language: _____

   The source of my motivation and strength: _____

4. **contemporary**

What I think about contemporary television shows: _____

A contemporary leader whom I'd like to meet: _____

5. **ratio**

The ratio of males to females in my family: _____

The ratio of work to fun in my life: _____

6. **theory**

How often I think of new theories: _____

A theory I have about life: _____

7. **retain**

How I best retain new vocabulary: _____

How I can retain my money: _____

8. **target**

A problem I wish my government would target: _____

A target that I have thrown a ball at: _____

9. **assess**

How I assess clothing that I might buy: _____

Someone I know who is good at assessing people: _____

10. **cease**

The year in which I will cease studying English: _____

Someone that never ceases to amaze me: _____

▌WORDS IN WRITING

Choose two topics and write a short paragraph on each. Try to use the key words.

1. How were you **assessed** in school as a child? Do you feel that this method was effective, or can you think of a better method of **assessment**?

2. Describe a **theory** that interests you.

3. Describe a topic you find it difficult to be **neutral** about.

4. When undeveloped land **ceases** to exist on Earth, should humans search for a new **source** of land in space? Explain why or why not.

5. What **contemporary** artist or musician would you most like to have dinner with? Explain why.

Key Words

adequate	demonstrate	indicate	relevant	transform
clarify	equivalent	potential	stable	utilize

▌ WORDS IN CONTEXT

*Use the sentences to guess what each key word means. Choose the meaning that is closest to that of the key word in **bold**.*

1. **adequate**
   /ˈædəkwɪt/
   -adjective

   • Because Vivek didn't get an **adequate** amount of sleep, he fell asleep during his English class.
   • How many pizzas are **adequate** to feed six hungry teenagers?

   Adequate means . . .   a. small   b. enough   c. important

2. **clarify**
   /ˈklærəˌfaɪ/
   -verb

   • Professor Edmonton found Jared's essay confusing, so she asked him to **clarify** his main argument.
   • Thank you for **clarifying** your ideas; now I understand.

   Clarify means . . .   a. to make something clear   b. to confuse   c. to talk about

3. **demonstrate**
   /ˈdɛmənˌstreɪt/
   -verb

   • The young players watched as the soccer coach **demonstrated** how to kick the ball.
   • We followed Tatiana into the kitchen and watched as she **demonstrated** how to make chicken noodle soup.

   Demonstrate means . . .   a. to show how to do something   b. to ask questions   c. to find a way

4. **equivalent**
   /ɪˈkwɪvələnt/
   -adjective

   • Two quarters are **equivalent** to 50 cents.
   • 32 degrees Fahrenheit is **equivalent** to 0 degrees Celsius.

   Equivalent means . . .   a. different   b. less   c. equal

5. **indicate**
   /ˈɪndəˌkeɪt/
   -verb

   • Black clouds **indicate** that it is going to rain.
   • The fuel light on my dashboard **indicates** when I need to get gasoline.

   Indicate means . . .   a. to show   b. to water   c. to hide

6. **potential**
   /pəˈtɛnʃəl/
   -adjective

   • Our company should advertise to teenagers; they do not buy our products now, but they are **potential** customers.
   • The project has been successful; there are some **potential** problems, but we know we can prevent them.

   Potential means . . .   a. unlikely   b. now   c. likely to develop

7. relevant
/ˈrɛləvənt/
-adjective

- Matteo needs excellent English to enter a good university; studying English is **relevant** to his plans for the future.
- When Kelsey asked the math teacher about his shirt during the lecture, the teacher said, "I have time only for questions that are **relevant** to mathematics."

Relevant means . . .   a. directly related   b. challenging   c. not important

8. stable
/ˈsteɪbəl/
-adjective

- Usually children don't like too much change; they like to be in a **stable** environment.
- If you sit on a chair that is not **stable**, you might fall on the floor.

Stable means . . .   a. new   b. exciting   c. strong and steady

9. transform
/trænsˈfɔrm/
-verb

- Ricardo **transformed** his life by moving to New York and becoming a professional singer.
- If we had $500 to buy new paint and furniture, we could **transform** this old room into a beautiful place.

Transform means . . .   a. to change completely b. to remain the same   c. to enjoy

10. utilize
/ˈyutḷˌaɪz/
-verb

- In her new job, Marta is **utilizing** her French and her Spanish skills.
- What tools would you **utilize** if you were going to build a house?

Utilize means . . .   a. to buy   b. to use   c. to have

WORDS AND DEFINITIONS

Read each definition and write the word it defines on the line.

1. _____ to change the appearance, character, etc. of someone or something completely, especially in a good way

2. _____ enough in quantity or of a good enough quality for a particular purpose

3. _____ to show or suggest something

4. _____ likely to develop into a particular type of person or thing in the future

5. _____ equal in value, purpose, rank, etc. to something or someone else

6. _____ to show or describe how to use or do something

7. _____ directly relating to the subject or problem being discussed

8. _____ strong, steady and not likely to move or change

9. _____ to use something

10. _____ to make something clear and easier to understand by explaining it in more detail

COMPREHENSION CHECK

Choose the best answer.

1. What is **equivalent** to a year?
   a. six months
   b. twelve months
   c. twelve days

2. Which of the following activities is probably **relevant** for an athlete who is training for the World Cup?
   a. sending e-mail
   b. eating pastries
   c. exercising

3. How can Bill **demonstrate** that he is well qualified for the new job?
   a. He can smile.
   b. He can explain how he was successful at a similar job.
   c. He won't be on time.

4. If a person's personality is **stable**, it
   a. changes wildly.
   b. is weak.
   c. is steady and remains the same.

5. Which of the following is a **potential** problem for Juan, who has just moved to the United States?
   a. He might learn how to play American football.
   b. He could learn English quickly.
   c. He might get homesick.

6. New flowers growing in a garden **indicate** that
   a. spring is beginning.
   b. the soil is dry.
   c. it is difficult to grow flowers.

7. Which CANNOT be **clarified**?
   a. an explanation
   b. an answer
   c. a pet

8. If a building has been **transformed**, it
   a. has had minor changes.
   b. has been destroyed.
   c. has changed greatly.

9. Which does a musician **utilize**?
   a. a hammer
   b. an instrument
   c. a calculator

10. Which piece of clothing is **adequate** protection for a person who is walking in a snowy forest?
    a. a T-shirt
    b. a sweater
    c. a warm coat

WORD FAMILIES

Now that you have studied the ten key words and their basic definitions, you are ready to learn words that belong to the same family as some of the key words. A word family includes words that look alike but have different functions (noun, verb, adjective, or adverb). Their meanings are related but different.

A. Look at each model phrase and decide whether the word in **bold** is used as a noun, verb, adjective, or adverb. Put a check (✓) in the correct column.

	NOUN	VERB	ADJECTIVE	ADVERB
1. **clarify**				
• **clarify** my suggestion				
• ask for **clarification**				
2. **demonstrate**				
• **demonstrate** how to cook				
• another **demonstration**				
3. **indicate**				
• what it **indicates**				
• a clear **indication**				
4. **potential**				
• **potential** boyfriend				
• the **potential** for change				
5. **relevant**				
• a **relevant** idea				
• explain the **relevance**				
• an **irrelevant** question				
6. **stable**				
• a **stable** job				
• a need for **stability**				
7. **transform**				
• **transform** a town				
• a remarkable **transformation**				

B. Ken is talking with his boss. Complete their conversation with words from the box.

clarification	indication	potential	stability
demonstration	irrelevant	relevant	transformation

KEN: I wish you'd given me a(n) _____ that you were unhappy with my job performance before you fired me! **1**

KEN'S BOSS: I gave you plenty of indications that I was unhappy. Every time you were late, I commented on it. You haven't gotten a promotion. That was a clear
_____ of my dissatisfaction.
2

KEN:	Maybe I was late a few times. I'm sorry, but is that really a good reason to fire me? I need some more _____ about what went wrong.
	3
KEN'S BOSS:	What went wrong is _____ now.
	4
KEN:	I disagree. It's very _____ to me! I need to know what the problem was!
	5
KEN'S BOSS:	You are lazy, slow, and difficult to work with. Until you change, you will never find job _____.
	6
KEN:	Am I really so difficult? If you let me keep my job, I'll have a complete _____. I'll become a star employee.
	7
KEN'S BOSS:	I'm sorry, but I don't think you have the _____ to be a star. I'm sorry, Ken. You're fired.
	8

▌ SAME WORD, DIFFERENT MEANING

*Most words have more than one meaning. Study the additional meanings of **adequate**, **demonstrate**, and **potential**. Then read each sentence and decide which meaning is used.*

a. **adequate** *adj.*	enough in quantity or of a good enough quality for a particular purpose
b. **adequate** *adj.*	fairly good but not excellent
c. **demonstrate** *v.*	to show or describe how to use or do something
d. **demonstrate** *v.*	to prove something clearly
e. **potential** *adj.*	likely to develop into a particular type of person or thing in the future
f. **potential** *n.*	a natural ability that could develop to make you very good at something

_____ 1. Ahmed's writing is **adequate**, but Gloria's is truly excellent; that's why his story received a B and hers got an A.

_____ 2. Watch me carefully. I am going to **demonstrate** how to feed a dolphin.

_____ 3. Meg was thrilled when her voice teacher said, "You have the **potential** to become a great singer."

_____ 4. I don't need another bottle of water. One is **adequate**.

_____ 5. I have an interview for a **potential** job tomorrow.

_____ 6. This experiment **demonstrates** that dogs can make conscious decisions.

WORDS IN SENTENCES

Complete each sentence with one of the words from the box.

adequate	demonstrate	indication	relevance	transform
clarification	equivalent	potential	stable	utilize

1. Because Nora has the _____ to be a successful businesswoman, she was accepted into the MBA program.

2. Before skydiving, the instructor will _____ how to open your parachute.

3. Twelve is _____ to a dozen.

4. It is important to build a house on _____ ground.

5. I understood the _____ of improving my vocabulary when I didn't understand everyone in my new office.

6. Micca asked his professor for _____ when he didn't understand part of the lecture.

7. Tom does _____ work, but he is not our best employee.

8. The good test results are a(n) _____ that the students were well prepared.

9. New businesses could _____ this neighborhood.

10. We can _____ new software to improve our business.

WORDS IN COLLOCATIONS AND EXPRESSIONS

Following are common collocations and expressions with some of the key words. Read the definitions and then complete the conversations with the collocations and expressions. You may have to change word forms for correct grammar.

1. **adequate**
   - **an adequate amount of time**   enough time to do something

2. **demonstrate**
   - **a political demonstration**   an event at which a lot of people meet to protest or support something political in public

3. **potential**
   - **potential for growth**   probability that something will grow

4. **relevant**
   - **a relevant question**   a question that relates to the topic being discussed

5. **stable**
   - **a stable relationship**   a peaceful relationship that you can trust will continue

6. **transform**
   - **a complete transformation**   a complete change in appearance or character, especially for the better

1.   **MOTHER:**   *(knocking on bathroom door)* Elizabeth, hurry up! We're going to be late.

     ELIZABETH: I need ten more minutes!

     MOTHER: But you've been getting ready for half an hour! That's _____ to prepare for a party.

     ELIZABETH: Are you kidding? I need at least an hour!

2.   **HARRY:**   Joe, is that you?

     JOE: Hello, Harry! What a surprise to see you here on Wall Street. The last time I saw you was at _____ in the 1960s. Are you a banker now, too?

     HARRY: Yes. Wow, I almost didn't recognize you! You have had _____.

     JOE: It's true. I lost fifty pounds, cut my long hair, and grew a moustache.

3.   **MARIA:**   How can I say "hello" in Chinese?

     ENGLISH TEACHER: That is not _____. This is an English lesson, Maria, not a Chinese class! Please focus on your English.

4.   **JESSICA:**   How is everything going with your girlfriend, Ben?

     BEN: Great. We've been together for two years now.

     JESSICA: It's wonderful to see that you are in _____.

5.   **BUSINESSMAN:**   Why should we buy that company? It's not very important.

     BUSINESSWOMAN: It's small now, but I think that could change. The company has real _____.

▌ WORDS IN A READING

Read this article about becoming a DJ. Complete it with words from the boxes.

adequate	demonstrated	equivalent	potential	relevant

DJ ACADEMY

Scratch DJ Academy in Greenwich Village offers a one-week program called DJ 101 to music lovers who believe they have the _____ to become DJs.
₁

Most DJs still learn their business informally, by watching other DJs in nightclubs and practicing on their own. Demonstrating one's abilities is usually _____ for landing a job at a small
₂
club. However, more and more people are learning how to DJ in classrooms. The University of California, Berkeley, started offering student-led DJ'ing courses in 1998, and in 2004 Berklee College of Music in Boston began offering formal instruction, too.

No one who has ever watched a DJ at work would be surprised by the seriousness of Scratch DJ Academy. Here, students learn through practical advice, music lab time, and _____
₃

homework assignments. They also benefit from guest lectures by famous DJs like Grandwizzard Theodore. Having Grandwizzard stop by your DJ lesson is the _____ of having Bill Gates stop by your computer class.

4

The first day of lessons at Scratch DJ Academy was devoted to the equipment, but Tuesday involved a bit of music theory: DJ Damage _____ how to count.

5

The students gathered around Damage's workstation, nodding their heads and saying, "1-2-3-4, 2-2-3-4," while out of the speakers came rap music. Damage was training his class to find the "one"—the downbeat—on any record, and soon the pupils were back at their workstations, learning how to stop a record exactly on the downbeat, pulling it slowly back and forth under the needle, listening for that dry, wooshing sound of a drum in slow motion.

clarify	indicates	stable	transform	utilize

While interest in becoming a DJ is growing, it's difficult to _____ what, exactly, a DJ is. Most serious DJs still use turntables to spin vinyl records, but some now _____ DJ-friendly CD and MP3 players, which are often built to resemble traditional turntables. Mixtape DJs can splice together tracks on a computer. Radio DJs often just talk; someone else spins. And at a typical house party, the DJ is often a laptop in the corner.

6

7

The popularity of Scratch DJ Academy _____ that the school's success will continue to grow. Not everyone who goes to DJ 101 will find (a) _____ job working as a DJ; nor can the class _____ a complete beginner into a professional DJ in one week. However, the class teaches all learners the basics of being a DJ and makes every student a better listener.

8

9

10

(Adapted from "Spin Doctorate: Learning How to be a DJ," The New York Times, August 8, 2004.)

WORDS IN DISCUSSION

Apply the key words to your own life. Read and discuss each question in small groups. Try to use the key words.

1. **utilize**

   Something I utilize every day: _____

   Something I hope to utilize soon: _____

2. **adequate**

   Something that is adequate in my life but not perfect: _____

   An adequate yearly salary for my next job would be $_____

3. **transform**

   Something in my life I want to transform: _____

   Someone I know who had a complete transformation: _____

4. **indicate**

My body indicates that it is hungry by _____

When I want to indicate that it's time for my guests to go home, I _____

5. **clarify**

How often I wish my teachers would clarify what they say : _____

How easy it is for me to clarify my main ideas when I write: _____

6. **potential**

Something I have the potential to be: _____

Something I wish I had the potential to be: _____

7. **stable**

If I had to choose between a stable but boring job and an exciting but unstable job, I'd choose

_____

The most important time of life for me to feel stable: _____

8. **relevant**

Something I have to do that is not relevant to my goals: _____

Something I do that is really relevant to my hopes and dreams: _____

9. **equivalent**

If you ask me if time is equivalent to money, I'll tell you _____

In my opinion, one hour of my free time is equivalent to $_____

10. **demonstrate**

Something I am good at and can demonstrate how to do: _____

By the way I live my life, I demonstrate to others that I am _____

▌WORDS IN WRITING

Choose two topics and write a paragraph on each. Try to use the key words.

1. In your opinion, what do bad grades **indicate** about a student?

2. If your home could have a complete **transformation**, would you want it? If yes, how would you change it?

3. April 1, also known as April Fools Day, is a fun holiday in the United States. On this day, people try to fool each other by telling funny lies. Do you have an **equivalent** holiday in your native country? If so, describe this holiday.

4. Who do you believe has the **potential** to change the world? This person might be a friend or a famous person. Explain why this person is special.

5. Is it as important for you to have a **stable** job as it is to have a **stable** family? Explain.

WORDS IN CONTEXT

*Use the sentences to guess what each key word means. Choose the meaning that is closest to that of the key word in **bold**.*

1. **assure**
   /əˈʃʊr/
   -verb

   - The salesman **assured** us that the necklace was real 14K gold.
   - When Cecilia's boss was not satisfied with her work, she **assured** him that she would work harder.

   Assure means . . .   a. to promise that something is true   b. to tell a lie   c. to make someone worry

2. **compatible**
   /kəmˈpæt̬ əbəl/
   -adjective

   - Laura was neat and quiet, but her roommate was messy and loud. Because they were not **compatible**, Laura decided to move.
   - The software that we use is **compatible** with both PCs and Macintosh computers.

   Compatible means . . .   a. having the same family   b. able to exist together without problems   c. costing a lot of money

3. **core**
   /kɔr/
   -noun

   - London is England's **core** of business.
   - The recipe called for five apples with their **cores** removed.

   Core means . . .   a. the most important or central part of something   b. the outside of something   c. the least important part of something

4. **enhance**
   /ɪnˈhæns/
   -verb

   - Add a pinch of salt to the pasta to **enhance** the flavor.
   - Planting flowers by the road would **enhance** the island's beauty.

   Enhance means . . .   a. to quickly change   b. to complicate   c. to make something better

5. **inevitable**
   /ɪˈnɛvət̬əbəl/
   -adjective

   - There are many things in life that we can avoid, but death and taxes are **inevitable**.
   - If you spend your entire life in a country, it is **inevitable** that you will learn the language.

   Inevitable means . . .   a. possible   b. impossible   c. certain to happen

6. interact
/ˌɪntəˈrækt/
-verb

- Jordan watched his daughter closely on the playground to see how she would **interact** with the other children.
- My aunt is a social person. She likes to **interact** with her coworkers.

Interact means . . .   a. to work alone   b. to talk to people and   c. to play
                                                     work with them

7. manual
/ˈmænyuəl/
-adjective

- On the farm, there is a lot of **manual** work, such as collecting eggs and picking fruit.
- Do you prefer to use a car with a **manual** transmission, in which you shift gears with a stick, or a car with an automatic transmission?

Manual means . . .   a. necessary   b. involving the use of   c. related to the mind
                                                     the hands

8. proceed
/prəˈsid, prou-/
-verb

- After the train stopped in Montreal, it **proceeded** to Quebec City.
- After complaining about the temperature of their room, the Smiths **proceeded** to tell the front desk clerk about the strange smell.

Proceed means . . .   a. to stop doing   b. to continue to do   c. to go back to doing
                             something or stop   something or do   something
                             going somewhere   something next

9. specify
/ˈspɛsəˌfaɪ/
-verb

- Burak is very careful with his money, so he asked his travel agent to **specify** the cost of each part of the trip.
- When I ordered a new dress on the Internet, I **specified** the color and size I wanted.

Specify means . . .   a. to state something   b. to guess   c. to state something in a
                             approximately   specific way

10. welfare
/ˈwɛlfɛr/
-noun

- Many people used to live on the government's money, but since the welfare reform bill was passed ten years ago, the number of people on **welfare** has gone down by half.
- Amanda was happy to go back to work when she recovered from her illness; she had not liked living on **welfare**.

Welfare means . . .   a. money a person wins b. stolen money   c. money paid by the
                             in the lottery   government to people
                                                                                      who are very poor

▌WORDS AND DEFINITIONS

Read each definition and write the word it defines on the line.

1. _____ the central or most important part of something

2. _____ to talk to other people and work together with them

3. _____ certain to happen and impossible to avoid

4. _____ to state something in a detailed and exact way

5. _____ involving the use of the hands

6. _____ to make someone feel less worried by promising that something is definitely true

7. _____ to make something better

8. _____ money paid by the government to people who are very poor or not working

9. _____ able to exist together or be used together without causing problems

10. _____ to continue to do something or do something next

▍COMPREHENSION CHECK

Choose the best answer.

1. Who is **interacting**?
   a. Bob is watching TV.
   b. Tracy and her husband are in different rooms.
   c. Sara and Kyle are chatting at a party.

2. Which is **inevitable**?
   a. The sun will set tonight.
   b. You will win the lottery tomorrow.
   c. You will spend a lot of money today.

3. Which situation does NOT relate to the meaning of **core**?
   a. Betty cut out the center of the apples while making the pie.
   b. A small team of important workers is responsible for the business's success.
   c. Greg decided that he wanted to live in the suburbs, outside the city.

4. Who is **assuring** someone?
   a. "Can I trust you?"
   b. "I am a responsible babysitter, and your kids will be safe with me."
   c. "I think this canoe may have a hole. Prepare yourself to sink."

5. If you ask someone to **specify** something, what do you want?
   a. exact details
   b. the general idea
   c. a guess

6. What CANNOT be used to **enhance** a room?
   a. new furniture
   b. flowers
   c. garbage

7. Amy's hairdryer from the United States is not **compatible** with the electrical system in England, so
   a. she can use it in England.
   b. it is exactly the same as English hairdryers.
   c. the hairdryer will not work if she plugs it into an outlet in England.

8. What kind of people CANNOT receive **welfare** from the government?
   a. the poor
   b. the wealthy
   c. the unemployed

9. If your boss tells you to **proceed** with a project, what does he mean?
   a. continue
   b. take a break
   c. stop

10. Which is a **manual** job?
    a. house cleaner
    b. lawyer
    c. teacher

WORD FAMILIES

Now that you have studied the ten key words and their basic definitions, you are ready to learn words that belong to the same family as some of the key words. A word family includes words that look alike but have different functions (noun, verb, adjective, or adverb). Their meanings are related but different.

A. *Look at each model phrase and decide whether the word in* **bold** *is used as a noun, verb, adjective, or adverb. Put a check (✓) in the correct column.*

	NOUN	VERB	ADJECTIVE	ADVERB
1. **assure**				
• completely **assure** you				
• quality **assurance**				
2. **compatible**				
• not **compatible** with				
• our **compatibility**				
3. **enhance**				
• **enhance** this product				
• significant **enhancements**				
4. **inevitable**				
• an **inevitable** result				
• **inevitably**, I was late				
5. **interact**				
• **interact** well				
• study the **interaction**				
6. **specify**				
• **specify** the time and place				
• give **specific** instructions				
• **specifically** for this purpose				

B. *Read the first half of each sentence and match it with the appropriate ending.*

_____ 1. There isn't much

_____ 2. Jairo knew he'd get a vegetarian meal on the flight because

_____ 3. After eating ice cream every night for two weeks

_____ 4. A strong message in the new marketing campaign is quality

_____ 5. Commuters will appreciate the

_____ 6. Luxury cars are wired for

_____ 7. Please tell me

a. **assurance**.

b. I **inevitably** gained weight.

c. **compatibility** with a range of computers, MP3s, and navigational systems.

d. **interaction** between the biology teacher and her students.

e. he'd made a **specific** request for one.

f. what happened, **specifically**, after you got home.

g. **enhancement** of the subway system.

SAME WORD, DIFFERENT MEANING

Most words have more than one meaning. Study the additional meanings of **interact**, **manual**, and **welfare**.
Then read each sentence and decide which meaning is used.

a.	**interact** v.	to talk to other people and work together with them
b.	**interact** v.	if two things interact, they have an effect on each other
c.	**manual** adj.	involving the use of the hands
d.	**manual** n.	instruction book
e.	**welfare** n.	money paid by the government to people who are very poor or not working
f.	**welfare** n.	a person's health, comfort, and happiness

_____ 1. The chemicals were combined to see how they would **interact**.

_____ 2. The government is working to reform the **welfare** system.

_____ 3. Yoon didn't understand how to use his new stereo, so he read the **manual**.

_____ 4. Ruth called her elderly neighbor because she was concerned about the old man's **welfare**.

_____ 5. Because Matt lives in a diverse neighborhood, he often **interacts** with people from different backgrounds.

_____ 6. The construction workers were exhausted after a day of hard **manual** labor.

WORDS IN SENTENCES

Complete each sentence with two of the words from the box.

assured	core	inevitable	manual	specifies
compatible	enhance	interact	proceed	welfare

1. Dr. Taylor _____ Mrs. Smith that the medication was very safe, so she agreed to _____ with the treatment.

2. If you are familiar with the way teenage boys _____, you know that it is _____ that they will fight once in a while.

3. Creating jobs to reduce the number of people on _____ was the _____ of the candidate's campaign message.

4. Let's check the _____ to see if this lens is _____ with our camera.

5. The recipe _____ the use of dark chocolate to _____ the flavor of the peppers.

WORDS IN COLLOCATIONS AND EXPRESSIONS

Following are common collocations and expressions with some of the key words. Read the definitions and then complete the conversation with the collocations and expressions. You may have to change word forms for correct grammar.

1. **assure**
   - **I can assure you (that)**   I can promise you (that)

2. **compatible**
   - **be compatible with**   able to be together without problems

3. **core**
   - **rotten to the core**   completely bad

4. **proceed**
   - **proceed to (do sth)**   to continue to do something or do something next

5. **specify**
   - **specify what**   to say exactly what

6. **welfare**
   - **on welfare**   receiving money from the government because you are unable to work

JULIE: I'm really worried about my future, Professor. I recently read about a starving artist who had to go _____ **1** to pay her bills. Do you think I will be able to make a living by selling my paintings?

ART PROFESSOR: Your paintings are beautiful, Julie, but they're not at a professional level yet.

JULIE: I want to be a professional artist. That's all I want to be. Could you _____ **2** I should change in my art to improve it?

ART PROFESSOR: For starters, you could enhance your colors. They're a bit too soft. If you _____ **3** paint in quiet pastels, no one is going to pay a lot of attention to your work. Try bolder colors. Why not talk to Jeff Kimball about his paintings? He uses color very well.

JULIE: _____ **4** I don't need advice from Jeff. He yells at everyone; he's mean and nasty. I think he's _____ **5** .

ART PROFESSOR: It's easy to criticize other people. It's more difficult to criticize your own work. Are you ready to do that?

JULIE: Well, I guess so. I need to sell my paintings for a lot of money, so I should do everything I can to improve. My dream is to be successful and buy a big house.

ART PROFESSOR: Unfortunately, expensive tastes _____ **6** the life of an artist. Most successful artists are not rich. My advice for you is to worry less about money now and focus on the quality of your art.

Read the article about lifestyle. Complete it with words from the boxes.

interact	manual	proceeded	welfare

TWO HOUSES, TWO VISIONS

Two contrasting images of the American home of the future were on display last week at the annual home builders' trade show in Orlando, which drew a record 105,000 attendees, including builders, architects, interior designers, and numerous curious homeowners.

The showcase house that is the center of the National Association of Home Builders show is called the New American Home 2006. The luxurious house is where housing products manufacturers display the latest and greatest in home fittings and fixtures, including side-shooting showers, two poolside fireplaces, a barbecue kitchen on the patio, room-size walk-in closets, a massage room, a pet alcove, four staircases, and an elevator. To live in such a house, a person would need an instruction _____ .
                        1

A sharply different portrait of the modern American lifestyle was visible outside the convention center, resting on a temporary foundation in a parking lot near the main convention building. It was a small, inexpensive cottage, simple and compact. Its little porch looked out to the street so that residents could sit on benches and _____ with passersby.
                                            2

The two houses spoke to different worlds, as well as different wallets. At 7,100 square feet, the New American Home dwarfs many American houses, though not as much as it once would have. Now even the houses of fairly ordinary Americans have grown noticeably. In 1950, the average new single-family house was 983 square feet; in 2005, the average new house was 2,349 square feet, even as family sizes have fallen.

The little yellow cottage in the parking lot was planned and built as a volunteer effort by architects, planners, home construction companies and appliance manufacturers, led by noted architect Andres Duany. These volunteers were concerned about the _____ of victims of Hurricane
                                                                          3
Katrina. They wanted to create a structure that could house very poor victims of natural disasters more attractively and affordably than many other kinds of manufactured housing. It was only 308 square feet, with one bedroom with four bunks, a thirty-square-foot bath, and a tiny kitchen. But a stream of visitors who _____ to visit, many of whom asked where they could purchase the house
                        4
themselves, made it clear that there is a strong market for such a house at a time when soaring prices have made homes unaffordable for moderate-income people in many parts of the country.

"I like to simplify my life and think about what's really necessary," said Jason Spellings of Jackson, Mississippi who built the small house. "Everybody coming through wants a house like this."

The designers described the house as a way people who are in difficult circumstances could live modestly but affordably and one day expand the house, making it a little larger as their finances improve. Various designs would allow homeowners to _____ the house by adding a

5

room or two, bringing the size up to perhaps 800 square feet. The designers _____

6

visitors that this is a permanent house, not a temporary mobile home of the kind used to house people cheaply for short periods of time.

"It's an adorable little house that everyone wanted to hug," said Marianne Casuto, the house's designer. She has designed it in a way that will allow the plan to be adapted to the local architectural styles in various regions. The roof, outward-facing porch, and bright yellow color were meant to be

_____ with traditional Mississippi Gulf Coast architectural styles. Casuto hopes builders

7

will use the model, whose plans will be available soon, to re-create houses that fit into the local landscape rather than copy the boring styles of many suburbs.

Conflicting visions of American life were apparent at the show in other ways, as well. For example, with energy prices rising, products that save consumers money on electricity or heating bills drew a lot of attention.

The New American Home is the first National Association of Home Builders showcase house to be a certified green home, meaning that it meets the _____ standards of environmental

8

friendliness. Among the energy-saving features are double-paned glass doors to reduce solar heat in the summer.

But even as they seek ways to save energy, Americans are looking at new ways to use it, as well. Even at a time of rising energy costs, it's _____; consumers are looking to buy more

9

products that consume electricity in new ways. So it all goes back to the _____ question:

10

Is less more, or is more, well, more?

(Adapted from "Two Houses, Two Visions," Washington Post, January 21, 2006.)

Read the questions and choose the best answers. Then discuss your answers in small groups.

1. Would you marry a person whom you loved deeply but were not **compatible** with?

   a. Yes, I would. I can't give up true love. I don't care if we have problems living together.

   b. I would date this person, but I would not marry her or him.

   c. No, I wouldn't. Love is not enough. I don't want to fight a lot with the person I marry.

2. Do you believe that it's **inevitable** that your English will be excellent?

   a. Yes, I am certain that my English will be excellent.

   b. I think it's probable, but not inevitable, that my English will be excellent.

   c. No, my English won't ever be excellent.

3. Which do you most want to **enhance**?

   a. my home

   b. my body

   c. my skills

4. Are you good at **manual** labor?

   a. No, I'm better at mental work.

   b. I am good at both mental and manual labor.

   c. Yes, I like working with my hands.

5. If it began raining when you had just begun a picnic, would you **proceed**?

   a. Yes. A little rain wouldn't ruin my fun.

   b. Maybe. I'd get in my car and wait fifteen minutes to see if the rain passed.

   c. No. I would pack up my food and go home.

6. If you lost your job, would you go on **welfare**?

   a. Yes, I would. I deserve my government's money.

   b. I would only go on welfare if I were sick and physically unable to work.

   c. No, I wouldn't.

7. How many people have you **interacted** with today?

   a. none

   b. one or two

   c. several

8. If you were going to run for president, what would the **core** message of your campaign be?

   a. Save the environment.

   b. End war.

   c. Lower taxes.

9. Do you think that you should have to **specify** your nationality, age, and gender when you apply to college?

   a. Yes. I think exact details can help the university understand who I am.

   b. I don't have a problem with specifying these details, but I don't think it's necessary.

   c. No. I want the college to accept me for my mind and talents, nothing else.

10. If you were to express worry about your life, who could **assure** you that everything would be OK?

    a. a person in my family

    b. a friend

    c. another special person

WORDS IN WRITING

Choose two topics and write a paragraph on each. Try to use the key words.

1. Describe a person (real or imaginary) with whom you are truly **compatible**. Give **specific** details to explain your **compatibility**.

2. If a family member suggested some ideas about how you could **enhance** your appearance, how would you **proceed** with the conversation? Would your **interaction** be friendly or cold?

3. How effective is the **welfare** system in your native country? Explain.

4. Describe the **core** beliefs that you hope your children (or younger relatives) will have.

5. What **manual** jobs, if any, should be done by computers? Explain why.

QUIZ 2

PART A

Choose the word that best completes each item and write it in the space provided.

1. The city looks completely different now. It has had a(n) _____.
   - a. indication
   - b. transformation
   - c. demonstration
   - d. retention

2. Carpenters _____ tools.
   - a. target
   - b. cease
   - c. utilize
   - d. proceed

3. Children don't like constant change. They need a _____ environment.
   - a. stable
   - b. relevant
   - c. potential
   - d. contemporary

4. Rick's dog is not _____ with his new cat, so he has to give the cat to his cousin.
   - a. potential
   - b. adequate
   - c. compatible
   - d. specific

5. Carol is nervous about trying Korean pickled cabbage, *kimchi,* so Ji Sun is _____ her that it will taste delicious.
   - a. proceeding
   - b. assuring
   - c. assessing
   - d. interacting

6. The lecturer didn't see the _____ of John's question, so he said, "I'll only answer questions that relate to this topic."
   - a. welfare
   - b. relevance
   - c. ratio
   - d. enhancement

7. A basketball hoop is the _____ at which players aim the ball.
   - a. manual
   - b. theory
   - c. assessment
   - d. target

8. Good music can _____ your mood.
   - a. enhance
   - b. assess
   - c. cease
   - d. interact

9. One inch is _____ to 2.54 centimeters.
   - a. adequate
   - b. equivalent
   - c. neutral
   - d. stable

10. Julia doesn't want old-fashioned furniture. She prefers a(n) _____ style.
    - a. equivalent
    - b. contemporary
    - c. compatible
    - d. manual

PART B

*Read each statement and write **T** for* true *and **F** for* false *in the space provided.*

_____ 1. Universities want students who have the **potential** to succeed.

_____ 2. An **inevitable** occurrence may not happen.

_____ 3. A person on **welfare** gives extra money to the government.

_____ 4. At the end of a hockey game, the players **cease** playing.

_____ 5. If you want to fix a problem, you should understand its **source**.

_____ 6. Clouds **indicate** that it might rain.

_____ 7. The **core** of an apple is red, thin, and shiny.

_____ 8. Every **theory** has been proven.

_____ 9. A doctor who is fine but not excellent could be called **adequate**.

_____10. If there are twice as many girls as boys in the class, the **ratio** is 2:1.

PART C

Match each sentence with the letter it describes.

_____ 1. If you want your boss to **clarify** something, you say this.

_____ 2. You do this to **demonstrate** sleepiness.

_____ 3. These are **specific** instructions.

_____ 4. A **neutral** person says this.

_____ 5. This person **assesses** a building.

_____ 6. If Sara and Jen **proceed**, they do this.

_____ 7. This person **interacts** with everyone who enters the office.

_____ 8. While Marian is describing the **highlight** of her vacation, she says this.

_____ 9. If a firm does not **retain** its banker, it must do this.

_____10. This person does **manual** labor.

a. "That was amazing!"

b. hire someone new

c. a construction worker

d. yawn

e. "Can you explain that more clearly?"

f. real estate agent

g. continue

h. a receptionist

i. Turn left after the third stoplight.

j. "I don't care who wins."

WORDS IN CONTEXT

*Use the sentences to guess what each key word means. Choose the meaning that is closest to that of the key word in **bold**.*

1. **acknowledge**
/əkˈnɑlɪdʒ/
-verb

   • At the meeting, Roger **acknowledged** that it was his fault that the product had failed.

   • My fifteen-year-old sister refuses to **acknowledge** that she still has more to learn about life.

   Acknowledge means . . .
   a. to deny something   b. to admit that something is true   c. to discuss

2. **apparently**
/əˈpærəntˀli/
-adverb

   • **Apparently**, I was supposed to call you. I'm sorry. I didn't realize it.

   • **Apparently,** Lizzie is a great cook now. Can you believe it?

   Apparently means . . .
   a. based on what you've heard is true   b. strangely   c. thankfully

3. **conform**
/kənˈfɔrm/
-verb

   • Greg wanted to wear a red shirt, but the director told him that he had to **conform** and wear black like the rest of the chorus.

   • In high school, were you an individual, or did you feel pressure to **conform**?

   Conform means . . .   a. to behave in the way most people do   b. to be different and unique   c. to follow your own style

4. **eliminate**
/ɪˈlɪməˌneɪt/
-verb

   • The Browns want to **eliminate** the mice from their house, so they adopted five cats.

   • Would it be difficult for you to **eliminate** sugar from your diet?

   Eliminate means . . .   a. to increase the amount of something   b. to decrease the amount of something   c. to get rid of something completely

5. **function**
/ˈfʌŋkʃən/
-noun

   • The **function** of a glass is to hold liquid.

   • Dennis's **function** at work is to protect the national park.

   Function means . . .   a. purpose or job   b. where something happens   c. the way that something is built

6. **insight**
/ˈɪnsaɪt/
-noun

- Marta gained **insight** into Austrian culture when she spent six months in Vienna.
- Reading about the Middle East gave me some **insight** into world history.

Insight means . . .
a. the ability to understand clearly
b. weak judgment
c. entertainment

7. **justify**
/ˈdʒʌstəˌfaɪ/
-verb

- Helena **justified** spending $500 on clothes by explaining that she hadn't bought anything new for more than five years.
- Martin could not **justify** being late to work again.

Justify means . . .
a. to give a poor explanation for
b. to tell a happy story
c. to give an acceptable explanation for

8. **perspective**
/pɚˈspɛktɪv/
-noun

- The child psychologist interviewed dozens of children to get their **perspectives** on life.
- Artists have unique **perspectives** of the world.

Perspective means . . .
a. a way of speaking
b. a way of thinking; point of view
c. a way of moving

9. **proportion**
/prəˈpɔrʃən/
-noun

- A significant **proportion** of adults in the world cannot read.
- A large **proportion** of a whale's body is fat.

Proportion means . . .
a. a complete amount
b. a part of a larger amount
c. a small amount

10. **shift**
/ʃɪft/
-verb

- Truck drivers **shift** into a low gear when going up and down hills.
- Have your ideas about politics **shifted** during your life?

Shift means . . .
a. to remain in the same position
b. to change; to move
c. to lose your position; to forget

WORDS AND DEFINITIONS

Read each definition and write the word it defines on the line.

1. _____ a way of thinking about something, influenced by the kind of person you are or by your experiences

2. _____ to get rid of something completely

3. _____ to behave in the way most people do

4. _____ to change your opinion or attitude, or to move something from one place to another

5. _____ the usual purpose of a thing, or a job that someone or something does

6. _____ to accept or admit that something is true

7. _____ a part of a larger amount or number

8. _____ the ability to understand clearly

9. _____ based on what you have heard is true, although you are not completely sure about it

10. _____ to give an acceptable explanation for something, especially when other people think it is unreasonable

▌COMPREHENSION CHECK

Choose the best answer.

1. If Joe decides to **eliminate** cigarettes from his life, he
   a. buys several cartons of cigarettes.
   b. smokes only occasionally.
   c. throws away all his cigarettes and quits smoking.

2. What is the **function** of a candle?
   a. A candle is inexpensive.
   b. A candle is made of wax.
   c. A candle lights a room.

3. Who **conforms**?
   a. Brandon, who has purple hair
   b. Sue, who has the same backpack as her three best friends
   c. Vince, who is twenty-one and drives a car that was made in 1965

4. What CANNOT be **shifted**?
   a. a flexible person's opinion
   b. a stubborn person's opinion
   c. a gear stick in a car

5. Who is **acknowledging** something?
   a. Azar says she has not lost the race.
   b. Henry denies that he was a lazy student.
   c. Julie admits that she was late to work three times this week.

6. My brother and mom like to eat French fries. Dad and I don't. What **proportion** of my family likes French fries?
   a. 30%
   b. 1/2
   c. .75

7. In which statement is the person **justifying** his or her behavior?
   a. "I didn't steal the money!"
   b. "I took the money because my children were starving."
   c. "If you ask me one more time about the money, I will beat you up."

8. What is NOT **apparent**?
   a. what kind of luck I will have in the future
   b. when I will have my next birthday
   c. where I am now

9. Who can best provide **insight** into how the human body works?
   a. an actor
   b. a politician
   c. a doctor

10. If we want to know a person's **perspective**, we are interested in the way he or she
    a. thinks and perceives.
    b. exercises.
    c. sleeps.

■ WORD FAMILIES

Now that you have studied the ten key words and their basic definitions, you are ready to learn words that belong to the same family as some of the key words. A word family includes words that look alike but have different functions (noun, verb, adjective, or adverb). Their meanings are related but different.

A. *Look at each model phrase and decide whether the word in **bold** is used as a noun, verb, adjective, or adverb. Put a check (✔) in the correct column.*

	NOUN	VERB	ADJECTIVE	ADVERB
1. acknowledge				
• **acknowledge** what's happening				
• his **acknowledgment**				
2. apparently				
• **apparently** the children know each other				
• our **apparent** mistake				
3. conform				
• pressure to **conform**				
• their **conformity**				
4. eliminate				
• **eliminate** a problem				
• her **elimination** from the game				
5. function				
• an important **function**				
• I **function** as the manager				
6. justify				
• **justify** your actions				
• no **justification**				

B. *Bill is talking with his mother about coming home late. Complete the conversation with words from the box.*

acknowledgment	apparent	eliminated	functions	justification

BILL'S MOM: Don't try to make excuses, Bill! Helping Mike is no _____ for
coming home at midnight. Your _____ lack of respect for our rules
surprises me. You've never made me worry like this before.

BILL: I'm sorry you worried. I made a mistake. I should have called you, but I had to
help Mike for the team. I promised the coach I'd do anything to help the team!

BILL'S MOM: I appreciate your _____ of making a mistake, but I don't understand
how helping Mike was necessary to help the team.

BILL: I was helping Mike with his U.S. Government project. Tomorrow he is giving a
presentation that explains how the Congress _____. If he fails his

presentation, he fails the class. The coach said if we fail a class, he'll take us off the team. Mike needed my help, and so did the team. Without Mike, we'll lose the next game and be _____ from the playoffs.

5

BILL'S MOM: Hmm. I see. Well, it was nice of you to help Mike, but next time you're going to be home after 10:00, you need to call me and explain things.

BILL: You're right, Mom. Next time I'll call.

SAME WORD, DIFFERENT MEANING

*Most words have more than one meaning. Study the additional meanings of **acknowledge**, **apparent**, and **proportion**. Then read each sentence and decide which meaning is used.*

a. **acknowledge** *v.*	to accept or admit that something is true
b. **acknowledge** *v.*	to show that you have seen, heard, or been helped by someone
c. **apparent** *adj.*	seeming to be true, although it may not really be
d. **apparent** *adj.*	easily seen or understood
e. **proportion** *n.*	a part of a larger amount of something
f. **proportion** *n.*	the correct relationship between the size or shape of the parts of something

_____ 1. Dan smiled at the pretty girl on the street, but she did not **acknowledge** him.

_____ 2. The **proportion** of students who smoke at the high school is lower than it was five years ago.

_____ 3. Emily's **apparent** confidence disappeared when her teacher asked her to explain the math problem to the class.

_____ 4. The architects **acknowledged** that their competitor's designs were more innovative than their own.

_____ 5. The mother's love for her baby was **apparent**.

_____ 6. Max's art teacher asked him to draw the house again because the picture was out of **proportion**; he had drawn the window larger than the door!

WORDS IN SENTENCES

Complete each sentence with one of the words from the box.

acknowledgments	Conformity	functions	justification	proportion
apparent	eliminate	insight	perspective	shift

1. This drawing is out of _____; the baby's head looks too small.

2. In her job, Janet _____ as a lawyer and a diplomat.

3. In the _____ at the beginning of the book, the author thanked his colleagues who had helped him to develop his theory.

4. Rachel believes that there is no _____ for one country attacking another country.

5. From Allison's _____ in the front row, the ballet was amazing.

6. _____ is the norm in most high schools; there is a lot of pressure to dress and act the same.

7. Ben had bought two houses, so he gave us valuable _____ into the process.

8. If you put high-quality screens on the windows, you can _____ your fly and mosquito problem.

9. Luke's _____ Spanish-language skills disappeared when we started speaking in the past tense.

10. The aerobics instructor told me to _____ my weight to my left foot.

▌ WORDS IN COLLOCATIONS AND EXPRESSIONS

Following are common collocations and expressions with some of the key words. Read the definitions and then complete the conversations with the collocations and expressions. You may have to change word forms for correct grammar.

1. **apparent**	
• **for no apparent reason**	without a clear reason
2. **conform**	
• **conform to (a rule, law)**	obey (a rule or law)
3. **insight**	
• **give (sb) insight into**	help someone understand something clearly
4. **perspective**	
• **keep this in perspective**	think about this sensibly so that it doesn't seem worse than it really is
5. **proportion**	
• **in proportion with/out of proportion with**	having the correct/incorrect relationship of size or shape
6. **shift**	
• **work the night shift**	work at night in a factory, hospital, etc.

1.   NATE: Why did you yawn? Am I boring you?

         MELISSA: Not at all! I have _____ at the factory this month, so I'm not getting enough sleep.

2.   HUSBAND: Don't you like the porch I built?

         WIFE: I do like it, but it's way too big. It's totally _____ the house! Can you make it smaller so that it's _____ the house?

3.   ANNE: Why did Peter break up with you?

            RACHEL: I have no idea! Everything was going great. He always told me he really loved me and that I was perfect for him. Then one day, _____, he dumped me.

4. COMPANY PRESIDENT: You didn't follow company policy, and we're losing $2 million on this deal!

            JOHN: Yes, sir, it looks that way. Let's _____, though. We're going to make $4 million on the Pensky deal.

COMPANY PRESIDENT: It's a good thing. Let's make sure we _____ the company investment policy at all times on this one.

            JOHN: Yes, sir. Absolutely.

5.   STUDENT: Can you _____ me some _____ the history of the Chinese writing system?

      PROFESSOR: Yes. I'll start by explaining how the writing system began about 3,500 years ago. Then I'll explain how it has changed over time.

▌ WORDS IN A READING

Read this passage about dogs and health. Complete it with words from the boxes.

apparent	function	perspective	proportion	shift

THERAPY DOGS SEEM TO BOOST HEALTH OF SICK AND LONELY

Three years ago, Marcia Sturm was walking her golden retriever, Bo, near her Los Angeles home. An employee from nearby Cedars-Sinai Medical Center approached her and asked if she would be interested in bringing Bo to the hospital's AIDS unit to visit with patients. She was—and she and Bo have been a part of the POOCH (Pets Offer Ongoing Care and Healing) program ever since.

Bo is one of a growing number of dogs who _____ as "therapy dogs," visiting people
                                      1
in hospitals, nursing homes, mental health centers, and shelters, where they do everything from lift spirits to assist with physical therapy.

Bo's love for his job is _____. He is happy to be dressed in his "uniform," a blue scarf
                             2
around his neck that identifies him as a member of the POOCH program. "Once I take the scarf out, he knows it's time for his _____ at the hospital," Sturm says.
                                3

Once at the hospital, Sturm checks the book that lists patients who have requested a visit, and she and Bo begin their rounds. Because he is a big dog, Bo rarely gets onto a patient's bed, but he's tall enough to rest his head on the bed for a good rub.

A notable _____ of elderly patients have few relatives and visitors and are
                     4
particularly charmed by Bo. While they may be too sick for lengthy visits, some are so happy to see him that it brings them to tears. Sturm says, "You'll hear them say, 'He likes me. He's my friend.'"

Not only does Bo cheer up patients in the units he visits, he's also a big hit with the staff, too. And from the _____ of family members in the waiting room, he helps break up tension by taking their minds off their troubles for just a few minutes. The families often shower Bo with affection.

acknowledges	conform to	eliminated	insight	justify

It's not all fun and games, however. Bo's work is serious business, and he knows it. Stress cannot be _____ from the dog's visit. Sturm pays close attention to signals that Bo might be stressed, such as the time they were visiting a dying patient and Bo nudged Sturm and headed for the door. But for the most part, Bo is happy to visit with anyone. "Dogs are not prejudiced," said Sturm. "They don't see color."

Most people are familiar with dogs that assist blind or otherwise disabled owners. Therapy dogs offer a different kind of help. Some pay informal social visits to people to boost their spirits, while others work in a more structured environment with trained professionals like physical therapists and social workers to help patients reach clinical goals, such as increased mobility or improved memory.

The POOCH program at Cedars-Sinai is an informal one, started six years ago by licensed social worker Barbara Cowen, who was working as the volunteer coordinator in the AIDS unit. In the program, a dog may stay with a patient for as little as five minutes or as long as an hour, depending upon the patient's needs. Currently there are about thirty volunteers in the program.

Therapy dogs must _____ the standards of the program. They can be of any size and breed. Temperament is key to being a good therapy dog. Being well trained is not enough to _____ a dog becoming a therapy dog; the animal must also be easygoing and patient, and comfortable with strangers.

Cowen said that nurses have noticed that after a POOCH visit, patients sometimes have slower heart rates and they require less pain medication. Evidence of positive responses to animal-assisted therapy is common in personal stories. Now a recent scientific study on elderly nursing home patients _____ that these stories might be right. The study shows that brief weekly visits from man's best friend can have a positive therapeutic impact.

The researchers in St. Louis completed a rigorous, scientifically controlled study showing that brief weekly visits with a therapy dog reduced the loneliness of elderly patients in a long-term care facility. They used a scientific measure known as the UCLA Loneliness Scale to test forty-five patients before and after the visits, concluding that patients who spent as little as half an hour a week with a therapy dog were significantly less lonely after only six weeks when compared to a control group.

What is it about the dogs that creates such a powerful effect?

William Banks offered this _____: "It's not that the animals have magic vibes coming
10
out of them. It's a quality-of-life issue. It's about giving people access to what they like and enjoy."
According to Banks, the elderly patients in the study were not confusing the therapy dogs with
childhood pets; they were being reminded of the joy animals had brought them in the past. "Their
response seemed to be, 'I had forgotten what a pleasure this was'"!

(Adapted from "Therapy Dogs Seem to Boost Health of Sick and Lonely," National Geographic News, August 8, 2002.)

▌WORDS IN DISCUSSION

Apply the key words to your own life. Read and discuss each question in small groups. Try to use the key words.

1. **eliminate**

   Something I want to eliminate from my life: _____

   Something I want to eliminate from my home: _____

2. **conform**

   How often I conformed when I was a teenager: _____

   How often I conform to the laws of my country: _____

3. **function**

   My function in my dream job: _____

   How much I understand about how the human body functions: _____

4. **justify**

   A time when I tried to justify my actions to my family: _____

   How I might justify spending $1,000 on a coat: _____

5. **apparent**

   A person whose feelings are apparent to me: _____

   Something about life that is apparent to me: _____

6. **perspective**

   How my perspective differs from my parents': _____

   How my perspective on work differs from my best friend's: _____

7. **acknowledge**

   Something I acknowledge about myself: _____

   A person I acknowledge for teaching me something important: _____

8. **shift**

   An issue about which I have shifted my opinion: _____

   How skillful I am at shifting with a manual transmission in a car: _____

9. **proportion**

   In an average day, the proportion of time I use the English language:

   _____

   A building I have visited that I feel is in perfect proportion: _____

10. **insight**

A person who has insight into many topics: _____

I wish I had more insight about _____

▌WORDS IN WRITING

Choose two topics and write a paragraph on each. Try to use the key words.

1. Describe a time when a person tried to **justify** his or her actions but failed to convince you. Why did you disagree with his or her **justifications**?

2. Explain how something **functions** (for example, the human body, your office, a light bulb, your government).

3. If you wanted **insight** into a topic that interests you, whose **perspective** would you ask for? Explain why you would choose this person.

4. Do you feel more comfortable **conforming** to a group or being an individual? Explain.

5. In your opinion, what problem that the world faces now can be **eliminated** in the next hundred years? Explain how you think this can happen.

Key Words

aspect	distinct	foundation	norm	scope
commit	extract	integrity	rely	trace

▌ WORDS IN CONTEXT

*Use the sentences to guess what each key word means. Choose the meaning that is closest to that of the key word in **bold**.*

1. **aspect**
/ˈæspɛkt/
-noun

- The speaker described several **aspects** of life in Taiwan.
- Pronunciation is the most difficult **aspect** of language learning for Riko.

Aspect means . . .   a. something whole   b. a part   c. the appearance of something

2. **commit**
/kəˈmɪt/
-verb

- Edward told the young couple, "You need to **commit** yourselves to your marriage if you want it to succeed."
- Perhaps we also can help in the spring, but we can **commit** to helping you only in the summer.

Commit means . . .   a. to promise to do something   b. to think about doing something   c. to change your mind about something

3. **distinct**
/dɪˈstɪŋkt/
-adjective

- The research group found five **distinct** groups of cell phone users.
- There is a **distinct** possibility that I'll live in Portugal next year, so I've bought some CDs that will help me learn Portuguese.

Distinct means . . .   a. clearly different; clearly understood   b. the same as all others   c. similar to others; good

4. **extract**
/ɪkˈstrækt/
-verb—formal

- The dentist **extracted** Hector's rotten tooth.
- Sap is **extracted** from a tree to make maple syrup.

Extract means . . .   a. to add   b. to remove   c. to find

5. **foundation**
/faʊnˈdeɪʃən/
-noun

- A house must be built on a **foundation**.
- Elementary school provided Irene with the **foundation** for her future learning.

Foundation means . . .   a. a base from which something develops   b. the top and final result of something   c. a challenge

6. integrity
/ɪnˈtɛgrəti/
-noun

- We can trust Ben; clearly, he has **integrity**.
- My grandfather said, "Don't marry a man unless he has **integrity**."

Integrity means . . .
a. having high moral principles
b. having a good sense of humor
c. being very good looking

7. norm
/nɔrm/
-noun

- In many countries, it is the **norm** for women to work.
- Is eating dinner at 7:00 P.M. the **norm** where you live?

Norm means . . .
a. a strange way of doing something
b. an original way of doing something
c. the usual way of doing something

8. rely
/rɪˈlaɪ/
-verb

- Elsa knows that she can **rely** on her parents when she needs help.
- I **rely** on my alarm clock to wake me up.

Rely means . . .
a. to trust or depend on someone or something
b. to be suspicious
c. to use someone or something

9. scope
/skoʊp/
-noun

- The question of the future of the universe is beyond the **scope** of this lecture.
- Chemistry is not within the **scope** of an eight-year-old's scientific knowledge.

Scope means . . .
a. idea
b. range
c. knowledge about everything

10. trace
/treɪs/
-verb

- Elizabeth was able to **trace** her family history back to fifteenth-century Ireland.
- Scientists have **traced** the origins of AIDS to a particular subspecies of chimpanzee in the central African rainforest.

Trace means . . .
a. to study or describe the history of something
b. to make a guess about something
c. to write in detail about something

WORDS AND DEFINITIONS

Read each definition and write the word it defines on the line.

1. _____ the quality of being honest and having high moral principles

2. _____ the range of things that a subject, activity, or book deals with

3. _____ an idea, system, or base from which something develops; the solid layer of material that is under a building to support it

4. _____ to study or describe the history, development, or origin of something

5. _____ one part of a situation, idea, or plan that has many parts

6. _____ the usual way of doing something

7. _____ clearly different; clearly seen, heard, or understood

8. _____ to promise to do something and use time, money, or effort to achieve it

9. _____ to remove an object or substance from the place where it belongs or comes from

10. _____ to trust or depend on someone or something

▌COMPREHENSION CHECK

Choose the best answer.

1. Where is walking in snow the **norm**?
   a. the deserts of Saudi Arabia
   b. the northern cities of Russia
   c. the beaches of Turkey

2. Where is the **foundation** of a building?
   a. below it
   b. above it
   c. around it

3. What is beyond the **scope** of science?
   a. biology
   b. chemistry
   c. poetry

4. Who has **integrity**?
   a. a person who lies
   b. a person who is very honest
   c. a person who is immoral

5. If something is **distinct**, it
   a. is different from one or more things.
   b. is almost the same as other things.
   c. is a copy.

6. If medicine is **extracted** from a flower, it
   a. is added to the flower.
   b. is created by the flower.
   c. is removed from the flower.

7. Which person **commits** himself or herself to running?
   a. Rafe, who jogs occasionally
   b. Angie, who runs five miles a day
   c. Tom, who runs when the weather is nice

8. If you **rely** on someone, do you trust him or her?
   a. yes
   b. usually
   c. no

9. Which is an **aspect** of the ocean?
   a. the sun
   b. waves
   c. tourists

10. Which CANNOT be **traced**?
    a. something in the future
    b. the history of something
    c. the origins of someone

WORD FAMILIES

Now that you have studied the ten key words and their basic definitions, you are ready to learn words that belong to the same family as some of the key words. A word family includes words that look alike but have different functions (noun, verb, adjective, or adverb). Their meanings are related but different.

A. *Look at each model phrase and decide whether the word in **bold** is used as a noun, verb, adjective, or adverb. Put a check (✓) in the correct column.*

	NOUN	VERB	ADJECTIVE	ADVERB
1. commit				
• **commit** to a relationship				
• make a **commitment**				
• a **committed** father				
2. distinct				
• the alligator is **distinct** from the crocodile				
• a **distinctive** flavor				
• a **distinction** between coffee and espresso				
3. extract				
• **extract** it painlessly				
• read an **extract** from *Pride and Prejudice*				
4. foundation				
• a solid **foundation**				
• plans to **found** a new state				
• the club's **founder**				
5. norm				
• it's the **norm**				
• not **normal**				
6. rely				
• **rely** on me				
• their **reliance** on their mother				
• a **reliable** friend				
• completely **unreliable** source of information				

B. *Read the first part of each sentence and match it with the appropriate ending. The exercise continues on page 78.*

_____ 1. I wanted to read the entire book after reading a(n)

_____ 2. I could recognize Fisal's voice anywhere; his voice is very

_____ 3. When the eighteen-year-old wanted to get married, his father asked if he was ready for such a serious

a. **founded** in 1607.

b. **distinctive**.

c. **normal** for dogs to bark when they are excited?

d. **committed** doctor.

_____ 4. Santa Fe, New Mexico, was

_____ 5. Petra works long hours at the hospital because she believes in helping as many people as possible; she is a

_____ 6. He was a drug addict; his life was ruined by his

_____ 7. Is it

_____ 8. Muhammad was the

_____ 9. I don't want to break down on a snowy highway, so I need a(n)

_____ 10. What is the

e. **distinction** between your plan and our plan?

f. **reliable** car.

g. **founder** of Islam.

h. **reliance** on drugs.

i. **extract** from it in the newspaper.

j. **commitment**.

▌SAME WORD, DIFFERENT MEANING

*Most words have more than one meaning. Study the additional meanings of **commit**, **foundation**, and **trace**. Then read each sentence and decide which meaning is used.*

a. **commit** *v.*	to promise to do something and use time, money, or effort to achieve it
b. **commit** *v.*	to do something wrong or illegal
c. **foundation** *n.*	an idea, system, or base from which something develops; the solid layer that is under a building to support it
d. **foundation** *n.*	an organization that gives or collects money for special purposes
e. **trace** *v.*	to study or describe the history, development, or origin of something
f. **trace** *v.*	to find someone or something that has disappeared

_____ 1. The National Historical **Foundation** collects money to preserve old buildings.

_____ 2. The elderly couple **committed** $10 million to finding a cure for cancer.

_____ 3. Bridget **traced** the missing package using the United Parcel Service's Web site.

_____ 4. Criminals **commit** crimes; the worst criminals **commit** murder.

_____ 5. A team of anthropologists is trying to **trace** prehistoric migration in Africa.

_____ 6. The building must be destroyed because its **foundation** is unstable.

WORDS IN SENTENCES

Complete each sentence with two of the words from the box.

aspect	distinctive	foundation	norm	scope
commit	extracted	integrity	rely	trace

1. Is it the _____ in your home town for children to _____ on their parents until they are twenty-one years old?

2. People who _____ their lives to helping others have a great deal of _____.

3. Local police tried to _____ the missing criminal, but the _____ of the investigation was too wide for them, so they called the FBI.

4. White truffles, which are _____ from the earth in northwestern Italy, sell for 30 Euros each because of their _____ taste.

5. A good _____ is one _____ of a well-designed house.

WORDS IN COLLOCATIONS AND EXPRESSIONS

Following are common collocations and expressions with some of the key words. Read the definitions and then complete the conversation on page 80 with the collocations and expressions. You may have to change word forms for correct grammar.

1. **commit**
   - **be committed to (sth)**   believe that something is important and work hard for it
   - **commit a crime**   to do something illegal

2. **distinct**
   - **a distinct possibility**   a definite possibility that should not be ignored

3. **rely**
   - **rely on (sb/sth)**   to trust or depend on somebody or something

4. **trace**
   - **disappear without a trace**   for something to be gone suddenly without any sign of where it may have gone
   - **no trace of**   no sign that someone or something has been in a place

GREG: I don't understand why I got an F on this essay. It's excellent!

PROFESSOR JONES: Yes, your essay gives an excellent analysis of what happened when the lost colony of Roanoke, Virginia, mysteriously _____ 1 in 1587. Unfortunately Greg, you didn't write this paper. It sounded too professional to have been written by a freshman Introduction to American History student. I decided that there was _____ 2 that you had copied it, so I looked online. Sure enough, I found several paragraphs from your paper in an article written by a professor in San Francisco in 2005.

GREG: Look, I didn't _____ 3 . I just borrowed some sentences from that article to support my ideas. You can't fail me for that!

PROFESSOR JONES: Yes, I can. Plagiarism is a serious problem, Greg. Is it really worth risking your integrity to try to get a good grade?

GREG: I'm sorry, Professor. I know it was stupid to copy so much from that article. I never copied anything in high school, but now that I'm in college I have so much more work to do. And I haven't been able to concentrate on anything because my girlfriend broke up with me last week.

PROFESSOR JONES: I'm sorry to hear that you've been having personal problems. But that's no excuse for cheating.

GREG: Please let me write the paper again. I really _____ 4 this class. I'll do anything to pass it. I promise you, Professor, there will be _____ 5 of anyone else's writing in my paper this time. From now on I will _____ 6 only myself to do the work. Please give me another chance.

PROFESSOR JONES: I'm not sure. I'll think about it.

▌WORDS IN A READING

Read this article about DNA technology. Complete it with words from the boxes.

committed	distinct	extracted	relying	scope	trace

DNA TESTING: IN OUR BLOOD

For Debra Anne Royer, DNA unlocked a deep mystery. Adopted at birth, Royer knew nothing about her biological parents. But certain physical traits—wide nose, dark skin—led people to guess that she was Iranian or even Cambodian. "I always wondered," she says. She paid $200 and _____ 1 a sample of her saliva from the inside of her cheek to get an answer: Royer's maternal ancestors were most likely Native American. The knowledge, she says, "makes you feel more of a person."

Our blood holds the secrets to who we are, and increasingly, individuals, families, and research scientists are _____ on genetic testing to tell us what we don't already know. Human genomes are 99.9 percent identical; we are far more similar than diverse. But that tiny 0.1 percent difference holds _____ clues to our ancestries, the roots of all human migration. Tens of thousands of Americans who are _____ to discovering their ancestry have mailed in their DNA to companies nationwide for testing. Distant cousins are finding each other; family legends are being overturned. Six years ago the term *genetic genealogy* was meaningless, says Bennett Greenspan, head of Family Tree DNA, which has 52,000 customers. "Now the interest is huge." So huge that celebrities like Whoopi Goldberg and Quincy Jones are signing on.

As individuals track down their personal family narratives, population geneticists are seeking to tell the larger story of humankind. Our most recent common ancestors—a genetic "Adam" and "Eve"—have been traced back to Africa, and other intriguing forebears are being discovered all over the map. The most ambitious effort by far is the National Geographic Society's $40 million Genographic Project, which aims to collect 100,000 DNA samples from indigenous populations around the world over the next five years. The goal: to _____ human roots from the present day back to the origin of our species. This will widen our _____ of understanding about human history and allow scientists to create something close to a DNA museum.

| aspects | foundation | integrity | norm |

History lives in our genes. The DNA in each of our cells not only dictates the color of our eyes, it also contains the footprints of our ancestors. A child's genome is almost entirely a mix of genetic material created by the union of mother and father. Only two _____ of the genome remain pure, untainted by the influence of a mate's DNA: the Y chromosome (passed down from father to son) and mitochondrial DNA (passed from mother to both sons and daughters). Occasionally, "spelling mistakes," or mutations, in these regions differ from the _____, creating unique sequences that serve as genealogical markers—providing links backward in time, not just to our ancestors but to the places they lived in the world. Scrape the inside of your cheek a few times, and for $100 and up, a testing company will put your DNA under its microscope, map your markers into your own genetic pattern, called a *haplotype,* then tell you which "haplogroup," or major branch of the human tree, you come from.

DNA testing is forcing some people to rethink their identities. Phil Goff, forty-two, of Naperville, Illinois, thought his heritage was pure English, but a Y chromosome test matched him at least partially to Scandinavia. Now he wonders if he has any Viking blood in him. Alvy Ray Smith, sixty-two, uncovered roots tracing back to the Puritans in 1633. "It was astonishing," says Smith, who thought his closest relatives were Irish potato farmers. "It gave me a whole different model of myself."

Online communities now allow people to compare genomes. Find a match, and you may be able to fill in branches on your family tree. Looking for relatives without your surname? You can also search within individual testing companies or in public databases like the Sorenson Molecular Genealogy _____, which has collected 60,000 DNA samples and ancestral charts over the past four
9
and a half years.

The more we discover our differences, the more we find connections. Wayne Joseph grew up a black American in Louisiana and Los Angeles. He heard about DNA testing several years ago and, seeking details about his mixed ancestry, sent away for a kit. "I figured I'd come back about seventy percent African and thirty percent something else," he says. When the results arrived in the mail he was shocked. The testing company said he was fifty-seven percent Indo-European, thirty-nine percent Native American, and four percent East Asian. No African blood at all! For almost a year, Joseph searched his soul, sifting in his mind the decisions he'd made based on his identity as a black man: his first marriage, his choice of high school, his interest in African-American literature. The results changed his self-perception but not his _____. Before the test, "I was unequivocally black," he says.
10
"Now I'm a metaphor for America." And not just for America but for all of us.

(Adapted from Newsweek, February 6, 2006.)

▌WORDS IN DISCUSSION

Read the questions and choose the best answers. Then discuss your answers in small groups.

1. Would you **commit** a crime to protect yourself?
   a. No. I would never commit a crime.
   b. Yes, but only if I were in serious danger.
   c. Yes. Committing a crime would not be difficult for me.

2. What is your most **distinct** feature?
   a. my hair
   b. my eyes
   c. other _____

3. On whom can you **rely** when you have a problem?
   a. my family
   b. my friends
   c. only myself

4. What **aspect** of your life would you most like to change?
   a. my career
   b. my love life
   c. my financial situation

5. How far back into history can you **trace** your roots?
   a. I know nothing about my family history.
   b. I know only my parents' and grandparents' names.
   c. I know about my relatives in the past hundred years.

6. How much **integrity** do you have?
   a. A lot. I am a very honest and moral person.
   b. Some. I am usually a good and honest person.
   c. None. I am a liar and an unreliable person.

7. Which of the following are the **norm** for your group of friends?

    a. smoking

    b. talking on the phone many times a day

    c. other _____

8. Which of the following do you feel should be part of the **foundation** of a child's education? (Choose as many as you like.)

    a. how to read

    b. how to fight

    c. how to dance

9. Which of these subjects is beyond the **scope** of your knowledge?

    a. cooking

    b. physics

    c. poetry

10. Imagine that you have five minutes to read a famous **extract** from a classic book. Which book would you choose?

    a. *Crime and Punishment,* by F. Dostoyevsky

    b. *The Adventures of Huckleberry Finn,* by Mark Twain

    c. *Frankenstein,* by Mary Shelley

WORDS IN WRITING

Choose two topics and write a paragraph on each. Try to use the key words.

1. What job must a person have a lot of **integrity** to do well? Explain.

2. Describe a **distinct** taste or smell which you feel strongly about. **Trace** your feelings back to an experience involving this taste or smell.

3. How do you think that the government should punish criminals who **commit** serious crimes?

4. Describe a person on whom you can always **rely**.

5. If you were given $100,000 to start a **foundation**, what type of foundation would you start?

▌ WORDS IN CONTEXT

*Use the sentences to guess what each key word means. Choose the meaning that is closest to that of the key word in **bold**.*

1. annual
/ˈænyuəl/
-*adjective*

- Henry's **annual** birthday party takes place each June.
- Was your **annual** income this year greater than it was last year?

Annual means . . .
a. happening every month
b. happening once a year
c. happening only once

2. bond
/bɑnd/
-*noun*

- The **bond** between a mother and baby is very strong.
- Kara, who is from Dublin, feels a **bond** with the Irish people she meets in her new home, New York.

Bond means . . .
a. a shared feeling or interest
b. a long friendship
c. a sudden curiosity

3. contribute
/kənˈtrɪbyut/
-*verb*

- After the 2004 tsunami hit Southeast Asia, people around the world **contributed** money to help the victims.
- Max **contributed** a lot of good ideas to our project.

Contribute means . . .
a. to take away or subtract
b. to give money, help, or ideas
c. to join or meet

4. expand
/ɪkspænd/
-*verb*

- The Korean-American population rapidly **expanded** after 1970.
- Because Marissa wants to **expand** her circle of friends, she is going to join two clubs at her college.

Expand means . . .
a. to become smaller or make smaller
b. to improve in an independent way
c. to become larger or make larger

5. incentive
/ɪnˈsɛntɪv/
-*noun*

- The factory manager offered the **incentive** of extra pay to workers who completed their work on time.
- The **incentive** of getting a good job motivates me to improve my English.

Incentive means . . .
a. something that encourages you to work harder
b. a gift given to people for working at a company for a long time
c. money

6. **modify**
/ˈmɑdəˌfaɪ/
-verb

- Although the computer program was very good, the students hoped to **modify** it to make it even better.
- Ollie, who is very tall, thinks that airplane seats should be **modified** so that they have more leg room.

Modify means . . .   a. to make big changes to something to improve it   b. to throw something away and start again   c. to make small changes to something to improve it

7. **presume**
/prɪˈzum/
-verb

- Although we hadn't received an answer from Jane, we **presumed** that she was coming to the party, so we set a place for her at the table.
- Do not **presume** that the weather in London will be nice; check the weather report before you leave home.

Presume means . . .   a. to think that something is true, although you are not certain   b. to know for a fact that something is true   c. to have no idea whether or not something is true

8. **subsequent**
/ˈsʌbsəkwənt/
-adjective—formal

- Mike's first business project was very difficult, but his **subsequent** projects were much easier.
- **Subsequent** to the publishing of his book, there were a lot more students who wanted to take Professor Brown's class.

Subsequent means . . .   a. coming before something else   b. coming after or following something else   c. happening at the same time as something else

9. **ultimate**
/ˈʌltəmɪt/
-adjective

- For American high school students, the **ultimate** test is the SAT, which they take in order to enter college.
- You may try many different jobs in your life, but what will be your **ultimate** career choice?

Ultimate means . . .   a first and least important   b. average   c. final and most important

10. **widespread**
/ˌwaɪdˈsprɛd/
-adjective

- Soccer's popularity is **widespread** and growing.
- **Widespread** illegal drug use has caused serious social problems in our city.

Widespread means . . .   a. happening in a few places   b. happening in many places   c. happening nowhere

▌WORDS AND DEFINITIONS

Read each definition and write the word it defines on the line.

1. _____ to give money, help, or ideas to something that other people are also giving to

2. _____ happening once a year

3. _____ coming after or following something else

4. _____ something that encourages you to work harder or start new activities

5. _____ final and most important

6. _____ happening in many places, among many people

7. _____ a shared feeling or interest that unites people

8. _____ to become larger or to make larger

9. _____ to think that something is true, although you are not certain

10. _____ to make small changes to something in order to improve it

▌COMPREHENSION CHECK

Choose the best answer.

1. How often does an **annual** conference meet?

   a. once a week

   b. once a month

   c. once a year

2. In which statement is the speaker **presuming** something?

   a. "Quinn isn't going to be in class. He told me."

   b. "I have no clue if Bella will accept my marriage proposal."

   c. "I see that you drive a Jaguar. You must be very rich."

3. What is NOT a **widespread** problem?

   a. pollution

   b. tiger attacks

   c. poverty

4. If Jen and her sister have strengthened their **bond** on their camping trip, what happened?

   a. They traded money.

   b. They made a fire together.

   c. They became closer friends.

5. Which is NOT an example of something **expanding**?

   a. The paper store's business remains steady.

   b. The Clarks add a new room to their house.

   c. Ben's knowledge grows as he gets closer to completing his degree.

6. James is in medical school. What is probably his **ultimate** reason for being there?

   a. He loves to study the human body.

   b. He wants to practice medicine.

   c. He decided not to become a teacher.

7. If Wendy wants to **modify** her business plan, what does she want to do?

   a. change it completely

   b. make small changes

   c. throw it away

8. Which month is **subsequent** to June?

   a. September

   b. January

   c. July

9. What do people usually NOT **contribute** when asked for help?

    a. complaints

    b. money

    c. time

10. What **incentive** motivates Jim to work late?

    a. He hates his job.

    b. He wants to earn overtime money to help feed his kids.

    c. His boss is watching him.

WORD FAMILIES

Now that you have studied the ten key words and their basic definitions, you are ready to learn words that belong to the same family as some of the key words. A word family includes words that look alike but have different functions (noun, verb, adjective, or adverb). Their meanings are related but different.

A. *Look at each model phrase and decide whether the word in* **bold** *is used as a noun, verb, adjective, or adverb. Put a check (✓) in the correct column.*

	NOUN	VERB	ADJECTIVE	ADVERB
1. **annual**				
• an **annual** fair				
• celebrate **annually**				
2. **contribute**				
• **contribute** to the European Union				
• a generous **contribution**				
3. **expand**				
• **expand** the computer market				
• the **expanding** population				
• the **expansion** of the airport				
4. **modify**				
• **modify** our plans				
• discuss the **modifications**				
5. **presume**				
• **presume** that is why				
• a reasonable **presumption**				
6. **subsequent**				
• the **subsequent** offer				
• **subsequently** we left				

B. *Read the first half of each sentence on pages 87 and 88 and match it with the appropriate ending.*

_____ 1. The cell phone company is getting more customers due to its

_____ 2. Between the ages of three and six, a child should visit the doctor

_____ 3. We'll find out why Della is late when she arrives; our

    a. **annually**.

    b. **contribution** to your academic field.

    c. **modifications**.

    d. **presumption** is that she's stuck in traffic.

_____ 4. Eddy began his career as a lawyer in the Houston office;

_____ 5. To become a famous scholar, you need to make a significant

_____ 6. To make more space for the athletic teams, the coach suggested

_____ 7. Before it is released to the public, this product needs some

e. **subsequently**, he moved to the New York branch of the firm.

f. **expanding** the playing fields.

g. **extended** network.

SAME WORD, DIFFERENT MEANING

Most words have more than one meaning. Study the additional meanings of **bond**, **presume**, and **ultimate**. Then read each sentence and decide which meaning is used.

a.	**bond** _n._	a shared feeling or interest that unites people
b.	**bond** _v._	to develop a special relationship with someone
c.	**presume** _v._	to think that something is true, although you are not certain
d.	**presume** _v._	to accept that something is true until it is proved untrue, especially in law
e.	**ultimate** _adj._	final and most important
f.	**ultimate** _adj._	an ultimate decision, responsibility, etc. is one that you cannot pass on to someone else

_____ 1. A love for music is a **bond** that Xander and Mariana share.

_____ 2. In the United States legal system, the court **presumes** that a person is innocent until proven guilty.

_____ 3. For mountain climbers, Mount Everest is the **ultimate** challenge.

_____ 4. Marco and his brother didn't use to get along, but they **bonded** on their trip to Spain.

_____ 5. Raymond accepts **ultimate** responsibility for the accident.

_____ 6. Because there is no public transportation near her house, I **presume** that Yetta has a car.

WORDS IN SENTENCES

Complete each sentence with one of the words from the box.

annual	contribution	incentive	presume	ultimate
bonded	expand	modifications	subsequently	widespread

1. The English language is _____.

2. I _____ that you forgot your key and that's why you're standing outside in the cold.

3. The _____ have improved the software.

4. Some people believe that a red rose is the _____ symbol of love.

5. During freshman orientation, Soo Jin _____ with her college roommate, so they got off to a good start.

6. "Alan's having another boring barbeque? I hope this doesn't become a(n) _____ tradition!"

7. The cellular phone company marketed a free phone as a(n) _____ to attract customers.

8. First Gina traveled to Tibet to complete her research. _____ she wrote her report.

9. There are too few dinner choices, so the chef is going to _____ the menu.

10. The Smiths' _____ of lemonade and iced tea was greatly appreciated by everyone at the picnic.

■ WORDS IN COLLOCATIONS AND EXPRESSIONS

Following are common collocations and expressions with some of the key words. Read the definitions and then complete the conversations with the collocations and expressions. One of them is used twice. You may have to change word forms for correct grammar.

1. **annual**
   - **annual checkup**   a yearly appointment with the doctor to check your health

2. **bond**
   - **a bond between (people)**   a shared feeling or interest that unites people

3. **contribute**
   - **contribute to/toward (sth)**   to give money, help, or ideas to something

4. **expand**
   - **expand rapidly**   to become larger quickly

5. **presume**
   - **presumed dead**   believed to be dead although it has not yet been proven

6. **ultimate**
   - **the ultimate in (sth)**   the best or most modern example of something

1. DOCTOR: What is the problem?

     PATIENT: I don't have any problems. I just came in for my _____.

     DOCTOR: Excellent. OK, let's get started. Please stick out your tongue.

2. MARGARET: How long have you known your husband?

     ELLEN: Ever since I was a child. Our parents were best friends. Because there was _____ our families, it was easy for me to fall in love with him.

3. **SOLDIER 1:** We've been waiting in this jungle for a month! When is someone going to discover where our plane crashed and rescue us?

   SOLDIER 2: I hate to be pessimistic, but I don't think it's going to happen, Sam. I'm sure we're _____.

   SOLDIER 3: I still have hope. I know that the men from our base camp are searching for us. Once more soldiers arrive at the camp, the search for us will _____, and we'll be rescued.

4. **STUDENT:** Good morning, Mr. Jones. Will you _____ some money _____ the school track team?

   MR. JONES: I _____ the track team a month ago.

   STUDENT: Yes, thanks. We really appreciate your help, but we need a lot more. We need all the help we can get!

5. **SALESMAN:** Congratulations! The vacuum cleaner you have bought is _____ advanced cleaning technology.

   CUSTOMER: Ah, so that's why it cost a fortune!

▌WORDS IN A READING

Read this article about soul food. Complete it with words and expressions from the boxes.

annual	contribute to	presume	ultimate	widespread

SAVING SOUL FOOD

Sylvia Woods knows her soul food. For the past forty-plus years, for everyday dining and _____ celebrations, she's been dishing out the best of it at her famous restaurant,
    1
Sylvia's, in Harlem—the fried chicken, the macaroni and cheese, the candied yams. But one recent

winter day, the _____ soul food queen wandered by a table occupied by her grandson,
    2
Lindsey Williams, and witnessed a culinary revolution. There, on a plate elegantly dusted with flecks of

parsley, sat two round lentil cakes with a swirl of tofu yogurt on top and Thai sesame dressing on the

side. "What's that?" Woods asked. "Veggie croquettes," said Williams. Woods popped a piece into her

mouth. "Mmm," she said, "that's good."

   And good for you, too, especially when compared with the down-home cooking that has nourished

the bodies and souls of African-Americans for decades. Soul food, with its heavy doses of salt, sugar,

and fat, can _____ toxic effects like high blood pressure and diabetes, both
    3
_____ problems for black Americans. Now entrepreneurs like Williams, nutritionists,
    4
and even pastors are on a mission to improve African-American diets, not by condemning their rich

culinary heritage, but by reinventing time-honored recipes. They are asking cooks not to

_____ that soul food requires unhealthy ingredients. Dietitians are teaching family chefs
    5
how to flavor collard greens with smoked turkey instead of pork fat. And around the country, black

churches are giving healthy homilies ("Your body is the temple of God") along with nutritious Sunday dinners: baked chicken and fruit, not fried chicken and biscuits.

| bond | expand | incentive | modify | subsequently |

Aunt Obie's Restaurant, in Waukegan, Illinois, is signing on. Last year chef Charlie Black teamed up with the Lake County Health Department to improve nutrition in the county's African-American population. Black, whose parents both died of heart attacks, eagerly agreed to _____ a
6
handful of items on his menu for a special "heart healthy" day. The numbers say it all: less than 1 gram of fat in his new and improved carrots (seasoned with honey and cilantro) compared with 5 grams in Aunt Obie's original recipe (margarine and sugar); 141 calories in the garlic mashed potatoes compared with 219. Most important for Black, his customers liked the taste; next month he's expanding his menu by offering the dishes as permanent options.

Lindsey Williams is going even farther. A caterer* and chef-in-training, Williams wants to make the cuisine as refined as sushi. As an overweight kid who grew up in his grandmother's restaurant, he and his family shared the _____ of soul food, but they suffered consequences; at his heaviest,
7
in 1997, he weighed 400 pounds. _____ he took the sugar and grease out of his food, and
8
today he is lean and muscular at about 180 pounds. Williams's goal is to _____ soul
9
food's appeal and inspire African-Americans to reclaim their culinary heritage in a healthy way. He is one of many who hope that the _____ of a longer and healthier life will inspire African-
10
Americans to rethink the way they prepare and serve soul food.

*caterer: *a business that provides food and drinks for a party*

(Adapted from "Saving Soul Food," Newsweek, February 6, 2006.)

WORDS IN DISCUSSION

Apply the key words to your own life. Read and discuss each question in small groups. Try to use the key words.

1. **widespread**

   A widespread problem I want to eliminate from the world: _____

   A widespread fashion I like: _____

2. **ultimate**

   My ultimate dream vacation is _____

   The ultimate challenge in my career is _____

3. **expand**

   What I hope to expand in my life: _____

   What I hope not to expand in my life: _____

4. **bond**

A person with whom I feel a close bond: _____

A person with whom I would like to develop a closer bond: _____

5. **presume**

What people might presume about me when they see me on the street:

_____

Someone I know who presumes too much: _____

6. **annual**

An annual tradition for me: _____

An annual holiday celebrated in my country: _____

7. **incentive**

An incentive that could motivate me to work harder: _____

An incentive I might offer children to make them study harder: _____

8. **modify**

Something in my life that I would like to modify: _____

Something perfect that should not be modified: _____

9. **subsequent**

What I will do in the week subsequent to this one: _____

What I will do in the year subsequent to this one: _____

10. **contribute**

Someone who contributed to my growth as a child: _____

What I hope to contribute to the world: _____

▌ WORDS IN WRITING

Choose two topics and write a paragraph on each. Try to use the key words.

1. Describe a person whom you feel **contributed** to **widespread** improvements in your country or the world.

2. What **incentives** would motivate you to make a significant change in your life? Explain in detail.

3. Explain how you would **modify** a typical car to suit your particular preferences.

4. Describe a **bond** that you feel with a person who is special to you. How did this **bond** develop?

5. Would you like to see your native country's population **expand**? Why or why not?

QUIZ 3

PART A

Choose the word that best completes each item and write it in the space provided.

1. Before we submit the proposal, we need to _____ it a bit.
   - a. function
   - b. extract
   - c. modify
   - d. bond

2. It is Juan Camilo's tradition to have a(n) _____ birthday party.
   - a. widespread
   - b. annual
   - c. apparent
   - d. reliable

3. Because of the _____ of a $500 bonus, the factory workers worked overtime.
   - a. extract
   - b. incentive
   - c. proportion
   - d. scope

4. In 1808, Dalton's theory of atoms was an important _____ to science.
   - a. contribution
   - b. extract
   - c. acknowledgment
   - d. norm

5. The explanation for a mysterious occurrence is not always _____.
   - a. subsequent
   - b. unreliable
   - c. distinct
   - d. apparent

6. To understand the Salem witch trials, it is important to consider the social, religious, and economic _____ of life in late seventeenth-century New England.
   - a. eliminations
   - b. aspects
   - c. extracts
   - d. proportions

7. As the car accelerated, the driver _____ from fourth gear to fifth gear.
   - a. expanded
   - b. bonded
   - c. shifted
   - d. conformed

8. Poverty and hunger are _____ problems.
   - a. widespread
   - b. annual
   - c. reliable
   - d. presumed

9. On the TOEFL test, I had to read a(n) _____ from a novel.
   - a. presumption
   - b. shift
   - c. extract
   - d. bond

10. The largest nonprofit organization in the United States is the Bill and Melinda Gates _____.
    - a. Scope
    - b. Aspect
    - c. Incentive
    - d. Foundation

PART B

*Read each statement and write **T** for true and **F** for false in the space provided.*

_____ 1. A rebel wants to **conform**.

_____ 2. If a person makes an **ultimate** decision, other people must agree with it.

_____ 3. You respect a person who has **integrity**.

_____ 4. Criminals **commit** crimes.

_____ 5. A dishwasher does not have a **function**.

_____ 6. An independent person **relies** on everyone else.

_____ 7. The moon's rotation around Earth is beyond the **scope** of an astronomy class.

_____ 8. There are **distinct** differences between a dog and a wolf.

_____ 9. 2008 is **subsequent** to 2009.

_____10. A child and a teenager have different **perspectives** on life.

PART C

Match each sentence with the letter it describes.

_____ 1. When Henry was **justifying** his actions, he said this.

_____ 2. If a university **eliminates** the French department, this happens to French courses.

_____ 3. This person can provide **insight** into the way that machines work.

_____ 4. If a store **expands** its shoe selection, this happens to the shoes there.

_____ 5. Samantha is **presuming** something when she says this.

_____ 6. It is the **norm** for this person to know the prices of new products.

_____ 7. Only a small **proportion** of employees in any company have this job.

_____ 8. If Mayra wants to **trace** her roots, she wants this.

_____ 9. If Larry is **acknowledging** what happened, he says this.

_____10. Rebecca has a **bond** with her parents, so they have this.

a. information about family history

b. a salesperson

c. They are no longer offered.

d. "Yes, I made a mistake."

e. a close relationship

f. a manager

g. "You must be from England."

h. More are available.

i. an engineer

j. "I didn't want to lay off the workers, but it saved a lot of money."

CHAPTER 10

Key Words

appropriate	confer	inherent	regulate	symbol
collapse	devote	minimize	sum	trend

WORDS IN CONTEXT

*Use the sentences to guess what each key word means. Choose the meaning that is closest to that of the key word in **bold**.*

1. appropriate
/əˈprouprɪɪt/
-adjective

- In many countries, it is not **appropriate** to wear a short skirt to a church.
- Singing loudly is usually not **appropriate** behavior on a train.

Appropriate means . . .
- a. correct for all situations
- b. correct for a particular situation
- c. fashionable

2. collapse
/kəˈlæps/
-verb

- When the large oak tree fell on the barn, the barn roof **collapsed**.
- The marathon runner was so exhausted that he **collapsed** after he crossed the finish line.

Collapse means . . .
- a. to fall down suddenly
- b. to be unaffected
- c. to have a small problem

3. confer
/kənˈfɚ/
-verb

- Jack, Jose, and Elaine wanted to **confer** before they answered the offer from the Tokyo office.
- My brother **confers** with his wife when he needs to make an important decision.

Confer means . . .
- a. to explain your opinion to someone
- b. to discuss something with other people
- c. to make a telephone call

4. devote
/dɪˈvout/
-verb

- Julie **devotes** her free time to volunteering at the hospital.
- How many hours a week do you **devote** to learning?

Devote means . . .
- a. to give your time, money, or energy to something or someone
- b. to waste your time, money, or energy on something
- c. to use your time, money, or energy for entertainment

5. inherent
/ɪnˈhɪrənt, -hɛr-/
-adjective

- Lakes are **inherent** in the landscape of Maine; driving toward Canada, you can see dozens of them.
- Because my plan had **inherent** problems, I gave up on it and started a new plan.

Inherent means . . .
- a. manmade and artificial
- b. able to change
- c. naturally and permanently a part of something

6. minimize
/ˈmɪnəˌmaɪz/
-verb

- The doctor wanted to **minimize** the risks to his patient, so he prescribed the lowest dose of the drug.
- A lot of people **minimize** their stress by listening to music.

Minimize means . . .   a. to schedule   b. to make as small as possible   c. to describe something clearly

7. regulate
/ˈrɛgyəˌleɪt/
-verb

- Towns **regulate** how fast people drive by posting speed limit signs.
- The government **regulates** the voting system.

Regulate means . . .   a. to be involved in something   b. to volunteer and help   c. to control an activity or process

8. sum
/sʌm/
-noun

- I can't believe that he spent such a large **sum** of money on his new sofa.
- The city spent a large **sum** of money on new sidewalks.

Sum means . . .   a. effort   b. amount   c. order

9. symbol
/ˈsɪmbəl/
-noun

- White doves are **symbols** of peace.
- For many Americans, the Statue of Liberty is a **symbol** of freedom.

Symbol means . . .   a. a copy of something   b. a gift at a special occasion   c. something that represents a particular idea

10. trend
/trɛnd/
-noun

- In Italy, there is a **trend** of parents having fewer children.
- Is there a **trend** toward more fast food in your native country?

Trend means . . .   a. a dream   b. the way a situation is generally developing or changing   c. the way something will be in the future

▌WORDS AND DEFINITIONS

Read each definition and write the word it defines on the line.

1. _____ to give your time, money, or energy to something

2. _____ to fall down suddenly

3. _____ correct or good for a particular time, situation, or purpose

4. _____ a natural part of something that cannot be separated from it

5. _____ to control an activity or process, usually by having rules

6. _____ to make the degree or amount of something as small as possible

7. _____ the way a situation is generally developing or changing

8. _____ an amount of money

9. _____ to discuss something with other people so that everyone can give his/her opinion

10. _____ a picture, person, or object that represents a particular idea or organization

COMPREHENSION CHECK

Choose the best answer.

1. Who **devotes** a lot of time to her homework?
   a. a lazy student
   b. a hard-working student
   c. a student who often skips class

2. Where is it **appropriate** to wear shorts?
   a. on a ski trip
   b. in a business meeting
   c. at the beach

3. Which of the following is NOT a **symbol**?
   a. love
   b. a flag
   c. H_2O

4. Which is an example of a **sum**?
   a. George gave a generous amount of money to Philip.
   b. Tara walked with her father on the beautiful beach.
   c. Frieda cooked dinner for the whole family.

5. Which is **inherent** in a child?
   a. eye color
   b. education
   c. friends

6. If a bridge **collapses**, what happens to it?
   a. It is built.
   b. It gets weaker.
   c. It falls down.

7. How could you **minimize** your spelling mistakes in an essay?
   a. Write quickly.
   b. Use the spell check on your computer.
   c. Don't bother to use a dictionary.

8. Who **regulates** the amount of food that chickens eat on a farm?
   a. a horse
   b. a farmer
   c. a cat

9. Whom does a rock star probably NOT **confer** with when planning a new show?
   a. his dog
   b. his manager
   c. his publicist

10. Which is a **trend**?
    a. Recently, many girls have become interested in hula dancing.
    b. Around the world, people drink water every day.
    c. Whales live in the ocean.

WORD FAMILIES

Now that you have studied the ten key words and their basic definitions, you are ready to learn words that belong to the same family as some of the key words. A word family includes words that look alike but have different functions (noun, verb, adjective, or adverb). Their meanings are related but different.

A. *Look at each model phrase and decide whether the word in **bold** is used as a noun, verb, adjective, or adverb. Put a check(✓) in the correct column.*

	NOUN	VERB	ADJECTIVE	ADVERB
1. appropriate				
• **appropriate** clothing				
• an **inappropriate** remark				
2. collapse				
• suddenly **collapse**				
• after the **collapse**				
3. confer				
• **confer** with my boss				
• an important **conference**				
4. devote				
• **devote** time and energy				
• total **devotion**				
5. inherent				
• **inherent** problems				
• **inherently** safer				
6. regulate				
• **regulate** gas prices				
• follow **regulations**				
7. symbol				
• a **symbol** of peace				
• a **symbolic** gesture				
• **symbolize** friendship				
8. trend				
• an interesting **trend**				
• a **trendy** girl				

B. *Ethan is talking with the governor about his design for the new museum. Complete the conversation with words from the box.*

collapse	inappropriate	symbolic
conference	inherently	symbolizes
devotion	regulations	trendy

GOVERNOR: Thank you for coming to this _____ 1, Ethan. Your design for the new museum was one of our favorites, and we want to talk to you about it.

ETHAN: It's a pleasure to be here, Governor. I hope I can explain why my design is _____ 2 better than all the others.

GOVERNOR: You don't need to explain the beauty of your design to us. It _____ 3 the spirit of the city! The only problem with the design is the arch on the top.

ETHAN: That's not an arch. It's a bridge, Governor. It's _____ 4 of the connection between different cultures in our city.

GOVERNOR: I don't care what it symbolizes; it looks unstable! I'm afraid it's going to _____ 5.

ETHAN: I can assure you that it's stable. I considered all building _____ 6 when I created this design.

GOVERNOR: Well, even if the bridge is safe, it's not the style we're looking for. We want the museum to look classic, not _____ 7. Something too modern is _____ 8 for the museum.

ETHAN: OK, Governor. I'll modify my design to take out the bridge. Your criticism has not stopped my _____ 9 to this project.

SAME WORD, DIFFERENT MEANING

*Most words have more than one meaning. Study the additional meanings of **collapse**, **sum**, and **trend**.*
Then read each sentence and decide which meaning is used.

a. **collapse** *v.*	to fall suddenly
b. **collapse** *v.*	to fail suddenly
c. **sum** *n.*	an amount of money
d. **sum** *n.*	the total when you add two or more numbers together
e. **trend** *n.*	the way a situation is generally developing or changing
f. **trend** *n.*	a current fashion

_____ 1. The **sum** of two and three is five.

_____ 2. The tunnel was closed after its ceiling **collapsed**.

_____ 3. The latest **trend** among teenage boys is wearing surfing shorts in the city.

_____ 4. According to many economists, it's very unlikely that the stock market will **collapse** as it did in 1929.

_____ 5. When Alfonso lost his wallet, he lost a small **sum** of cash.

_____ 6. As gasoline prices rise, the **trend** among consumers is to buy more fuel-efficient cars.

WORDS IN SENTENCES

Complete each sentence with two of the words from the box.

appropriate	confer	inherently	regulate	symbol
collapsed	devote	minimize	sum	trend

1. The senator asked his public relations advisor if it would be _____ for him to _____ an hour of his time to appearing on the television show.

2. The _____ in states with tobacco prevention programs shows a decrease in high school students who smoke, but attempts to _____ youth marketing of tobacco products continue to be blocked in Congress.

3. Eagles are _____ strong, fast, and independent, so Jill and her advertising team plan to use an eagle as the _____ of a new hybrid car.

4. To _____ the risk of getting lost, please _____ with the other members of the bike trip about when and where you plan to meet up on the route.

5. It will take a large _____ of money to rebuild Longfellow Bridge, which _____ in an ice storm last winter.

WORDS IN COLLOCATIONS AND EXPRESSIONS

Following are common collocations and expressions with some of the key words. Read the definitions and then complete the conversation with the collocations and expressions. You may have to change word forms for correct grammar.

1. **appropriate**	
• **appropriate for**	correct for a situation, time, or purpose
2. **confer**	
• **confer with**	to discuss with other people
3. **devote**	
• **devote yourself to (sth)**	to do everything you can to achieve something or help someone
4. **minimize**	
• **minimize the risk of (sth)**	to make the risk of something as small as possible
5. **symbol**	
• **symbol of**	something that represents a particular idea
6. **trend**	
• **fashion trend**	the current style in fashion

JOB CENTER COUNSELOR: Your resume looks great, Sean, and I believe you're ready to answer the questions in your interview successfully. Now you've got about an hour to go home and change your clothes before the recruiter arrives.

SEAN: Change my clothes? Why?

JOB CENTER COUNSELOR: You're wearing red pants.

SEAN: So? Red is the latest _____. Besides, I'm
₁ interviewing for a computer job. Everyone knows that computer programmers are very relaxed. We can wear anything.

JOB CENTER COUNSELOR: I have to disagree with you. Over the years, I have

_____ a few recruiters about the importance of
₂
professional clothing at an interview. They have told me that they want to hire someone who looks serious. This means that red pants are not

_____ an interview.
₃

SEAN: Come on! Red is the _____ strength and passion.
₄
If I wear red, the interviewer will know that I am a strong candidate for this job.

JOB CENTER COUNSELOR: Or she many think you're completely inappropriate for a professional position in her company. Please, Sean, take my advice. You've

_____ studying computers for four years. Don't
₅
waste all those years of hard work by insisting on wearing red pants to this interview.

SEAN: I guess you've got a point. I think the pants are OK, but to

_____ making a bad impression, I'll change them.
                             6

JOB CENTER COUNSELOR: I think that's a wise decision.

▌WORDS IN A READING

Read this article about community service. Complete it with words from the boxes.

collapsed	confer with	devote	minimize	sum	symbolizes

VOLUNTEERS CATCH PICKPOCKETS IN VENICE

For most visitors, Venice, Italy, _____ romance. Every year, 12 million visitors come
                                              1
to enjoy the legendary beauty of the water city. However, there is a small group of people who come for
a different reason: to steal from the tourists. Anton, a migrant pickpocket from Romania, arrived in
Venice with hopes of snatching purses and wallets. However, Anton's hopes _____ when,
                                                                                    2
in just five days, the seventeen-year-old Romanian was arrested twice. "Venice is beautiful, but not for
work," he complained as police booked him.

But it wasn't the police who caught him. This pickpocket was caught both times by a civilian
antipickpocket patrol called Cittadini Non Distratti, or Undistracted Citizens. Members, who call
themselves the "Cittadini," the "Citizens," walk around Venice looking for pickpockets. This group of
volunteers aims to _____ pickpocketing in their city. The Cittadini Non Distratti look for
                          3
a number of giveaways. Most pickpockets are men, they travel in small teams behind tourists, they
stop when tourists stop, and their eyes focus on vulnerable pockets and bags—not gondolas and pretty
buildings. The presence of a teenager is another clue (minors risk lighter punishment). Sudden
distractions are an even bigger signal: a person holding a map tries to _____ a tourist
                                                                                      4
about directions; food is spilled on a tourist by an apologetic stranger; a heated argument diverts
attention.

More than 200 Venetians have paid a small _____ for a Cittadini Non Distratti
                                                        5
membership card. Fewer _____ time to frequently searching the city for pickpockets.
                                  6
The group is legal, as long as members are unarmed and grab suspects only *after* they've slipped a
hand into another's pocket. They must then call the cops immediately.

appropriate	inherent	regulate	trend

Initially, the police were worried that the Cittadini might be targeting foreigners (in Venice, 96 percent
of arrested pickpockets come from outside the European Union). But the police soon warmed up, realizing
that the group simply was acting to help _____ the safety of the city and its visitors.
                                                    7

City Hall, however, has refused Cittadini Non Distratti's requests for official recognition and support. The city government does not feel that it is _____ for these citizens to be

8

working against crime. The Cittadini couldn't care less that they don't have the government's support. They feel that they are responsible for the fact that pickpocketing is down by half from last year's level.

The Cittadini enjoy wide popular support and regular praise in the local press (an unofficial Venice Web site nicknamed them the "Guardian Angels of Tourists"). Remaining anonymous is

_____ to the success of their work, so members won't let newspapers photograph them.

9

Still, many strangers know who they are and stop them in the street to give thanks. Members refuse thank-you money from people they have saved and bribes from trapped pickpockets desperate to keep out of jail.

Rome Police Chief Aldo Zanetti says that this "participative security" is increasingly common in Italy, and this new culture seems to be working. According to numbers in a 2005 Interior Ministry report, pickpocketing and purse-snatching have declined nationwide every year since 1997. The report attributes part of this success to cooperation among the citizens, police, and other institutions.

This raises two questions: Will this _____ of citizens protecting their cities from

10

pickpockets continue to grow in Italy, and will it spread to other countries?

(Adapted from "The Curse of the Venetian Pickpockets," Slate.com, February 20, 2006.)

▌WORDS IN DISCUSSION

Read the questions and choose the best answers. Then discuss your answers in small groups.

1. What would you do if you were camping during a strong windstorm, and your tent **collapsed** in the middle of the night?

   a. I would go into the windy night and try to set up my tent again.

   b. I would lie awake, scared and unmoving.

   c. I would run to my car and drive away.

2. Which animal would be the best **symbol** for your work habits?

   a. a cat, to symbolize how I am smart but a bit lazy

   b. a lion, to symbolize how I am strong and serious

   c. a turtle, to symbolize how slow I am

3. How could you best **minimize** your stress?

   a. spend more time with people I love

   b. exercise more

   c. spend more time doing activities that are fun or meaningful for me

4. How much time do you **devote** to improving your English every day?

   a. over 3 hours

   b. 1–3 hours

   c. under an hour

5. What do you most wish you could **regulate**?

   a. my salary

   b. the weather

   c. my weight

6. With whom would you first **confer** if you were thinking about moving to a new country?

   a. someone in my family

   b. a person I love

   c. my boss

7. In your opinion, is it **appropriate** to talk on a cell phone in a restaurant?

   a. Yes, of course! I do it all the time.

   b. No, but I've done it once or twice.

   c. No, it is totally inappropriate. People who talk on phones in restaurants are rude.

8. Which characteristic do you most hope will be **inherent** in the personality of your child?

   a. honesty

   b. kindness

   c. a sense of humor

9. If the **sum** of your life's savings adds up to only $100 when you are very old, how will you feel?

   a. great, if I have enjoyed my life

   b. a bit disappointed that I could not have saved more

   c. miserable—all that hard work for nothing

10. What do you think about the warming **trend** in the world's climate?

   a. It's great. I live in a cold place, so I'm happy that the weather is getting warmer.

   b. I don't know very much about environmental issues, so I don't have an opinion.

   c. I am very worried that this warming trend could cause serious problems for our planet.

▌ WORDS IN WRITING

Choose two topics and write a paragraph on each. Try to use the key words.

1. Describe something that is a **symbol** of your native country. Do you feel that it is the most **appropriate symbol**, or can you suggest something else that would better **symbolize** your country?

2. Describe a person whom you admire who is completely **devoted** to someone or something that she or he loves. (This person might be **devoted** to a husband or wife, a job, or a religion, for example.)

3. What part of your personality do you feel is **inherent** and what part have you acquired through experience? Explain.

4. Whom would you like to **confer** with about **minimizing** world problems? What is the main issue you would like to **confer** about with this person?

5. Describe a **trend** that you notice happening where you live. What is this **trend**, and why does it interest you?

Key Words

anticipate	detect	evaluate	overlap	resource
capable	estimate	fund	primary	terminate

▌ WORDS IN CONTEXT

*Use the sentences to guess what each key word means. Choose the meaning that is closest to that of the key word in **bold**.*

1. anticipate
/æn'tɪsə,peɪt/
-verb

- Many department stores in the United States **anticipate** large numbers of shoppers on the day after Thanksgiving, so they plan to open early on that day.
- Jack **anticipated** a cold winter, so he bought a warm coat.

Anticipate means . . . a. to expect something to happen b. to make a plan c. to discuss the future

2. capable
/'keɪpəbəl/
-adjective

- If you could speak several languages fluently, you would be **capable** of working as a translator.
- An elementary school teacher must be **capable** of leading and controlling a large group of children.

Capable means . . . a. having many talents b. having the power or skill needed to do something c. being interested in a specific job

3. detect
/dɪ'tɛkt/
-verb

- If you step off a train in Antalya, Turkey, you may **detect** the smell of the sea in the air.
- Few people could figure out what the secret ingredient was in Emily's cookies, but Jared was able to **detect** the taste of cardamom.

Detect means . . . a. to notice or discover something b. to taste something c. to enjoy

4. estimate
/'ɛstə,meɪt/
-verb

- Companies often **estimate** their yearly profits at the beginning of the year; if they don't do as well as **estimated**, their stocks usually lose value.
- Art dealers **estimate** that Van Gogh's painting *Self-Portrait without Beard* is worth at least $70 million.

Estimate means . . . a. to sell something b. to discuss something expensive c. to calculate something approximately

5. evaluate
/ɪ'vælyu,eɪt/
-verb

- In the Olympics, judges **evaluate** figure skaters using a ten-point system.
- Food critics use several criteria when **evaluating** a restaurant, such as quality, freshness, creativity, presentation, and price.

Evaluate means . . . a. to view or experience something entertaining b. to carefully judge how good someone or something is c. to make a choice

6. fund
/fʌnd/
-verb

- Several local businesses are **funding** the children's art festival.
- Listeners, rather than advertisers, **fund** National Public Radio.

Fund means . . . a. to provide money for b. to be involved in a cultural activity c. to make an announcement

7. overlap
/ˌoʊvɚˈlæp/
-verb

- If you put a piece of paper partially on top of a book, the paper is **overlapping** the book.
- I don't like how the picture **overlaps** the frame; it looks weird!

Overlap means . . . a. two things share the exact same space b. part of one thing covers part of another thing c. to be inside something else

8. primary
/ˈpraɪˌmɛri, -məri/
-adjective

- Jang's **primary** reason for improving his English is preparing for his new job, but he also wants to improve his English to understand movies better.
- Biology is my **primary** interest, but I am also studying chemistry.

Primary means . . . a. bright b. interesting c. most important; main

9. resource
/ˈrisɔrs/
-noun

- The Internet can be an excellent **resource** for students; it helps them find information quickly.
- Peter often takes his company's shuttle bus from San Francisco to his office in Silicon Valley; he appreciates this **resource** because he doesn't like to drive.

Resource means . . . a. something that makes an activity easier b. something free c. a kind of technology

10. terminate
/ˌtɚməˌneɪt/
-verb

- When the bank **terminated** its Saturday hours, the customers were upset.
- Emma **terminated** her relationship with her accountant when she learned that he was going to jail.

Terminate means . . . a. to continue b. to make longer c. to end

▌ WORDS AND DEFINITIONS

Read each definition and write the word it defines on the line.

1. _____ most important; main

2. _____ to provide money for an activity, organization, or event

3. _____ to carefully judge how good, useful, or successful someone or something is

4. _____ to end

5. _____ something that can be used to make a job or activity easier

6. _____ having the power, skill, or other qualities needed to do something

7. _____ to expect something to happen

8. _____ part of one thing covers part of another thing; to share some parts

9. _____ to calculate the approximate value or size of something

10. _____ to notice or discover something, especially something that is not easy to see, hear, etc.

▌COMPREHENSION CHECK

Choose the best answer.

1. Who usually **funds** a young child's karate class?
   a. the karate teacher
   b. the child's mother or father
   c. the classmates

2. Which animal is **capable** of living in the desert for a week?
   a. a polar bear
   b. a camel
   c. a chimpanzee

3. Who could best **evaluate** a teenager's writing skill?
   a. his friends
   b. his English teacher
   c. his girlfriend

4. If two carpets **overlap**, it means
   a. one partly covers the other
   b. their colors match exactly
   c. they cover the entire floor

5. What is the **primary** reason for eating?
   a. hunger
   b. entertainment
   c. routine

6. Which is NOT a **resource** for a writer?
   a. a computer
   b. a library
   c. a window

7. If you **estimate** the number of people who will come to your party,
   a. you know the exact number
   b. you have no idea how many people will come
   c. you have an idea of the approximate number of people who will come

8. If a road **terminates** in New Orleans, the road
   a. begins there.
   b. ends there.
   c. divides into two new roads there.

9. If Harriet **anticipates** no problems moving to her new house, she feels
   a. happy.
   b. worried.
   c. confused.

10. If a police inspector looks carefully at the mud, what might he **detect**?
    a. a dog
    b. a big puddle
    c. a footprint

WORD FAMILIES

Now that you have studied the ten key words and their basic definitions, you are ready to learn words that belong to the same family as some of the key words. A word family includes words that look alike but have different functions (noun, verb, adjective, or adverb). Their meanings are related but different.

A. *Look at each model phrase and decide whether the word in **bold** is used as a noun, verb, adjective, or adverb. Put a check (✓) in the correct column.*

	NOUN	VERB	ADJECTIVE	ADVERB
1. **anticipate**				
• **anticipate** success				
• our **anticipation**				
2. **detect**				
• **detect** a fingerprint on the glass				
• the **detective** investigates				
• a smoke **detector**				
3. **estimate**				
• **estimate** the distance				
• give me an **estimate**				
4. **evaluate**				
• **evaluate** a building				
• a poor **evaluation**				
5. **fund**				
• how to **fund** the school play				
• donate money to a **fund**				
6. **primary**				
• the **primary** election				
• **primarily**, I hope to learn				

B. *Read the first half of each sentence and match it with the appropriate ending.*

_____ 1. While we waited for the bride to appear, the church was filled with

_____ 2. If you want to find out who stole your car, hire a private

_____ 3. Every home should have a smoke

_____ 4. Sometimes I speak Spanish and Italian, but I

_____ 5. At the end of the diving course, we filled out a(n)

_____ 6. Kevin asked the carpenter for a(n)

_____ 7. UNICEF is a(n)

a. **primarily** speak English.

b. **evaluation** that expressed our opinions about it.

c. **anticipation**.

d. **fund** that helps children.

e. **detector** to alert people if there is a fire.

f. **estimate** of the cost to repair the roof.

g. **detective**.

SAME WORD, DIFFERENT MEANING

Most words have more than one meaning. Study the additional meanings of **anticipate**, **overlap**, and **resource**. Then read each sentence and decide which meaning is used.

a. **anticipate** v.	to expect that something will happen
b. **anticipate** v.	to think about something good that is going to happen
c. **overlap** v.	part of one thing covers part of another thing
d. **overlap** v.	two subjects, activities, or ideas share some but not all of the same parts or qualities
e. **resource** v.	something that can be used to make a job or activity easier
f. **resource** v.	something such as land, minerals, or natural energy that exists in a country and can be used to increase the country's wealth

_____ 1. Oil is a **resource** of Saudi Arabia.

_____ 2. The letters are **overlapping** the newspaper on the dining room table.

_____ 3. After six months of winter, my family was **anticipating** the arrival of spring.

_____ 4. The Internet is a valuable **resource** for students.

_____ 5. The weather forecaster **anticipates** many hurricanes this year.

_____ 6. The subjects of algebra and geometry **overlap**; they contain some of the same material, but otherwise are different.

WORDS IN SENTENCES

Complete each sentence with one of the words from the box.

| anticipation | detective | evaluation | overlap | resource |
| capable | estimate | Fund | primarily | terminates |

1. After the ruby necklace disappeared mysteriously in the middle of the night, the duke and his wife hired a(n) _____ to find out who had stolen it.

2. The World Wildlife _____ provides money to rescue and care for animals.

3. After hearing the doctor's _____ of her health, Jen decided to start exercising.

4. As the crowd waited for the three tenors to come on stage, the theater was filled with _____.

5. A stamp dealer told Henry that his stamp collection was worth about $500, but Henry felt that this _____ was too low.

6. An infant isn't _____ of deceiving his or her parents.

7. Paulo is _____ interested in antique cars from the 1920s, but he also likes cars from the 1950s.

8. A guidance counselor is an important _____ for high school students who are planning their future.

9. Natalie's trip to Rome is going to _____ with Yukiko's trip there, so they are planning to meet for a day.

10. The Trans-Siberian railroad begins in Russia and _____ in China.

WORDS IN COLLOCATIONS AND EXPRESSIONS

Following are common collocations and expressions with some of the key words. Read the definitions and then complete the conversations with the collocations and expressions. You may have to change word forms for correct grammar.

1. **capable**	
• **capable of**	having the power or skill needed to do something
2. **estimate**	
• **estimate (sth) to be**	judge something to be
• **a rough estimate**	a calculation that is not very exact
3. **overlap**	
• **overlapping subjects**	subjects that share some but not all of the same content
4. **primary**	
• **primary care**	the main medical help that you get before your doctor decides that you need to see a specialist
5. **resource**	
• **natural resources**	things such as land, minerals, or natural energy that exist in a country and can be used to increase the country's wealth

1.   CARLY: How much will it cost to build my porch?

     CARPENTER: I'm not sure exactly.

     CARLY: That's OK. Can you give me _____?

2.   COMPANY
     PRESIDENT: I believe we are _____ selling more furniture.

     JIM: How much more?

     COMPANY
     PRESIDENT: If we follow my sales plan, I _____ our profits next year _____ twice what they are now.

3.   ELDERLY WOMAN: Will you be performing my eye surgery, Dr. Smith?

DR. SMITH:	No, Mrs. Lee. I'm just your _____ doctor. A specialist will take care of your eye. Don't worry, I'll make sure that you get the best care.
ELDERLY WOMAN:	Thank you.

4.
MIKE:	Want to study with me tonight, Lucy?
LUCY:	Why would I want to study with you?
MIKE:	Because you're studying physics and I'm studying geometry. Those are _____. Maybe we could help each other.
LUCY:	Thanks, but no thanks.

5.
BO:	What are some of the _____ in Venezuela?
HECTOR:	Oil, sun, and land.

▮ WORDS IN A READING

Read this article about space. Complete it with words and expressions from the boxes.

capable of	detect	estimates to be	funding	primary

FIVE STARS THAT COULD SUPPORT LIFE ON OTHER PLANETS

In an atmosphere of looming* federal _____ cuts, the search for intelligent life on
other planets is still capturing the imaginations—and research interests—of astronomers.

Scientists already know that only a tiny fraction of the 200 to 400 billion stars in our galaxy seem
to be _____ supporting life on orbiting planets. Now researchers think they know where
such potential habitable** stars—or "habstars"—hang in the sky.

Margaret Turnbull, of the Carnegie Institution in Washington, D.C., recently released her list of the
top five potential habstars in our galaxy, three of which can be seen from Earth with the unaided eye.

Locating these sunlike stars, she says, is a step toward the eventual search for life on other
planets—intelligent or otherwise. "What we are thinking about now is how to _____ the
stars, then the planets, and then life," Turnbull said.

Scientists have spent years identifying and studying the basic characteristics of stars in our galaxy,
the Milky Way. They have found that stars vary in their characteristics and that some probably have
"habitable zones." Astronomers use this phrase to describe both the region around a star that may
support life on planets and areas on planets that are friendly to life.

Turnbull studied vast amounts of information about stars to come up with an initial catalog of
17,129 potential habstar systems, which she released in 2003. From this catalog she further narrowed
the search.

The list was prepared for the SETI (Search for Extraterrestrial Intelligence) Institute. Scientists at
SETI are listening for radio signals from other intelligent civilizations in our galaxy. Stars that SETI

might want to aim radio scanners at, Turnbull said, would probably be similar to our sun and should therefore meet several key criteria.

A star's age is a _____ factor: It should be old enough for planets to form and
                              4
complex life to arise, an age Turnbull _____ at least 3 billion years.
                                                        5

A star's size and brilliance can indicate its age, so Turnbull chose small, stable, dim stars with no other stars orbiting them.

| anticipate | evaluating | overlap | resource | terminate |

Activity is also important when _____ a star: "Some stars do a lot of flaring. Our sun
                                                    6
has big flares, but nothing like flares of other stars in our neighborhood," she said. Huge flares could
_____ life on nearby planets.
          7

But if any of Turnbull's picks turn out to have planets that are worth a closer look, it may be a long while before anyone on Earth could make the voyage. The closest is about five light-years away.

Another NASA team plans to shoot a giant telescope dubbed Kepler into space in 2008 to detect suns with planets.

"It will be the first time that this will be done," said Dimitar Sasselov, an astronomy professor at the Harvard-Smithsonian Center for Astrophysics in Cambridge, Massachusetts.

The Kepler telescope is a(n) _____ that will help answer the question "How many
                                          8
stars like the sun have planets orbiting them like the Earth?" said Sasselov, who is assisting with the project.

Named after the medieval astronomer Johannes Kepler, the telescope will be aimed at stars in and around the constellation Cygnus, which contains many stars like our sun. Kepler will take photographs continuously for five years, documenting when orbiting planets pass in front of their stars.

The Kepler research will _____ nicely with Turnbull's work, Sasselov said. Of the
                                      9
hundred thousand stars Kepler will observe, he expects two to three thousand to have planets circling them and about thirty of these planets to be like Earth.

Since stars in Cygnus are about a thousand light-years away, researchers do not _____
                                                                                              10
any trips to potentially habitable planets found there in our near future. But that doesn't worry Sasselov. He believes that we can do remote sensing and that one day we will be able to visit them.

*looming: *likely to happen soon.*

**habitable: *suitable for people to live in*

(Adapted from *"Top Five Stars That May Support Life Announced," National Geographic News, February 23, 2006.*)

WORDS IN DISCUSSION

Apply the key words to your own life. Read and discuss each question in small groups. Try to use the key words.

1. **capable**

   Something I am capable of doing: _____

   Something I wish I were capable of doing: _____

2. **evaluate**

   Something (music, clothing, cars, etc.) I often evaluate with my friends:

   _____

   How I feel when someone evaluates my English: _____

3. **primary**

   My primary reason for living where I do: _____

   The primary language I speak in my home: _____

4. **fund**

   An organization I would fund if I had a lot of money: _____

   An organization I would never fund: _____

5. **detect**

   A smell I can detect in the air now: _____

   What I think about becoming a detective: _____

6. **resource**

   A resource that helps me do my job or study: _____

   A resource that I imagine will help my grandchildren work
   fifty years from now: _____

7. **estimate**

   What I estimate the value of all my clothing to be: $_____

   The estimated amount of time I need to perfect my English: _____

8. **terminate**

   Something I do that I plan to terminate: _____

   How many times I have seen the movie *The Terminator:* _____

9. **overlap**

   Two things I can see now that are overlapping:_____

   Two overlapping subjects that interest me: _____

10. **anticipate**

    Something I anticipate will happen to me tomorrow: _____

    A time when I felt nervous and excited with anticipation:_____

WORDS IN WRITING

Choose two topics and write a paragraph on each. Try to use the key words.

1. Do you feel that the government of your native country **funds** the arts too much, the correct amount, or not enough? Explain why.

2. Describe the natural **resources** of your native country and **estimate** how the resources could affect the country's future if used correctly.

3. **Evaluate** your ability at one of your **primary** hobbies.

4. Describe a sport which many people in your country are **capable** of doing well. Do you feel that their **capability** is genetic or learned? Explain.

5. If the high school in your town wanted to use a metal **detector** to check whether students were bringing weapons to school, would you support this decision? Why or why not?

WORDS IN CONTEXT

*Use the sentences to guess what each key word means. Choose the meaning that is closest to that of the key word in **bold**.*

1. **compensate**
   /ˈkɑmpənˌseɪt/
   -verb

   - Jim tried to **compensate** for being late to dinner by bringing flowers for his wife.
   - If you are studying a subject at which you are not naturally talented, do you **compensate** by working harder?

   Compensate means . . .

   a. to give a gift
   b. to do something to reduce a bad effect
   c. to deny that you have a probem

2. **controversy**
   /ˈkɑntrəˌvɚsi/
   -noun

   - In Tracy's high school, there is a **controversy** over school uniforms; everyone is arguing because a lot of students want them, and a lot of students don't.
   - Diana always expresses her opinion about a **controversy**, but her sisters would rather not speak about emotional or divisive subjects.

   Controversy means . . .

   a. a small problem you can easily fix
   b. differences of opinion among family or friends
   c. a serious disagreement among many people

3. **distort**
   /dɪˈstɔrt/
   -verb

   - Hank Smith, a dishonest reporter, **distorted** the story in the newspaper article; he said a seven-year-old girl drove a car through New York City, when in fact the child drove only to the end of her driveway.
   - Helen **distorted** the politician's comments in her report; he'd been joking, but she wrote that his remark was serious.

   Distort means . . .

   a. to show something clearly
   b. to make something seem more beautiful
   c. to make something seem to mean something different from what it really means

4. **emerge**
   /ɪˈmɚdʒ/
   -verb

   - In the spring, crocuses are one of the first flowers to **emerge** from the soil.
   - A good swimmer can stay underwater for several seconds before needing to **emerge** and breathe air.

   Emerge means . . .

   a. to appear after being hidden
   b. to grow
   c. to breathe

5. facilitate
/fəˈsɪləˌteɪt/
-verb

- Learning a new language is difficult, but a good teacher can **facilitate** the process.
- A skillful employee can **facilitate** a business meeting.

Facilitate means . . .   a. to talk to a group   b. to make it easier for something to happen   c. to talk about difficult things

6. identical
/aɪˈdɛntɪkəl/
-adjective

- Mike and his **identical** twin, Joe, like to fool people; sometimes Mike skips class and Joe goes in his place.
- Are your eyes **identical**, or is one slightly different from the other?

Identical means . . .   a. similar   b. quite different   c. exactly the same

7. intense
/ɪnˈtɛns/
-adjective

- Because of the **intense** heat, the street was almost empty on that summer day.
- In medical school, there is **intense** pressure to work hard.

Intense means . . .   a. having a very strong effect   b. quiet   c. having a relaxing effect

8. phase
/feɪz/
-noun

- In an early **phase** of the project, the team planned for the hotel to use electricity for all its power, but in a later **phase** they decided that they could get half its energy from solar power.
- The cycle of the moon has eight **phases.**

Phase means . . .   a. the beginning of something   b. light   c. one part of a process

9. reverse
/rɪˈvɚs/
-verb

- The Supreme Court **reversed** the lower court's decision about Sam Jones; he was no longer considered guilty. Instead, he was proclaimed innocent.
- When leaving a parking spot, you usually need to **reverse** the direction of your car.

Reverse means . . .   a. to change something so that it is the opposite of what it was before   b. to discuss the direction of something   c. to move something for a good reason

10. scheme
/skim/
-noun

- Although Fred and Pete were not invited to the rock star's party, Fred had a **scheme**: they would dress as waiters to get inside.
- Instead of working on his essay, Patrick came up with a **scheme** for getting out of writing it.

Scheme means . . .   a. a plan, especially to do something bad or illegal   b. a quick decision to do something helpful   c. an important idea

WORDS AND DEFINITIONS

Read each definition and write the word it defines on the line.

1. _____ exactly the same

2. _____ to appear after being hidden

3. _____ to explain something in a way that makes it seem to mean something different from what it really means

4. _____ a plan, especially to do something bad or illegal

5. _____ to do something to reduce or balance the bad effect of something

6. _____ one part of the process in which something develops

7. _____ to change something so that it is the opposite of what it was before

8. _____ a serious disagreement among many people

9. _____ to make it easier for something to happen

10. _____ having a very strong effect or felt very strongly

COMPREHENSION CHECK

Choose the best answer.

1. An **intense** musician plays
   a. softly.
   b. with strong emotion.
   c. with mild interest.

2. If you are driving north and then **reverse** your direction, you drive
   a. east.
   b. south.
   c. northeast.

3. If a bird **emerges** from its nest, the bird
   a. hides within the nest.
   b. looks out of the nest.
   c. flies out of the nest.

4. Which of the following is **identical** to ☺?
   a. a good mood
   b. ☺
   c. ☹

5. Which of the following is NOT a **phase** of a butterfly's life?
   a. birth
   b. living as a caterpillar
   c. living in the ocean

6. Who **facilitates** learning in the classroom?
   a. a teacher
   b. a noisy student
   c. an entertainer

7. If Kenny **distorts** the truth, he
   a. tells a true story.
   b. tells an enjoyable story.
   c. tells a story inaccurately.

8. How can Joe best **compensate** for crashing and destroying his brother's car?

    a. He can pretend that he was not involved in the car crash.

    b. He can say that his brother is lucky to be rid of the old car.

    c. He can apologize, and buy his brother a new car.

9. What kind of opinions do people have about a **controversy**?

    a. identical

    b. strong and emotional

    c. sweet and gentle

10. If Jen has a **scheme** to make money, she has

    a. a partner.

    b. a plan.

    c. a photocopier.

WORD FAMILIES

Now that you have studied the ten key words and their basic definitions, you are ready to learn words that belong to the same family as some of the key words. A word family includes words that look alike but have different functions (noun, verb, adjective, or adverb). Their meanings are related but different.

A. *Look at each model phrase and decide whether the word in **bold** is used as a noun, verb, adjective, or adverb. Put a check (✔) in the correct column.*

	NOUN	VERB	ADJECTIVE	ADVERB
1. **compensate**				
• **compensate** for my mistake				
• adequate **compensation**				
2. **controversy**				
• a major **controversy**				
• a **controversial** subject				
3. **distort**				
• **distort** the truth				
• obvious **distortion** of the facts				
4. **emerge**				
• new details are **emerging**				
• the **emergence** of a new artist				
5. **intense**				
• an **intense** storm				
• **intensify** the colors				
6. **reverse**				
• **reverse** directions				
• a **reversal** of fortune				
7. **scheme**				
• a get-rich-quick **scheme**				
• quietly **scheme**				

B. *Daphne is talking with her lawyer about a court case. Complete the conversation with words from the box.*

compensation	distortion	intensify	scheme
controversial	emergence	reversal	

LAWYER: Daphne, we need to come up with a strategy for your trial tomorrow. The _____ of the photos showing you stealing the diamond have hurt our case.

1

DAPHNE: I can't believe you trust the newspaper that published those photos! The pictures are a(n) _____ of the truth.

2

LAWYER: Sorry, Daphne, but you and I both know that the photos are real. You took the diamond from the jewelry store. If you deny this in court, you'll only _____ the judge's disapproval and worsen your punishment.

3

DAPHNE: OK, so I took the diamond. Let's offer the store _____ for it—$50,000, and then I won't have to go to court.

4

LAWYER: The jewelry store won't be satisfied with money. You stole the diamond, and robbery is a crime. Because you are a famous actress, it would be _____ for them to allow you to go free without punishment.

5

DAPHNE: What kind of punishment? Do you mean I'll have to go to jail? I'm paying you a lot of money. You're supposed to come up with a(n) _____ to get me out of this mess.

6

LAWYER: Don't worry, Daphne. If the judge sentences you to jail time, we'll appeal and ask for a _____ of the decision. Everything is going to be okay.

7

SAME WORD, DIFFERENT MEANING

Most words have more than one meaning. Study the additional meanings of **compensate, emerge,** and **intense**.
Then read each sentence and decide which meaning is used.

a.	**compensate** *v.*	to do something to reduce or balance the bad effect of something
b.	**compensate** *v.*	to pay someone money because he or she has suffered injury, loss, or damage
c.	**emerge** *v.*	to appear after being hidden
d.	**emerge** *v.*	to have a particular quality or position after experiencing a difficult situation
e.	**intense** *adj.*	having a very strong effect, or felt very strongly
f.	**intense** *adj.*	serious and having very strong feelings or opinions

____ 1. Anne is really **intense**; I'm not surprised that her poetry is so emotional.

____ 2. The black bear **emerged** from its cave when spring began.

____ 3. The teacher **compensated** for being late by staying late at the end of class.

____ 4. An **intense** storm ripped the roof off the restaurant.

____ 5. The oil company will **compensate** the victims of the oil spill.

____ 6. A surprise winner **emerged** from the golf championship.

WORDS IN SENTENCES

Complete each sentence with two of the words from the box.

compensate	distorted	facilitate	intense	reversed
controversy	emerge	identical	phase	scheme

1. In the first _____ of their _____ to make $1 million, Greg and Olivia needed to find investors who would give them money to build the new casino.

2. If you look in a mirror, your reflection will be almost _____ to you, but if you look in a lake, your reflection will be _____.

3. Because there is usually _____ discussion about a _____, it is usually considered impolite to debate controversial subjects at a dinner party.

4. After the United States _____ segregation in the 1960s, ending the separation of blacks and whites, many people believed that more needed to be done to _____ for the years of discrimination that African-Americans had faced.

5. When new health facts _____, becoming known to doctors and patients, they can _____ healthy living.

WORDS IN COLLOCATIONS AND EXPRESSIONS

Following are common collocations and expressions with some of the key words. Read the definitions and then complete the conversation with the the collocations and expressions. You may have to change word forms for correct grammar.

1. **compensate**
   - **compensate for**   to do something to reduce or balance the bad effect of something

2. **controversy**
   - **controversy over**   emotional disagreement about a subject that people have strong opinions about
   - **controversial subject**   a subject that causes a lot of disagreement because many people have strong opinions about it

3. **identical**
   - **identical to**   exactly the same as

4. **intense**
   - **intense person**   a serious person who has very strong emotions or opinions

5. **phase**
   - **going through a phase**   to act in an unusual way for a short time while growing up

RA (RESIDENT ASSISTANT):   What's the matter, Rosie?

ROSIE: My roommate talks too much. I can't relax or study in the room. Half the time she's on the phone having emotional conversations with her boyfriend, and the other half, her friends from the philosophy club are in our room debating a(n) _____ 1 . Last night they were arguing about the _____ 2 women fighting in the military.

RA: Wow, she sounds like a(n) _____ 3 . Have you asked her to talk less?

ROSIE: Yes, and she told me I should talk more! She said that I'm too quiet and that it's good for me to have a roommate who isn't _____ 4 me. She says she has to talk a lot to _____ 5 my silence!

RA: Are you really quiet?

ROSIE: Yes. It's strange, I used to talk a lot, but ever since I started college, I haven't felt like talking. My mom says I'm just _____ 6 .

RA: Maybe it's because you feel uncomfortable in your room. I'd like to talk to your roommate and you together. I hope we can all come up with a solution.

Read this article about bottled water. Complete it with words and expressions from the boxes.

controversial	distorted	emerged	identical to	reverse

IS BOTTLED WATER REALLY HEALTHIER THAN TAP WATER?

A bottle of spring or mineral water has become the lifestyle accessory of the health conscious. No longer a luxury item, the beverage has become a common sight worldwide. But according to campaigners who hope to _____ this trend, the planet's health may be suffering as a
1
result.

A new report has _____ that warns that people's thirst for bottled water is producing
2
unnecessary garbage and consuming vast quantities of energy, even in areas where perfectly good drinking water is available on tap.

The report, released earlier this month by the Earth Policy Institute (EPI) of Washington, D.C., says that global consumption of bottled water doubled between 1999 and 2004, reaching forty-one billion gallons (154 billion liters) annually. Bottled water is often no healthier than tap water, but it can be 10,000 times more expensive, costing more per liter than gasoline, says Emily Arnold, a researcher with the Washington-based nonprofit.

Most of this extra cost is driven by transportation and packaging, as almost a quarter of all bottled water must cross national borders to reach consumers. The report lists the United States as the world's biggest drinker of bottled water, consuming seven billion gallons (twenty-six billion liters) annually. Mexico has the second highest consumption, followed by China and Brazil. Italians drink the most per person, equivalent to about two glasses a day.

For many developed nations, environmental groups make the _____ challenge that
3
water from the tap is as healthy as water from a bottle. The Natural Resources Defense Council, which carried out a four-year review of the bottled water industry, estimated that twenty-five percent of bottled water is _____ tap water; in fact, it is "really just tap water in a bottle—
4
sometimes further treated, sometimes not."

In Great Britain, the Chartered Institution of Water and Environmental Management recently published a report questioning the quality, labeling, and environmental cost of bottled water. "Branding and bottling of water where there already exists a wholesome and safe supply of . . . drinking water cannot be seen as a sustainable use of natural resources," said Nick Reeves, the institution's executive director.

He says that people have the _____ perception that the bottled product is purer than
5
tap water. They are not aware that the high mineral content in some bottled waters is not good for babies or young children.

| compensate for | facilitates | intense | phase | scheme |

But the International Bottled Water Association (IBWA) says that the product _____
6
healthy living by providing a convenient, healthy alternative to calorie-laden portable drinks or those
containing caffeine and artificial additives. In the association's opinion, the health benefits bottled
water provides _____ the environmental stress it causes.
7

The IBWA points out that bottled water is fully regulated by government agencies, such as the U.S.
Food and Drug Administration, to be guaranteed safe to drink. Meanwhile, in many developing
countries, tap water is either unavailable or unsafe, making bottled water a better option.

Even when bottled water is safer to drink, campaigners say that the packaging puts

_____ pressure on environmental health. Worldwide some 2.7 million tons (2.4 million
8
metric tons) of plastic are used to bottle water each year, according to EPI.

About 86 percent of plastic water bottles in the United States become garbage or litter, according to
the Container Recycling Institute in Washington, D.C. In this garbage _____, a water
9
bottle in the environment can take between 400 and 1,000 years to degrade.

To help reduce environmental harm some companies are adopting a more eco-friendly bottling

_____. For example, Colorado-based BIOTA bottles its spring water in a container made
10
from a biodegradable plastic called polylactic acid (PLA), which comes from corn. The bottling
company says that given the right conditions, the container will disappear in seventy-five to eighty
days.

(Adapted from "Bottled Water Isn't Healthier Than Tap, Report Reveals," National Geographic News, February 24, 2006.)

Read the questions and choose the best answers. Then discuss your answers in small groups.

1. Which of the following do you have **intense** feelings about?

   a. love

   b. my career

   c. sports

2. If you could **reverse** an important decision you made in your past, would you?

   a. Yes. I made a big mistake, and I'd like to reverse the decision.

   b. No. I made some bad decisions, but they helped me grow.

   c. No. All my decisions have been good ones.

3. What **phase** of your life are you most looking forward to?

   a. getting married

   b. being financially independent

   c. being retired and enjoying my old age

4. In your opinion, can a husband or wife who is not physically attractive **compensate** for his or her looks by having a great personality?

   a. Definitely. Outer beauty is not as important as a good personality.

   b. Yes, usually.

   c. No. The romance will die if the husband or wife is unattractive.

5. Do you enjoy talking about a **controversy**?

   a. Yes. I enjoy discussing controversial subjects.

   b. Sometimes.

   c. No. Controversial subjects upset me.

6. How often do you think of **schemes** to get rich?

   a. Often. I have many creative plans.

   b. Sometimes, when I am bored.

   c. Never.

7. Whom would you like to hire to **facilitate** your daily life?

   a. a cook

   b. a housekeeper

   c. a secretary

8. What is your general opinion of modern art that **distorts** images?

   a. interesting

   b. too strange

   c. beautiful

9. Do you notice when flowers **emerge** from the Earth in the spring?

   a. Yes, immediately.

   b. I notice only really bright or big flowers.

   c. No. I never notice spring flowers.

10. Would you like to have an **identical** twin?

    a. Yes, definitely. That would be cool.

    b. I wanted an identical twin when I was younger, but I don't anymore.

    c. No. It would be stressful to live with someone who looked the same as me!

WORDS IN WRITING

Choose two topics and write a paragraph on each. Try to use the key words.

1. Describe a **controversy** that is currently in the news and give your opinion about it.

2. Create a **scheme** that would allow you to retire at age forty-five. Explain how this **scheme** would work.

3. Do you want your close friends to have interests and opinions that are **identical** to yours? Explain why this would or would not **facilitate** your friendship.

4. Imagine that you were offered $200,000 a year to live and work in a small town in Alaska. Could the high salary **compensate** for the **intense** cold? Explain why you would or would not accept the offer.

5. If you had the power to **reverse** an existing law, would you? If so, explain what law you would **reverse.** If not, explain why not.

QUIZ 4

PART A

Choose the word that best completes each item and write it in the space provided.

1. The professor gave a final exam to _____ the students' knowledge.
   - a. facilitate
   - b. regulate
   - c. evaluate
   - d. compensate

2. Mom told us to take vitamins to _____ our chance of getting sick.
   - a. detect
   - b. minimize
   - c. anticipate
   - d. collapse

3. Due to zoning problems, the committee has _____ plans to create a new park on Western Avenue.
   - a. distorted
   - b. emerged
   - c. terminated
   - d. symbolized

4. Wood is a natural _____ of the U.S. state Maine.
   - a. trend
   - b. phase
   - c. resource
   - d. emergence

5. The Internet company was bought by a larger company for a significant _____.
   - a. sum
   - b. distortion
   - c. scheme
   - d. controversy

6. The _____ heat prevented us from hiking into the Grand Canyon.
   - a. appropriate
   - b. capable
   - c. primary
   - d. intense

7. Nick shows that he is a loving father by _____ much of his time to his children.
   - a. conferring
   - b. overlapping
   - c. devoting
   - d. reversing

8. Before buying a house, it's wise to read about the latest housing _____.
   - a. symbols
   - b. trends
   - c. compensations
   - d. conferences

9. Neighbors argued passionately about the _____.
   - a. estimate
   - b. trend
   - c. controversy
   - d. phase

10. Education is the _____ reason Jacques moved to New York.
    - a. inherent
    - b. primary
    - c. intense
    - d. controversial

PART B

*Read each statement and write **T** for true and **F** for false in the space provided.*

_____ 1. After watching a movie, the audience feels **anticipation**.

_____ 2. It is **appropriate** to wear jeans to a formal business meeting.

_____ 3. A flag is a **symbol**.

_____ 4. Truck drivers are **capable** of driving long distances.

_____ 5. It is possible for a boy and a girl who are twins to be **identical** to each other.

_____ 6. Leaves **emerge** in the fall.

_____ 7. Paul can **compensate** for being late for dinner by taking his wife flowers.

_____ 8. The subjects of drama and literature **overlap**.

_____ 9. Education is **inherent** to a person.

_____ 10. The moon goes through many **phases** each month.

PART C

Match each sentence with the letter it describes.

_____ 1. A bridge can **collapse** when this happens.

_____ 2. When Greg told me to **reverse** direction, he meant that I should do this.

_____ 3. An excellent reporter **distorts** news stories this many times a year.

_____ 4. This person **facilitates** Thomas's vacation in San Francisco.

_____ 5. Annie is **estimating** when she says this.

_____ 6. This person **detects** who was responsible for the robbery.

_____ 7. The police officer was **regulating** the speed limit when she said this.

_____ 8. When Joey creates a **scheme**, he says this.

_____ 9. When a president needs advice, he usually **confers** with this many advisors.

_____ 10. This person **funds** a new start-up business.

a. zero

b. an investor

c. turn around

d. "We'll earn about $50,000, more or less."

e. a private investigator

f. "Do you know how fast you were going?"

g. a tour guide

h. several

i. an earthquake

j. "We'll be dishonest to rich people and get a lot of money."

WORDS IN CONTEXT

*Use the sentences to guess what each key word means. Choose the meaning that is closest to that of the key word in **bold**.*

1. **alter**
    /ˈɔltɚ/
    -verb

    • Rachel is buying a needle and thread because she plans to **alter** her blouse so that it will fit her better.
    • If it rains on the day of the picnic, we will **alter** our plans.

    Alter means . . .   a. to return   b. to change   c. to repeat

2. **consequently**
    /ˈkɑnsəˌkwɛntli/
    -adverb

    • A levee was built to hold the river back; **consequently**, the town no longer got flooded.
    • Albert needed to lose ten pounds. **Consequently**, he went on a diet.

    Consequently means . . .   a. however   b. also   c. as a result

3. **decline**
    /dɪˈklaɪn/
    -verb

    • The mayor of New York City took credit for the fact that crime **declined** last year.
    • If house prices **decline** in your area, will you buy a new house?

    Decline means . . .   a. to decrease   b. to remain the same   c. to increase

4. **dominate**
    /ˈdɑməˌneɪt/
    -verb

    • Yao Ming **dominates** the basketball court.
    • Throughout history, Great Britain has **dominated** several countries.

    Dominate means . . .   a. to have power and control over someone or something   b. to have talent   c. to have a competitive relationship with someone or something

5. **innovation**
    /ˌɪnəˈveɪʃən/
    -noun

    • Nobel Prizes are given to reward people whose **innovations** have influenced science, the arts, and world peace.
    • There have been many **innovations** in telecommunications since the telephone was invented.

    Innovation means . . .   a. a great leader   b. a new invention   c. something old

6. **impact**
    /ˈɪmpækt/
    -noun

    • Good teachers have a great **impact** on the lives of young children.
    • Carla's decision to skip work had an **impact** on the entire team.

    Impact means . . .   a. education   b. discussion   c. effect

7. occupy
/ˈɑkyəˌpaɪ/
-verb

- A music student **occupies** the room next to mine in the dorm.
- If someone is using the bathroom on an airplane, a sign on the door shows that the bathroom is **occupied**.

Occupy means . . .   a. to enter a room   b. to be in a particular   c. to open a door
                                                      place

8. precede
/prɪˈsid/
-verb

- May and June **precede** July.
- A presentation will **precede** the discussion at noon; you should arrive at 11:30.

Precede means . . .   a. to happen or exist   b. to happen or exist   c. to happen or exist in
                                      after something else   before something else   the same year

9. release
/rɪˈlis/
-verb

- When Kim and her child were safely away from the busy street, she **released** his hand.
- Have you ever **released** a balloon and seen it float up into the sky?

Release means . . .   a. to stop holding   b. to look at something   c. to hold something
                                      something

10. technique
/tɛkˈnik/
-noun

- In order to improve his golf skill, Mike studied Tiger Woods's **technique**.
- Nori uses an interesting **technique** when carving ice sculptures.

Technique means . . . a. talent   b. a special way of   c. concentration
                                                        doing something

▌WORDS AND DEFINITIONS

Read each definition and write the word it defines on the line.

1. _____ as a result

2. _____ to have power and control over someone or something

3. _____ to live, work, or be in a particular place

4. _____ to let go or to stop holding something or someone

5. _____ a special way of doing something

6. _____ to change

7. _____ to decrease

8. _____ to happen or exist before something else

9. _____ a new idea, method, or invention

10. _____ the effect that an event or situation has

Choose the best answer.

1. Which number **precedes** 11?
   a. 21
   b. 10
   c. 12

2. If Larry **releases** a bird in nature, the bird is
   a. free.
   b. captured.
   c. followed.

3. What CANNOT **decline**?
   a. the number of fish in the sea
   b. taxes
   c. the number of days in a year

4. Does the sun have an **impact** on a flower?
   a. yes
   b. no
   c. rarely

5. Which best describes Leah's **technique** at drawing?
   a. She makes quick and light marks on the paper.
   b. She draws in art class.
   c. Her drawings are expensive.

6. If Jack **altered** his appearance, he
   a. changed his appearance.
   b. thought about his appearance for a long time.
   c. photographed himself.

7. If Yen ate five chocolate bars, what probably happened **consequently**?
   a. He got hungry.
   b. He got a stomachache.
   c. He unwrapped the chocolate bars.

8. Which might be an **innovation** in the year 2020?
   a. a car that flies
   b. a mobile telephone
   c. a flat-screen television

9. Who **dominates** the business world?
   a. a very successful businessman or woman
   b. an average businessman or woman
   c. an untalented businessman or woman

10. What usually **occupies** a chair?
    a. a table
    b. a person
    c. a footstool

WORD FAMILIES

Now that you have studied the ten key words and their basic definitions, you are ready to learn words that belong to the same family as some of the key words. A word family includes words that look alike but have different functions (noun, verb, adjective, or adverb). Their meanings are related but different.

A. *Look at each model phrase and decide whether the word in* **bold** *is used as a noun, verb, adjective, or adverb. Put a check (✓) in the correct column.*

	NOUN	VERB	ADJECTIVE	ADVERB
1. **consequently**				
• to take place **consequently**				
• a **consequence** of her actions				
2. **decline**				
• interest rates are **declining**				
• the **decline** of civilization				
3. **dominate**				
• **dominate** the country				
• the **dominant** dog				
4. **impact**				
• **impact** it had				
• **impact** your grades				
5. **innovation**				
• an **innovation** that changed the world				
• a talented **innovator**				
• an **innovative** idea				
6. **occupy**				
• **occupy** a room				
• an unusual **occupation**				
7. **release**				
• **release** the steering wheel				
• Fred's **release** from prison				

B. *Read the first part of each sentence and match it with the appropriate ending. The exercise continues on page 132.*

_____ 1. The landlord prepared for his tenants'

_____ 2. We were fifteen minutes late; as a

_____ 3. Successful inventors have

_____ 4. I was surprised by the

_____ 5. The National Seal Sanctuary in Cornwall, England, provides seal rescue, rehabilitation, and

a. **consequence**, we missed the beginning of the movie.

b. **decline** in gas prices.

c. **dominant** team in the playoffs, winning the most games.

d. **impact** the amount of traffic near the school.

e. **innovative** ideas.

_____ 6. The high school graduation ceremony tonight will

_____ 7. The design was created by a famous

_____ 8. The New York Giants were the

f. **innovator**.

g. **occupation** of the new apartment.

h. **release**.

SAME WORD, DIFFERENT MEANING

*Most words have more than one meaning. Study the additional meanings of **decline**, **occupy**, and **release**. Then read each sentence and decide which meaning is used.*

a. **decline** *v.*	to decrease
b. **decline** *v.*	(formal) to say no to something, usually politely
c. **occupy** *v.*	to live, work, or be in a particular place
d. **occupy** *v.*	to enter a place and get control of it, especially by military force
e. **release** *v.*	to let something go free or to stop holding something or someone
f. **release** *v.*	to make news, a record, or a movie available to the public

_____ 1. You cannot use the bathroom because it is **occupied**.

_____ 2. The new James Bond movie will be **released** in theaters this week.

_____ 3. The admiral explained his plan to **occupy** the country and end the civil war there.

_____ 4. When asked to describe his competition, the chess player **declined** to comment.

_____ 5. The zookeeper **released** the monkey from the cage.

_____ 6. The birth rate is **declining** in much of Europe.

WORDS IN SENTENCES

Complete each sentence with one of the words from the box.

| alter | declined | impact | occupied | released |
| consequence | dominant | innovators | precede | technique |

1. Changing our marketing strategy could _____ our sales.

2. Leonardo da Vinci was one of the greatest _____ of all time.

3. Tess asked the architect to _____ his design for her house; she wanted him to add another bathroom.

4. In the United States, smoking rates have _____ from their peak in the mid-1990s by fifty-six percent among tenth-graders.

5. Tickets to *King Kong* were sold out on the weekend when the movie was _____.

6. Elizabeth is the _____ person in that relationship.

7. Ben began gambling too much and, as a _____, lost his house.

8. The band will _____ the dancers in the parade.

9. The teacher admired Ryoji's _____ at writing Japanese characters.

10. The army _____ the city for ten months.

▌ WORDS IN COLLOCATIONS AND EXPRESSIONS

Following are common collocations and expressions with some of the key words. Read the definitions and then complete the conversations with the collocations and expressions. You may have to change word forms for correct grammar.

1. **consequently**
   - **as a consequence**   as a result

2. **decline**
   - **to decline**   to politely refuse

3. **impact**
   - **to have an impact on (sth)**   to affect something

4. **innovation**
   - **an innovative approach**   a new and creative approach

5. **occupy**
   - **occupies most of my time**   keeps me busy

6. **release**
   - **release (sb) from**   to allow someone or something to be free

1. SENATOR WILLIAMS: Wasn't Senator Nelson invited to this party?

   SENATOR SMITH: Yes he was, but he had _____ the invitation. He is in New York this week for his daughter's graduation.

2. TEACHER: Why do you want to do your report on Mother Teresa, Kim?

   KIM: Because I think she _____ the world. By helping poor and sick people, she made ordinary people like us also think about helping.

3. PUBLICIST: You signed to work with that record company for two years, Rocky. I can't believe they just canceled the deal!

   ROCK STAR: I'm happy that my record company decided to _____ me _____ my contract. Now I can make the kind of music I really love. I'd rather take _____ to my music than follow other people's directions.

4. ANNA: Why do you want to buy a house in Siberia?

   PASHA: Global warming is shortening the winters there. _____, I think that Siberia will become a comfortable place to live.

5. Shakespeare's Wife: Why do you never have time to come home to visit me, Will? Do you have a girlfriend in London? What are you spending all that time doing?

Shakespeare: Of course I don't have a girlfriend. I'm busy acting, but actually writing _____.

▌WORDS IN A READING

Read this article about film. Complete it with words from the boxes.

innovations	occupies	preceded	technique

THE INFLUENCE OF *STAR WARS*

The film critic Robert Ebert explains how Star Wars *has influenced film*:

To see *Star Wars* again after twenty years is to revisit a place in the mind. George Lucas's space epic _____ a part of our imaginations, and it is hard to stand back and see it simply as a
(1)
motion picture because it has so completely become part of our memories.

Like two great films that _____ it, *The Birth of a Nation* and *Citizen Kane*, *Star Wars*
(2)
brought technical _____ that influenced many of the movies that came after. These films
(3)
have little in common except for the way they came along at an important moment in cinema history.
The Birth of a Nation brought together the developing language of shots and editing. *Citizen Kane*
combined special effects, advanced sound, a new photographic _____, and a freedom
(4)
from linear storytelling. *Star Wars* combined a new generation of special effects with the high-energy
action picture; it linked space opera and soap opera, fairy tales and legend, and packaged them as a
wild visual ride.

altered	consequently	decline	dominate	impact	release

The _____ of *Star Wars* brought the _____ of the golden era of early
(5)   (6)
1970s personal filmmaking. *Star Wars* _____ moviemakers' goals, focusing the industry
(7)
on big-budget special effect blockbusters, which still _____ Hollywood. All the big
(8)
studios have been trying to make another *Star Wars* ever since (pictures like *Raiders of the Lost Ark*,
Jurassic Park, *Independence Day*, and *The Matrix* are its heirs). It located Hollywood's center of
attention at the intellectual and emotional level of a bright teenager.

The film has simple, well-defined characters, beginning with the robots C-3PO (fastidious), and R2-
D2 (childlike, easily hurt). The evil Empire has almost triumphed in the galaxy, but rebel forces are
preparing to attack the Death Star. Princess Leia has information about the Star's vulnerable point and
feeds it into C-3PO's computer. When her ship is captured, the robots escape from the Death Star and

find themselves on Luke Skywalker's planet, where Luke _____ meets the wise, old,
                                                                         9
mysterious Ben Kenobi. Next, they hire the freelance space jockey Han Solo to carry them to Leia's
rescue.

The films that will live forever are the simplest-seeming ones. They have profound* depths, but their surfaces are as clear to an audience as a beloved old story. The way I know this is because the stories that seem immortal are all the same: a brave but flawed** hero, a journey, colorful people and places, and the discovery of life's underlying truths. If I were asked to say with certainty which movies

_____ us so deeply that they will still be widely known in a century or two from now, I
        10
would list *Star Wars* for sure.

*profound: *having a strong effect*

**flawed: *having a weakness*

▌WORDS IN DISCUSSION

Apply the key words to your own life. Read and discuss each question in small groups. Try to use the key words.

1. **consequently**

   If I won a hundred dollars, I would consequently _____

   If a lost puppy followed me home, I would consequently _____

2. **innovation**

   An innovation I wish someone would make: _____

   How innovative I am: _____

3. **technique**

   A sports or music star I would like to teach me his or her technique: _____

   My technique for improving my vocabulary: _____

4. **decline**

   The price of something that I wish would decline: _____

   Something I hope will never decline: _____

5. **precede**

   A person in my family whose birthday precedes mine: _____

   An event which I hope will precede my thirty-fifth birthday: _____

6. **alter**

   Something I would like to alter about myself: _____

   How I would like to alter my environment: _____

7. **occupy**

   A person who often occupies my thoughts: _____

   How I usually occupy my time on the weekends: _____

8. **dominate**

A dominant player in my favorite sport : _____

A competition I would like to dominate: _____

9. **release**

How long it would take me to release a burning hot pan: _____

A movie I want to see when it is released: _____

10. **impact**

How my classmates have impacted my life: _____

The impact I hope to have on the world: _____

▌WORDS IN WRITING

Choose two topics and write a paragraph on each. Try to use the key words.

1. Do you think there would be a **decline** in crime if all criminals were never **released** from prison? Explain why or why not and tell whether you support the idea of **altering** the prison system in this way.

2. Imagine that you are waiting in line at the movies when you notice that the person **preceding** you in line is your favorite television star. What would you do?

3. When you ride on the subway or train, do you put your bag on the seat next to you so that a person is not likely to **occupy** the seat, or do you feel this is rude? Explain why.

4. What recent **innovation** has had the greatest **impact** on your life? Explain why.

5. Do you have a **technique** for making friends? Explain.

Key Words

aware	diversity	period	role	statistics
correspond	ethnic	promote	significant	theme

▌ WORDS IN CONTEXT

*Use the sentences to guess what each key word means. Choose the meaning that is closest to that of the key word in **bold**.*

1. aware
/əˈwɛr/
-adjective

- Because Kelly is only four years old, she is not **aware** that her father is writing a computer program.
- The woman on the subway looked at me coldly and said, "Excuse me, sir. Are you **aware** that you are standing on my coat?"

Aware means . . .

a. not understanding the reason something happens

b. realizing that something is happening

c. being a part of a project

2. correspond
/ˌkɔrəˈspɑnd, ˌkɑr-/
-verb

- The decrease in mice on farmer Brown's farm **corresponds** with his purchase of a new cat.
- My hopes for a good job **correspond** with my interest in improving my English.

Correspond means . . .

a. to spend money for a good reason

b. for two things to be related to each other

c. to plan

3. diversity
/dəˈvɚsɪti, daɪ-/
-noun

- There is a lot of **diversity** in California: people move from many different states and countries to live there.
- The university welcomes **diversity**; people from all religions are invited to pray or meditate in its spiritual space.

Diversity means . . .

a. excitement

b. a large amount of something

c. variety

4. ethnic
/ˈɛθnɪk/
-adjective

- There are many different **ethnic** restaurants in London, such as Indian, Chinese, and Thai.
- What **ethnic** groups were your ancestors from?

Ethnic means . . .

a. relating to a particular race, nation, tribe, etc.

b. the family you come from

c. a place where you feel comfortable

5. period
/ˈpɪriəd/
-noun

- The Egyptians built the Great Pyramid of Giza during a **period** of twenty years, concluding around 2560 B.C.
- If you are not happy with this product, you can return it for a refund within a **period** of twelve days.

Period means . . .

a. a length of time

b. a long time

c. more than a week

6. **promote**
   /prə'moʊt/
   -verb

   - A group of concerned parents will meet on Tuesday night to discuss how they can **promote** peace in their violent neighborhood.
   - Daniel's gym teacher **promoted** his growth as a basketball player.

   Promote means . . .   a. to stop something harmful   b. to work together   c. to help something develop and be successful

7. **role**
   /roʊl/
   -noun

   - As the architect, Olaf has played an important **role** in the construction of the new gym.
   - The secretary of state played a key **role** in developing Chinese foreign policy.

   Role means . . .   a. something or someone important   b. a position, job, or function   c. responsibility

8. **significant**
   /sɪg'nɪfəkənt/
   -adjective

   - When Greg asked Dr. Jones if he needed to go on a diet, Dr. Jones said, "No. I don't think you need to worry. You haven't gained a **significant** amount of weight."
   - What people have been **significant** in your education?

   Significant means . . . a. noticeable or important   b. dangerous   c. unhealthy

9. **statistics**
   /stə'tɪstɪks/
   -noun

   - **Statistics** in the *Old Farmer's Almanac* show the typical amount of rainfall in each month of the year.
   - If we study the **statistics** provided by the U.S. Census, we can see that the number of Latinos in the United States is increasing.

   Statistics means . . .   a. unusual information   b. numbers that represent facts   c. guesses

10. **theme**
    /θim/
    -noun

    - Hans liked the characters in the movie, but he was bored by the science fiction **theme**.
    - Have you ever had a difficult time thinking of an interesting **theme** when planning an essay?

    Theme means . . .   a. the main subject or idea   b. supporting details   c. vocabulary

WORDS AND DEFINITIONS

Read each definition and write the word it defines on the line.

1. _____ a variety or range of different people or things

2. _____ to help something develop and be successful

3. _____ relating to a particular race, nation, or tribe

4. _____ a length of time

5. _____ numbers that represent facts or measurements

6. _____ realizing that something is true, exists, or is happening

7. _____ the position, job, or function someone or something has in a particular situation

8. _____ the main subject or idea in a book, movie, or speech

9. _____ for two things to be related to each other; to match

10. _____ noticeable or important

▌COMPREHENSION CHECK

Choose the best answer.

1. Which is an **ethnic** group?
   a. the Beatles
   b. the Humane Society
   c. the Swedes

2. Who is **aware** that it is raining when leaving for work?
   a. Elizabeth, who is wearing sunglasses
   b. Julian, who is dressed for the beach
   c. Drake, who is carrying an umbrella

3. What usually **corresponds** with studying all the time?
   a. parties
   b. academic success
   c. relaxation

4. Where can you probably NOT find **statistics**?
   a. in an encyclopedia
   b. in a poem
   c. on the news

5. If the L.A. Lakers are trying to **promote** a new basketball player, how do they probably feel about him?
   a. They do not think he is good enough to play in the NBA.
   b. They believe he has potential.
   c. They want to test his skills.

6. Which is NOT an example of a **period**?
   a. a clock
   b. the Middle Ages (476 A.D.–1450 B.C.)
   c. seven minutes

7. Who has the most important **role** in a restaurant's kitchen?
   a. the dishwasher
   b. the bartender
   c. the cook

8. If there is a **significant** change in Roy's appearance, what will his friends say?
   a. "You look a little bit different, Roy. Did you get a haircut?"
   b. "Wow, Roy! What happened to you?"
   c. "Did you lose a pound or two, Roy?"

9. Where is there NOT a lot of **diversity** of plants and animals?
   a. the Amazon River
   b. the moon
   c. the Nile River

10. Which is the most common **theme** in movies?
    a. love
    b. sports
    c. transportation

WORD FAMILIES

Now that you have studied the ten key words and their basic definitions, you are ready to learn words that belong to the same family as some of the key words. A word family includes words that look alike but have different functions (noun, verb, adjective, or adverb). Their meanings are related but different.

A. *Look at each model phrase and decide whether the word in **bold** is used as a noun, verb, adjective, or adverb. Put a check (✓) in the correct column.*

	NOUN	VERB	ADJECTIVE	ADVERB
1. **aware**				
• **aware** of what's happening				
• **unaware** of the problem				
• **awareness** of				
2. **diversity**				
• a lot of **diversity**				
• a **diverse** town				
3. **ethnic**				
• an **ethnic** group				
• your **ethnicity**				
4. **promote**				
• **promote** an idea				
• a sales **promotion**				
5. **significant**				
• a **significant** influence				
• an **insignificant** problem				
• the **significance** of her comment				
• **significantly** late				
6. **statistic**				
• a surprising **statistic**				
• the **statistical** probability				
• **statistically** highly unlikely				

B. *Read the first half of each sentence and match it with the appropriate ending.*

_____ 1. When my boss forgot my name, I felt

_____ 2. Visiting Malaysia raised Emily's

_____ 3. In your essay on Dostoevsky, please explain the

_____ 4. The doctor told Ted that the chances that he'd get the disease were nearly

_____ 5. I'm sorry. I was completely

a. **statistically** impossible.

b. **ethnicity**.

c. **insignificant**.

d. **promotion**.

e. **significantly** faster than its natural relatives.

f. **unaware** that you were mad at me.

_____ 6. If we want children to read more of our books, the books need

_____ 7. Rhonda has a lot of African art in her home because she is proud of her

_____ 8. A genetically altered fish grows

_____ 9. In your business report, you need to provide

_____10. Sean and Elise want to raise their children in a

g. **statistical** evidence.

h. **awareness** of life in developing countries.

i. **diverse** neighborhood.

j. **significance** of dreams in *The Brothers Karamazov.*

SAME WORD, DIFFERENT MEANING

*Most words have more than one meaning. Study the additional meanings of **correspond**, **period**, and **role**. Then read each sentence and decide which meaning is used.*

a.	**correspond** *v.*	for two things to be similar or related to each other
b.	**correspond** *v.*	to write letters to each other
c.	**period** *n.*	a length of time
d.	**period** *n.*	the mark used in writing that shows the end of a sentence (.)
e.	**role** *n.*	the position, job, or function someone or something has in a particular situation
f.	**role** *n.*	a character played by an actor

_____ 1. In history class, we are studying the Early Republic **period** of Chinese history.

_____ 2. An announcer told the theater audience, "In tonight's performance of *Cinderella,* the **role** of the prince will be played by William Dell."

_____ 3. Your writing is very creative, but you're missing some punctuation: commas and **periods**.

_____ 4. In *Letters to a Young Poet,* the famous poet Rilke **corresponds** with a young writer, offering him advice about writing and life.

_____ 5. Paula's guidance counselor played a major **role** in helping her get into college.

_____ 6. The president's opinion does not **correspond** with the opinion of many of the senators.

WORDS IN SENTENCES

Complete each sentence on page 142 with two of the words from the box.

aware	diversity	periods	roles	statistics
correspond	ethnic	promote	significant	theme

1. When Irene visited Vancouver, she was surprised by its _____; she had never realized how many different _____ groups lived there.

2. Lucia has had many _____ throughout different _____ of her life: daughter, friend, sister, teacher, wife, mother, and grandmother.

3. _____ show that motorcycle helmets _____ with riders' safety.

4. Anger appears to be a(n) _____ _____ in Picasso's paintings.

5. When teachers became _____ that poor children were coming to school hungry, they arranged a meeting with the principal to _____ a free lunch program.

▌WORDS IN COLLOCATIONS AND EXPRESSIONS

Following are common collocations and expressions with some of the key words. Read the definitions and then complete the conversation with the collocations and expressions. You may have to change word forms for correct grammar.

1. **aware**
   - **not that I'm aware of**   not that I know about

2. **correspond**
   - **correspond with**   to be related to; to match

3. **period**
   - **a period of (noun)**   a length of time

4. **promote**
   - **be promoted**   to be given a better position at work

5. **role**
   - **to play a major role in**   to be an important part of an activity

6. **significant**
   - **significance of**   the importance or meaning of something

ADMISSIONS COUNSELOR:	During this interview, I'd like to ask you some questions about your application to get an idea of whether you are the kind of student we're looking for at Langley University.
JONG LEE:	Great.
ADMISSIONS COUNSELOR:	First, I noticed that you have excellent grades except for your freshman year. Why don't your grades from the beginning of high school _____ your grades later on?
	1
JONG LEE:	I moved to the United States from Korea that year. Since I didn't speak English, I had _____ adjustment that first year.
	2
ADMISSIONS COUNSELOR:	Let's talk about the _____ language in your extracurricular activities. Has learning English as a second language made joining teams or clubs more difficult for you?
	3

JONG LEE:	_____. For the last few years, I've felt very comfortable speaking English. I'm a member of the chess team and the soccer team. Last year I was even my class president.
ADMISSIONS COUNSELOR:	It's excellent that you got involved and _____ student government. Would you like to be a politics major?
JONG LEE:	No, international business. After that I hope to get my MBA. I want to work for a large international bank and eventually _____ to an executive position.
ADMISSIONS COUNSELOR:	Your plans are impressive.

▌WORDS IN A READING

Read this article about multiculturalism. Complete it with words from the boxes.

diversity	ethnic	period	significant	themes

AMERICAN KIDS SOAK UP SPANISH TV

Each episode of the children's cartoon *Dora the Explorer* starts with the girl running from her family's home, waving to her Mami and Papi, and going off to explore the jungle. The brave and curious seven-year-old greets her viewers in both English and Spanish. "Ready to explore? *Vamos arriba!*"

Just about everyone in Dora's world speaks fluent English and Spanish, their adventures are punctuated by salsa rhythms—and young TV viewers can't get enough of the mix. Her Nickelodeon show was the top-rated preschool program for a four-year _____, and when she finally lost this position, it was to a new spin-off featuring her cousin, Diego.

If you're looking for television that spotlights Latino characters and _____, don't bother with prime time—those shows mostly ignore the nation's largest _____ group. Today, Latino programs are the ones children are watching.

"These programs are making _____ a natural part of kids' understanding of the world around them," said Phillip C. Serrato, a professor of children's literature at California State University at San Diego.

Multicultural children's TV used to start—and mostly end—with PBS's *Sesame Street*. For thirty-seven years, the show has been a United Nations of characters, including a Puerto Rican family and a Mexican monster named Rosita.

But now children's television is experiencing a _____ change. PBS Kids changed its show *Dragon Tales* to highlight Latino issues and include Enrique, an immigrant who is Puerto Rican and Colombian. PBS Kids Go!, a twenty-four-hour cable station to launch this fall, will include two hours a day of shows in Spanish with English subtitles. The Disney Channel and the Cartoon Network also have plans to include Spanish in some programs.

Chapter 14   143

What's driving the trend? Producers say it's demographics. _____ in Census 2000
₆
showed that Latino communities are the United States' fastest growing—and the biggest five-year
Latino age group is infants to preschoolers. Data have long shown that the representation of Latinos
on prime-time TV does not _____ the percentage of Latinos living in the United States.
₇
In fact, prime-time TV mostly excludes Latinos—UCLA research found that four percent of characters
in 2004 were Latino—but few researchers had focused on children's shows. Then studies in the late
1990s showed that Latino youth almost never saw themselves on-screen and it made them feel society
ignored them. A 1999 Annenberg Public Policy Center report said, "Latino American preschoolers
ought to and deserve to see greater representation of their own culture."

Cyma Zarghami, president of Nickelodeon Television, said that the message got through: "It felt
like an audience was being underserved." After reading the studies, her producers decided to
_____ a Latino character. They created Dora. Every detail of Dora's _____,
₈   ₉
her appearance, family background, and speech, was carefully considered to reflect her Latino
heritage. Experts urged Nickelodeon to make the show's songs more Latino and to incorporate
Spanish. *Dora the Explorer* was the first mainstream show to try to teach Spanish by blending it into
dialogue, as opposed to translating vocabulary.

Soon, Dora's cousin, Diego Marquez, who rescues animals, was a popular guest on her show, and
the spinoff *Go, Diego, Go!* became an instant hit.

Not only Latino children love these shows. The shows can help all children be more
_____ of diversity in the world. One Brooklyn mother described how her preschool-age
₁₀
son adores Diego: "Even though we're not Hispanic, he loves learning the language. It teaches him that
there's a bigger world full of wonderful things."

Now many people are hopeful that television will grow up with today's preschoolers and make
prime-time television more diverse.

(Adapted from "Se Habla 'Dora'? TV Shows Have Children Absorbing Spanish Language and Culture," Lowell Sun, February 24, 2006.)

▮ WORDS IN DISCUSSION

Read the questions and choose the best answers. Then discuss your answers in small groups.

1. If you were acting in a play, what type of
   role would you probably have?

   a. a funny role

   b. a musical role

   c. a dramatic role

2. Do you have friends from different **ethnic**
   groups?

   a. Yes, many.

   b. Yes, some.

   c. No, none.

3. Imagine that you run an advertising agency. If a business offered you a large sum of money to **promote** a new kind of cheese which you thought tasted disgusting, what would you do?

   a. I would accept the money and promote the cheese.

   b. Unless the cheese made me ill, I would promote it.

   c. I would decline the offer. I could not promote a bad product.

4. What **period** of your life has been your favorite?

   a. my childhood

   b. my teenage years

   c. other

5. When you visit friends' homes, how **aware** are you of the music they play?

   a. Quite aware. I love music and always notice it.

   b. Somewhat aware. If the music is loud or memorable, I notice it.

   c. Unaware. Music isn't important to me, and I never notice it.

6. If you were to write a novel, what **theme** would it probably have?

   a. humor

   b. anger

   c. beauty

7. How much **diversity** is there in the town where you live?

   a. A lot. Many different kinds of people live here.

   b. Some.

   c. None. Everyone is the same ethnicity.

8. If you were writing to ask friends to donate money to a good cause, would you include **statistics** in your letter?

   a. Yes, many. Giving facts would help my friends understand the cause.

   b. Yes, a few.

   c. No. Including statistics in a letter to friends is too formal.

9. Does the amount you work **correspond** with your success?

   a. Yes. The more I work, the more successful I am.

   b. No. No matter how much I work, I am always successful.

   c. No. No matter how much I work, I always fail.

10. If someone gave you a **significant** amount of money to improve your home, what would you do?

    a. paint the walls

    b. buy new furniture

    c. move

▌ WORDS IN WRITING

Choose two topics and write a paragraph on each. Try to use the key words.

1. Is it important for you to be environmentally **aware** (that is, to be aware of environmental issues)? Explain why or why not.

2. What invention in the last hundred years do you believe was the most **significant**? Explain why.

3. Describe a person who helped you during a difficult **period** in your life. How did this person **promote** a positive change in your life?

4. Do the people in your city or town respect **diversity**? Explain why or why not.

5. Do you believe that happiness **corresponds** with money? Explain why or why not.

CHAPTER 15

Key Words

attribute	constrain	element	isolated	reluctant
circumstances	domain	expose	principal	valid

WORDS IN CONTEXT

*Use the sentences to guess what each key word means. Choose the meaning that is closest to that of the key word in **bold**.*

1. attribute
/ˈætrəˌbyut/
-noun

- Helpfulness is one of Mary's many **attributes**.
- E-mail's greatest **attribute** is its speed.

Attribute means . . .
a. a negative or harmful quality
b. a goal or ambition
c. a good or useful quality

2. circumstances
/ˈsɚkəmˌstænsz/
-noun

- Due to the **circumstances**, I think we can understand why Rico was so upset.
- Some of Natalie's success was because of hard work, but some was the result of her **circumstances**.

Circumstances means . . .
a. the facts or conditions that affect a situation
b. something you plan and work for
c. good relations with other people

3. constrain
/kənˈstreɪn/
-verb

- Our deadline **constrains** the amount of research we can do; we have time to find out only the basic facts.
- Hugo's financial problems **constrained** his choices when he was applying to college.

Constrain means . . .
a. to be a reason for something
b. to limit something
c. to make a decision

4. domain
/doʊˈmeɪn, də-/
-noun

- Film direction is a predominantly male **domain**.
- In this school, dance lessons are Instructor Lopez's **domain**.

Domain means . . .
a. an activity that someone is interested in
b. a place where you feel comfortable
c. an activity that is controlled by one person or group

5. element
/ˈɛləmənt/
-noun

- The most interesting **element** of the project involves working on a submarine.
- Mrs. Jones told Irene that **elements** of her singing were beautiful but other parts needed work.

Element means . . .
a. something positive
b. one part of something
c. a plan

6. expose
/ɪk'spoʊz/
-*verb*

- After the long winter, Anita put on her sandals and walked on the beach; it felt good to **expose** her feet to the sun.
- The newspaper **exposed** the private life of the actress by publishing pictures of her vacation.

Expose means . . .   a. to show something that is usually covered or hidden   b. to go outside and exercise in the sun   c. to take photographs outside

7. isolated
/'aɪsəˌleɪt̬ɪd/
-*adjective*

- Allen was the only child in his small farming village, so he felt **isolated**.
- Would you prefer to live in an **isolated** cabin in the middle of the forest or in an apartment in the center of a busy city?

Isolated means . . .   a. part of a big family   b. far away from other things   c. near animals

8. principal
/'prɪnsəpəl/
-*adjective*

- The **principal** speaker at the meeting will be the president.
- Jim's **principal** reason for quitting smoking was to improve his health.

Principal means . . .   a. secondary   b. oldest   c. main

9. reluctant
/rɪ'lʌktənt/
-*adjective*

- When Sam's mother asked him to clean up his room, he was **reluctant**; Sam said, "Not today. I don't like cleaning."
- Because she is **reluctant** to try new foods, Anne did not accept her friends' invitation to the Tibetan restaurant.

Reluctant means . . .   a. eager and helpful   b. unwilling and slow to do something   c. talkative and enthusiastic

10. valid
/'vælɪd/
-*adjective*

- Dan needs to go to the Department of Motor Vehicles to renew his driver's license by January 15; if he does not, his license will no longer be **valid**.
- It is necessary to take a **valid** photo ID to the polling place in order to vote.

Valid means . . .   a. legal   b. long   c. useful

▌WORDS AND DEFINITIONS

Read each definition and write the word it defines on the line.

1. _____ unwilling and slow to do something

2. _____ a particular place or activity that is controlled by one person or group

3. _____ one part of something

4. _____ legal or acceptable

5. _____ a good or useful quality that someone or something has

6. _____ most important; main

7. _____ to limit what someone or something can do or become

8. _____ the facts or conditions that affect a situation

9. _____ far away from other things or lonely

10. _____ to show something that is usually covered or hidden

▮ COMPREHENSION CHECK

Choose the best answer.

1. What is an **attribute** of a laptop computer?
   a. It is expensive.
   b. It is portable.
   c. It will break if you drop it.

2. What is a **valid** excuse for missing a class?
   a. I slept late.
   b. I was in the hospital.
   c. I skipped class so that I could eat breakfast.

3. Who is **isolated**?
   a. Mark, who lives with two roommates and a cat
   b. Karen, who lives in New York City with her husband
   c. Juliette, who lives alone in Siberia

4. If there is an **element** of romance in a novel,
   a. the entire novel is romantic.
   b. the book has no romance.
   c. part of the story is romantic.

5. If a newspaper **exposes** the truth, it
   a. hides a story.
   b. reports on a story that everyone already knows about.
   c. reveals information that was previously hidden.

6. Who is usually the **principal** person in a dog's life?
   a. its neighbor
   b. its owner
   c. its vet

7. Which of the following is NOT a part of **circumstances**?
   a. luck
   b. uncontrollable events that happen to you
   c. plans

8. In which statement is the speaker **reluctant**?
   a. "Listen to me!"
   b. "I'd love to tell you the story."
   c. "I'd rather not talk about it."

9. In which country's **domain** does Antarctica lie?
   a. Antarctica is in no country's **domain**.
   b. France
   c. Portugal

10. What **constrains** Jason from driving too fast?
    a. the gas pedal
    b. the speed limit
    c. his seat belt

WORD FAMILIES

Now that you have studied the ten key words and their basic definitions, you are ready to learn words that belong to the same family as some of the key words. A word family includes words that look alike but have different functions (noun, verb, adjective, or adverb). Their meanings are related but different.

A. *Look at each model phrase and decide whether the word in **bold** is used as a noun, verb, adjective, or adverb. Put a check (✔) in the correct column.*

	NOUN	VERB	ADJECTIVE	ADVERB
1. **circumstance**				
• difficult **circumstances**				
• **circumstantial** evidence				
2. **constrain**				
• her budget **constrains** her shopping				
• two **constraints** to our plan				
3. **isolated**				
• an **isolated** campsite				
• in total **isolation**				
• police **isolate** a dangerous criminal				
4. **reluctant**				
• he was **reluctant** to do his homework				
• clear **reluctance**				
• **reluctantly** leave				
5. **valid**				
• a **valid** argument				
• question the **validity**				

B. *Mrs. Mills is talking with a police officer about her dog. Complete the conversation with words from the box.*

circumstantial	isolate	reluctance
constraint	isolation	validity

POLICE OFFICER: We're taking Fluffy because your neighbor complained that the dog is sick and dangerous. She couldn't give any solid proof, but based on the _____ evidence, we need to take the animal.
1

MRS. MILLS: Don't take my dog, Officer. There is no _____ to my neighbor's complaint! She's never liked Fluffy.
2

POLICE OFFICER: We are going to see if your neighbor is correct. Our plan is to _____ your pet for forty-eight hours and observe him.
3

MRS. MILLS:	Fluffy is a very social animal. The _____ will depress him.
POLICE OFFICER:	Don't worry, your dog will be okay. Confinement from other animals is the only _____ we'll place on him. He'll be able to run, play, and eat.
MRS. MILLS (reluctantly):	OK, Officer, I'll let you take Fluffy, but only if I can go with him.
POLICE OFFICER:	I understand your _____, and I appreciate your cooperation. Let's go.

SAME WORD, DIFFERENT MEANING

Most words have more than one meaning. Study the additional meanings of **attribute**, **element**, *and* **principal**. *Then read each sentence and decide which meaning is used.*

a. **attribute** *n.*	/ˈætrəbyut/ a good or useful quality that someone or something has
b. **attribute** *v.*	/əˈtrɪbyut/ to believe or say that someone or something is responsible for something
c. **element** *n.*	one part of something
d. **element** *n.*	a simple chemical substance such as oxygen or gold that is made up of only one type of atom
e. **principal** *adj.*	most important; main
f. **principal** *n.*	someone who is in charge of a school

_____ 1. In chemistry class, students must memorize about a hundred symbols for the **elements**, such as H for hydrogen.

_____ 2. Miranda Richards is the **principal** of Hope Elementary School.

_____ 3. Intelligence is one of Adam's strongest **attributes**.

_____ 4. For a romantic date, you might want to include an **element** of surprise.

_____ 5. I **attribute** my love of music to my guitar teacher.

_____ 6. Please explain your **principal** objective in greater detail.

WORDS IN SENTENCES

Complete each sentence on page 151 with one of the words from the box.

attribute	constraint	elements	isolation	reluctance
circumstances	domain	exposed	principal	valid

1. The bright light _____ the dust on the bookcase.

2. You should ask Jeff about how to file your taxes; in our house, finances are his _____ .

3. Chemistry students learn combinations of _____, which are compounds like H_2O.

4. Sara's _____ to help really bothered me; she didn't have anything else she needed to do.

5. Wisdom is a(n) _____ of old age.

6. The library and the Internet will be our _____ sources of information, but we will also interview a few people.

7. The bad weather was a(n) _____ on our vacation plans, but we managed to enjoy ourselves nevertheless.

8. Julia is an extrovert, so she could never live in total _____ .

9. If _____ were different, I would join you on your trip driving across the country, but as it is, I need to work to pay my bills.

10. Your information is outdated; to be convincing, you need to present _____ proof.

■ WORDS IN COLLOCATIONS AND EXPRESSIONS

Following are common collocations and expressions with some of the key words. Read the definitions and then complete the conversations with the collocations and expressions. One expression is used twice. You may have to change word forms for correct grammar.

1. **attribute**		
	• **attribute (sth) to (sb/sth)**	to say that someone or something is responsible for something
2. **circumstance**		
	• **due to/under the circumstances**	used to say that a particular situation makes an action or decision necessary or acceptable
	• **under no circumstances**	used to emphasize that something must not happen
3. **element**		
	• **an element of truth (in sth)**	a small amount of truth
	• **expose (sb) to (sth)**	(positive) to help someone experience new ideas (negative) to put someone in a dangerous situation
4. **isolated**		
	• **an isolated case (or event)**	an event or situation that happens only once

1. TEACHER: Why were you late to class?

   STUDENT: My car broke down. I had to wait for fifteen minutes for help. Really, I tried to be on time, but _____, I couldn't.

TEACHER: You've never been late before. This is a(n) _____, so I'll let it go this time.

2. FAN: Congratulations on winning your second Grammy. What is your secret to success?

CONCERT PIANIST: Thank you very much. I _____ my success _____ the piano lessons I took when I was six years old. My teacher, Mrs. Holmes, would not let me leave until I had every note perfect.

3. WALTER: What was the best part of working in the White House?

JUAN: Working in the White House _____ me _____ working processes of government that I hadn't known about before.

4. JENNY: Uncle Zach told me that he was a pilot and flew around the world when he was sixteen!

DAD: What?! Honey, _____ should you believe the stories Uncle Zach tells. He has a distorted memory of the past, and he likes to embellish the truth.

JENNY: So he wasn't a pilot?

DAD: Well, there is _____ in what he says. He went to flight school, but he flunked out.

5. BABYSITTER: I took Jack to see *Carjacked*. He loved it.

MOTHER: What?! That's R-rated! You _____ my six-year-old _____ violence and adult content. Why would you think that was appropriate?

BABYSITTER: Oops. I didn't think about that. Sorry.

▮ WORDS IN A READING

Read this article about wildlife. Complete it with words from the boxes.

attribute	domain	isolated	reluctant	valid

AS MOOSE POPULATION FALLS, WOLVES STRUGGLE

Chewing on the remains of a moose, a wolf pack's alpha male seemed unaware that his life was in danger. Suddenly an eight-member rival pack burst into view. The alpha male jumped to his feet, but too late. Howling and barking, the enemy chased him down and killed him within a couple of minutes.

It is not unusual for the gray wolves on Isle Royale National Park to fight each other, said John A. Vucetich, a wildlife biologist at Michigan Technological University who witnessed the attack from an airplane in January. But the rival pack's brazen invasion of another's _____ was unusual.
1
Usually a wolf is _____ to invade another wolf's territory. This rival pack had a
2
_____ reason for their invasion, however; Dr. Vucetich explains that the wolves are
3
hungry. "One of the ways the wolves struggle through a food shortage is to try and usurp territory from their neighbors," he said.

Scientists _____ the wolves' hunger to a steady decline of moose, now at their lowest
4
numbers in the forty-eight years that scientists have studied the two species in Isle Royale's closed
environment. Dr. Vucetich and a fellow researcher, Rolf O. Peterson, estimated the moose population
at 450 this winter, down from 540 last year. Only four years ago, there were 1,100 in the park, located
on a(n) _____ island in northwestern Lake Superior accessible only by boat or airplane.
5

circumstances	constrained	elements	exposed	principal

The wolf census held at thirty for the second consecutive year. But their number is sure to drop
because there will not be enough moose to feed them all, the scientists said. There are now about
fifteen moose for every wolf. The usual ratio is forty to fifty moose per wolf. If a young and strong
moose is _____ to a wolf, it can fight the wolf off, so most of the moose population is
6
safe. Wolves feast mostly on calves and elderly moose, both of which are in short supply under the
_____ now, Dr. Peterson explained.
7

The moose population decline results from many causes. A _____ reason is the aging
8
of a "baby boom" generation of moose that was born in the early 1990s, when wolf numbers dropped
because of a disease outbreak, Dr. Peterson said. Also, a tick infestation in recent years weakened the
moose, making them easy prey for wolves.

Also, the moose are _____ because their main food supply has gradually declined as
9
the island's forests have evolved from primarily birch and aspen to less nutritious spruce and balsam
fir, Dr. Vucetich said.

The changing forest cover has also caused a sharp drop in the number of beaver, an alternative
food source for the wolves, Dr. Peterson said.

Though the moose population is at a low, it is not in danger of disappearing, Dr. Peterson said. Its
decline will enable other _____ of nature to recover. Vegetation will recover from
10
overbrowsing that occurred when the herd was thriving, and fewer moose will be killed as wolf
numbers fall.

(Adapted from "As Michigan Park's Moose Population Falls, Wolves Struggle," The New York Times, March 11, 2006.)

▌WORDS IN DISCUSSION

Apply the key words to your own life. Read and discuss each question in small groups. Try to use the key words.

1. **circumstance**

Something I would do under NO circumstances: _____

Circumstances under which I would sing in public: _____

2. **expose**

   Something positive that I wish all children could be exposed to: _____

   Something I don't think children should be exposed to: _____

3. **constrain**

   Something that constrains my choices: _____

   Something that will never constrain me: _____

4. **valid**

   A piece of ID I have that is valid: _____

   A person whom I believe makes valid arguments: _____

5. **reluctant**

   A famous person I would be reluctant to marry: _____

   A food I am reluctant to eat: _____

6. **domain**

   A place that is my domain: _____

   An activity that is my domain: _____

7. **principal**

   My principal reason for getting a job: _____

   The number of times I have been sent to the principal's office: _____

8. **isolated**

   The amount of time I would like to spend on an isolated island: _____

   A time when I felt isolated: _____

9. **element**

   How many chemical elements I have memorized: _____

   How often there is an element of humor in my speech: _____

10. **attribute**

   One positive attribute that people tell me I have: _____

   Who or what I attribute my success to: _____

▌ WORDS IN WRITING

Choose two topics and write a paragraph on each. Try to use the key words.

1. Under what **circumstances**, if any, would you lie? Explain why you feel that lying would be **valid** under these **circumstances**.

2. What **elements** of life in your native country do you feel that people in other countries don't know about? Describe these **elements** and explain whether or not you think that people in other countries should be **exposed** to them.

3. Describe your **attributes**. You do not need to be modest.

4. Would you feel **isolated** if you were living in a different country? Explain why or why not.

5. Do you think dogs should be **constrained** from running free in public parks? Explain why or why not.

QUIZ 5

PART A

Choose the word that best completes each item and write it in the space provided.

1. A major storm was predicted. Due to the _____, we canceled our trip.
   - a. innovations
   - b. statistics
   - c. circumstances
   - d. attributes

2. Yuka _____ with her coworkers in Sweden via e-mail.
   - a. corresponds
   - b. promotes
   - c. isolates
   - d. declines

3. The train compartment was _____ by a Russian family.
   - a. promoted
   - b. released
   - c. occupied
   - d. exposed

4. I love to eat food from different countries, so I am happy to try any _____ food.
   - a. isolated
   - b. ethnic
   - c. significant
   - d. valid

5. Michael _____ his skill at chess to the lessons his older sister gave him.
   - a. occupies
   - b. constrains
   - c. impacts
   - d. attributes

6. The politician included _____ in his speech because the facts strengthened his message.
   - a. principals
   - b. statistics
   - c. constraints
   - d. domains

7. We won the championship. _____, we celebrated.
   - a. Significantly
   - b. Reluctantly
   - c. Consequently
   - d. Statistically

8. Cross-cultural friendship was the _____ reason for Jill's visit to China.
   - a. valid
   - b. principal
   - c. isolated
   - d. ethnic

9. Reading with young children can _____ their interest in books.
   - a. decline
   - b. dominate
   - c. occupy
   - d. promote

10. _____ of the film were interesting, but overall it bored me.
   - a. Elements
   - b. Domains
   - c. Statistics
   - d. Constraints

PART B

*Read each statement and write **T** for true and **F** for false in the space provided.*

_____ 1. An **isolated** house is surrounded by buildings.

_____ 2. Weather never **impacts** traffic.

_____ 3. There is more **diversity** in London than in a small English farming village.

_____ 4. All films are **released** before their actors are chosen.

_____ 5. The temperature **declines** in the winter.

_____ 6. If a photograph **exposes** something, it shows what everyone knew before.

_____ 7. Dance is a ballerina's **domain**.

_____ 8. A mother's pregnancy **precedes** the birth of her baby.

_____ 9. Having too much money is a common **constraint**.

_____ 10. If you are **unaware** of a problem, you can fix it.

PART C

Match each sentence with the letter it describes.

_____ 1. This person can explain the **technique** of self-defense.

_____ 2. This is a common **theme** in movies.

_____ 3. A **period** describes an amount of this.

_____ 4. This person plays a key **role** in a child's development.

_____ 5. Every **innovation** is this.

_____ 6. When Rose wants to know the **significance** of the reports, she asks this.

_____ 7. A **valid** ID is NOT this.

_____ 8. Dana thinks that the plans should be **altered**, so he asks this.

_____ 9. Carla, who is **reluctant** to change the plan, says this.

_____ 10. This person **dominates** the boxing ring.

a. a parent

b. new

c. "Why don't we change them?"

d. "Why are they important?"

e. time

f. a heavyweight champion

g. love

h. "Hmm. I'm not sure about that. Let's reconsider."

i. fake

j. a karate instructor

| conduct | emphasize | invest | range | strategy |
| contact | input | policy | secure | undertaking |

WORDS IN CONTEXT

*Use the sentences to guess what each key word means. Choose the meaning that is closest to that of the key word in **bold**.*

1. conduct
/kənˈdʌkt/
-verb

- Dr. Emoto **conducted** the experiment using water from different sources.
- Have you ever **conducted** research in a science lab?

Conduct means . . .
- a. to do something scientific
- b. to do something to find out something
- c. to do academic work

2. contact
/kantækt/
-noun

- At the university, Wen has **contact** with professors, teaching assistants, and researchers.
- If you would like to get in **contact** with me, write me a letter.

Contact means . . .
- a. communication
- b. friendship
- c. work

3. emphasize
/ˈɛmfəˌsaɪz/
-verb

- To **emphasize** her idea, Julie underlined it.
- The doctor **emphasized** that the medication could be taken only twice a day.

Emphasize means . . .
- a. to mention something
- b. to give instructions
- c. to show that an idea is important

4. input
/ˈɪnpʊt/
-noun

- Peter valued his brother Steve's carpentry experience, so when Peter was planning to build a new shed, he asked for Steve's **input**.
- If you needed ideas for a paper you were writing for a business course, would you like to ask Bill Gates for his **input**?

Input means . . .
- a. talent
- b. something original
- c. ideas or advice

5. invest
/ɪnˈvɛst/
-verb

- When Google was a new company, Ben **invested** a thousand dollars in its stock; he hoped that as the company grew, he would make a lot of money.
- Amy **invested** a lot of time and energy in her accounting class so that she would learn a lot and receive an excellent grade.

Invest means . . .
- a. to give money, time, or effort to get a profit or success later
- b. to give money, time, or effort to get a profit or success now
- c. to give money, time, or effort because you admire a company, class, or project

6. policy
/ˈpɑləsi/
-noun

- The company's **policy** is that you cannot take more than five sick days a year.
- If you want to be a diplomat, you need to understand the government's foreign **policy**.

Policy means . . .

a. advice from an organization or political party

b. an official way of doing things

c. communication

7. range
/reɪndʒ/
-verb

- In Boston, the price of a cup of coffee **ranges** from 50 cents to $5.00.
- The models of cars that BMW makes **range** from station wagons to sport cars.

Range means . . .

a. to vary between particular limits

b. to always be the same

c. to follow a pattern

8. secure
/sɪˈkyʊr/
-adjective

- William's parents worry about his temporary freelance work; they wish he would find a **secure** job.
- Ester feels **secure** in her marriage, so she doesn't worry when her husband comes home late.

Secure means . . .

a. wealthy

b. safe or confident

c. enjoyable

9. strategy
/ˈstrætədʒi/
-noun

- A company cannot succeed without a good business **strategy**.
- Before we play, we need to discuss our **strategy**; how can we win this soccer game?

Strategy means . . .

a. financial or physical support

b. team spirit

c. a plan

10. undertaking
/ˈʌndərˌteɪkɪŋ/
-noun

- Organizing the United Nations conference was a major **undertaking**.
- Building a new space station will be a massive **undertaking** for NASA.

Undertaking means . . .

a. a normal project

b. something impossible

c. an important job or activity

WORDS AND DEFINITIONS

Read each definition and write the word it defines on the line.

1. _____ not likely to change or be at risk; confident

2. _____ to do something in order to find out or prove something

3. _____ ideas, advice, money, or effort that you put into a job to help it succeed

4. _____ to show that an opinion, idea, quality, etc. is important

5. _____ a way of doing things that has been officially agreed on and chosen by a political party or organization

6. _____ to vary between particular limits

7. _____ communication with a person, organization, country, etc.

8. _____ an important job, piece of work, or activity

9. _____ a planned series of actions for achieving an aim

10. _____ to give money, time, or effort to get a profit or success later

▌COMPREHENSION CHECK

Choose the best answer.

1. Which person is NOT **investing** something?
   a. Julie, who buys stock in an oil company
   b. Andrew, who puts a lot of energy into the project
   c. Rick, who gives no money to the new company

2. If Joe is **conducting** an experiment, he
   a. is part of the experiment.
   b. is watching the experiment.
   c. is doing the experiment.

3. If a company has a **secure** financial standing,
   a. it is financially weak.
   b. its president feels confident.
   c. its workers could lose their jobs soon.

4. Whom should you ask for **input**?
   a. someone who has good ideas
   b. someone who follows your directions
   c. someone who can sing

5. Which is a large **undertaking**?
   a. starting a new company
   b. having dinner with your family
   c. finding a parking spot

6. If bouquets of roses **range** in price from $5 to $15, which of the following could be the cost of a bouquet of roses?
   a. $10
   b. $15
   c. both a and b

7. Which form of **contact** is possible through a telephone?
   a. touch
   b. writing
   c. speech

8. What does a tour guide usually **emphasize**?
   a. little details about the country
   b. the most beautiful places in the city
   c. where McDonald's is in the city

9. What **policy** does a business usually NOT have for its employees?
   a. a dress policy
   b. a snack policy
   c. a no-smoking policy

10. Which is a **strategy**?
    a. First we will chat for five minutes. Then we will ask the difficult questions.
    b. The meeting is starting, but we're unprepared.
    c. How should we start the meeting?

▌ WORD FAMILIES

Now that you have studied the ten key words and their basic definitions, you are ready to learn words that belong to the same family as some of the key words. A word family includes words that look alike but have different functions (noun, verb, adjective, or adverb). Their meanings are related but different.

A. *Look at each model phrase and decide whether the word in **bold** is used as a noun, verb, adjective, or adverb. Put a check (✔) in the correct column.*

	NOUN	VERB	ADJECTIVE	ADVERB
1. contact				
• in **contact** with her				
• **contact** me immediately				
2. emphasize				
• put an **emphasis** on an idea				
• **emphasize** your best features				
• an **emphatic** "no"				
3. invest				
• **invest** your money in a project				
• a wise **investment**				
4. range				
• **range** from 1 to 10				
• within the normal **range**				
5. secure				
• a **secure** family				
• the bank's **security**				
• an **insecure** teenager				
6. strategy				
• what's our **strategy**?				
• a **strategic** move				
7. undertaking				
• an impressive **undertaking**				
• she is **undertaking** a new role				

B. *Read the first half of each sentence and match it with the appropriate ending.*

_____ 1. Gisele will do well in business because she has a(n)

_____ 2. When I asked Stan if he wanted frog legs for dinner, he answered with a(n)

_____ 3. Please feel free to

_____ 4. After losing her boyfriend and her job in the same week, Ellen felt

_____ 5. Building a house is a major

a. **security** in his life.

b. **undertaking**.

c. **insecure**.

d. **range** of friends.

e. **emphatic** "no!"

f. **contact** me if you have any questions.

_____ 6. I have a wide

_____ 7. Buying real estate is often a wise

_____ 8. Luca wants to settle down because he needs more

_____ 9. During the job interview, try to

g. **emphasize** your best qualities.

h. **investment**.

i. **strategic** mind.

SAME WORD, DIFFERENT MEANING

*Most words have more than one meaning. Study the additional meanings of **conduct**, **policy**, and **range**. Then read each sentence and decide which meaning is used.*

a.	**conduct** v.	/kən'dʌkt/ to do something to get information or prove facts
b.	**conduct** v.	/kən'dʌkt/ to stand in front of a group of musicians or singers and direct their playing or singing
c.	**conduct** n.	/'kandʌkt/ the way someone behaves
d.	**policy** n.	a way of doing things that has been officially chosen
e.	**policy** n.	a particular principle that you believe in
f.	**range** v.	to vary between particular limits
g.	**range** v.	to deal with a large number of subjects

_____ 1. Ester's cousins **range** in age from two to thirty-three.

_____ 2. It is Jill's **policy** never to laugh at people's mistakes.

_____ 3. Howard was kicked out of the army because of his bad **conduct**.

_____ 4. My interests **range** from British literature to Hawaiian hula dancing.

_____ 5. The music teacher **conducted** the high school band.

_____ 6. Charles disagrees with the government's **policy** on immigration.

_____ 7. Every week we **conduct** an experiment in biology lab.

WORDS IN SENTENCES

Complete each sentence with one of the words from the box.

conducted	emphasis	investment	ranged	strategic
contact	input	policy	security	undertaking

1. Tonight's symphony will be _____ by Theodore Jones.

2. In my opinion, honesty is the best _____.

3. If you want to beat me at chess, you need to be _____.

4. The president is preparing a speech on national _____.

5. An optimist puts a(n) _____ on what is positive in life.

6. Harriet was happy when her _____ paid off; with the money, she was able to travel to India.

7. Writing a novel is a(n) _____.

8. You know a lot about this. Could I ask you for your _____?

9. If you are able to _____ Jin, please ask her to call me.

10. Our conversation _____ from religion to philosophy to art.

■ WORDS IN COLLOCATIONS AND EXPRESSIONS

Following are common collocations and expressions with some of the key words. Read the definitions and then complete the conversations with the collocations and expressions. You may have to change word forms for correct grammar.

1.	**contact**	
	• **a business contact**	someone you know who may be able to help you
	• **stay in contact with**	to speak or write to someone regularly
2.	**input**	
	• **thanks for your input**	thank you for your ideas or advice
3.	**invest**	
	• **invest in**	to put money, time, or effort into something
4.	**range**	
	• **out of my price range**	too expensive for me
5.	**secure**	
	• **financially secure**	not needing to worry about having enough money

1. CAR SALESMAN: Let me show you the Porsche. It's the most beautiful car we have.

   JOE: Unfortunately, a Porsche is _____.

2. MRS. XU: Do you like my Picasso? It's an original painting.

   RON: Wow! You must be a real art lover to have paid for that.

   MRS. XU: Actually, no. I just like to _____ art. Since I bought this painting five years ago, it has doubled in value. I'll make a lot of money when I sell it.

3. TESSA: I've got no money! It's really stressful not being _____.

   MARY: If you could find a new job, you might be able to get out of debt. I know some people who work for the World Bank. If I introduce you to some _____ I've got there, you might be able to get an interview.

   TESSA: Thank you so much.

4. PROFESSOR BROWN: Have you spoken with Dr. Campbell since the conference?

   PROFESSOR SMITH: Yes. We've managed to _____ each other despite our busy schedules.

5. NEIGHBOR 1: If you want to plant a garden, you should probably put up a fence. Otherwise the deer will eat everything you plant.

   NEIGHBOR 2: _____. I'll do that.

▌WORDS IN A READING

Read this article about business. Complete it with words from the boxes.

conducted	contacts	input	investing	secure

HOW TO TURN AN INTERNSHIP INTO A JOB

When trying to find their first job after university, many people struggle with the lack of work experience on their resumes. One solution that is popular with recent graduates is an internship. While this temporary job is unpaid or low-paying, a good internship can lead to a full-time position or to important business _____.

1

In late 2004, Jamie Fedorko was working difficult and long hours as an intern on the ill-fated CNBC show *McEnroe,* hoping through hard work to turn the internship into a full-time job. The failing talk show did not lead to the _____ job he was hoping for, but he turned the experience

          2
into a moneymaker anyway.

Like many interns, Fedorko, then a senior at New York City's New School University, hoped that _____ time and work in an internship would give him professional contacts and help

  3
pay the bills after graduation. What he got was a hard lesson on the difficult New York media business. His internship led him nowhere professionally, but it gave him seeds for a book idea.

Rather than chasing another job in the industry, the budding writer decided to turn his experiences into a handbook for student interns. Thinking of his time on *McEnroe* and three years of working at other internships as a list of dos and don'ts, he gives interns his _____ in the book *The*

                4
Intern Files: How to Get, Keep, and Make the Most of Your Internship.

In addition to using his own experiences on *McEnroe* and at *Vibe* and *Paper* magazines, Fedorko, now twenty-four, _____ a survey of other interns in his university's internship program

     5
and learned from the experiences of friends and acquaintances across the country. What he found was that many had gone through similar experiences and had entered their first professional work setting with similar feelings—uncertainty about how best to make a lasting, positive impression.

The Intern Files touches on subjects _____ from how to apply for internships and
                                              6

what to wear on the job to how best to make a good impression without looking as if you are trying too
hard. It includes an index of popular companies who employ interns and a listing of intern resources,
Web sites, and other books.

The book starts with a guide on how to find the right internship. It explains that, before

_____ an internship, students should read between the lines of the job posting to
        7

understand the quality of the job. Fedorko says some internships can be really helpful professional
tutorials, while others are just the result of overworked office managers looking for cheap labor.

"Pay attention to the wording of the posting for the internship. Are they looking to help you, or are
they looking for a couple months of slave labor?" he said.

Similarly, he noted that once on the job, it's a good _____ to take care of the most
                                                                8

menial tasks first to give the impression of being a capable person. Once the easy, boring stuff is out of
the way, it frees up time to volunteer for more challenging tasks.

What _____ should interns follow to be successful? Fedorko recommends that they
          9

should do extra work and never say no to any work. He even thinks it is a good idea to stay a half hour
late at work. While other interns disappear at 5:00, you will be the only person available if a new project
appears after 5:00, and people will appreciate that you are the only one who is there to do the work.

The book _____ that the most important thing an intern can learn is how to blend in
              10

with coworkers while at the same time doing the little things that will make his or her work stand
out—following directions, even if the work is dull, and communicating to supervisors that more
challenging work is welcome.

And even if the internship doesn't turn out the way you expect, like Fedorko's *McEnroe* experience,
there are still positive things to take away. You will have learned about the working world, improved
your resume, and also made business contacts.

(Adapted from "How to Turn an Internship into a Job," ABC News, February 28, 2006.)

▌WORDS IN DISCUSSION

Apply the key words to your own life. Read and discuss each question in small groups. Try to use the key words.

1. **contact**

   A person with whom I am in contact every day: _____

   A famous person whom I would like to contact: _____

2. **strategy**

   My strategy for being successful in life: _____

   How often I have a strategy when I play a game: _____

3. **input**

How good I usually am at giving input about a math or science problem:_____

A person whose input I trust: _____

4. **undertaking**

The greatest undertaking I have ever worked on: _____

An undertaking I hope to attempt some time in the future: _____

5. **invest**

The amount of time I invest in learning vocabulary every week: _____

A good investment I have made: _____

6. **secure**

A place where I feel secure: _____

The amount of money I need to earn every year to feel secure: _____

7. **conduct**

The number of times I have conducted a scientific experiment:_____

How successful I would be at conducting an orchestra: _____

8. **emphasize**

How often I emphasize what I'm saying by using hand gestures: _____

How often I emphasize my ideas by shouting: _____

9. **policy**

The percentage of time I follow the policy of my school or business: ___

How much I know about the government's policies:_____

10. **range**

My favorite subjects range from _____ to _____

A person with whom I often discuss a wide range of topics:_____

▌WORDS IN WRITING

Choose two topics and write a paragraph on each. Try to use the key words.

1. What is the best **investment** you have made in your life? (It could be a financial **investment** or an **investment** of time, energy, or love.)

2. Describe a person from your past whom you have not kept in **contact** with but would like to meet again. Why did you lose **contact**, and where would you like to meet again?

3. Imagine that you want to get on the national news tomorrow without doing anything violent or outside the **range** of legal behavior. What would be your **strategy** for achieving this goal?

4. Do schools put too much **emphasis** on tests? Explain why or why not.

5. Which country's **policies** would you most like to understand? Explain why you chose this country.

CHAPTER 17

Key Words

commission	evident	integrate	obtain	reinforce
contrary	hierarchy	mutual	prospect	substitute

WORDS IN CONTEXT

*Use the sentences to guess what each key word means. Choose the meaning that is closest to that of the key word in **bold**.*

1. commission
/kəˈmɪʃən/
-noun

- The government has appointed a **commission** to investigate the effects of global warming.
- Members of the **commission** checked the votes to make sure that they had been counted correctly.

Commission means . . .

a. an important person in the government
b. a group of voters
c. a group whose job is to find out about something

2. contrary
/ˈkɑnˌtrɛri/
-adjective

- A pacifist is a peaceful person who will never be violent because fighting is **contrary** to his or her beliefs.
- My professor welcomed the expression of views and opinions **contrary** to her own.

Contrary means . . .
a. a bit similar
b. completely opposite
c. the same

3. evident
/ˈɛvədənt/
-adjective

- Louisa's happiness was **evident**; I could see her smile from across the room.
- The answer was **evident**; we could all see what we needed to do.

Evident means . . .
a. agreed on by everyone
b. easily noticed or understood
c. interesting

4. hierarchy
/ˈhaɪəˌrɑrki/
-noun

- Dan, the assistant who gets everyone coffee, is at the bottom of the company **hierarchy**; Xen Xen, the company president, is at the top of the **hierarchy**.
- If you want to achieve a high position in the **hierarchy** of the army, you need to work hard.

Hierarchy means . . .
a. a system in which people have higher and lower ranks
b. a group of people in a business or the military
c. a manager of a group

5. integrate
/ˈɪntəˌgreɪt/
-verb

- After the ESL students have studied English for six months, we plan to **integrate** them into classes of American students.
- How easy is it for you to **integrate** into a new culture?

Integrate means . . .
a. to observe a group that you don't belong to
b. to separate two groups of people
c. to join in the life and customs of a group or society or to help someone do so

6. mutual
/ˈmyutʃuəl/
-adjective

- Jim and I sometimes disagree, but we have **mutual** respect.
- Jane and I were surprised to discover that we have a **mutual** friend: Elsa Jones.

Mutual means . . .
a. friendly
b. not serious
c. shared

7. obtain
/əbˈteɪn/
-verb

- To **obtain** a driver's license, you must pass a test at the Department of Motor Vehicles.
- Builders must **obtain** a permit before they construct a new house.

Obtain means . . .
a. to get something that you want or need
b. to do business
c. to create something

8. prospect
/ˈprɑspɛkt/
-noun

- This business has excellent **prospects** for growth.
- The **prospect** of becoming an actor was exciting for Joe and made him work hard to prepare for the future.

Prospect means . . .
a. something that is happening now
b. something that is possible or likely to happen in the future
c. something that happened in the past and affects the present

9. reinforce
/ˌriɪnˈfɔrs/
-verb

- The fisherman attached an extra board to the bottom of the boat to **reinforce** it.
- You can **reinforce** your knowledge of a new word by reviewing it the day after you learn it.

Reinforce means . . .
a. to do a great amount of work
b. to make something stronger
c. to use something too much

10. substitute
/ˈsʌbstəˌtut/
-verb

- If you run out of baking powder when you are making a cake, don't worry; you can **substitute** 1 teaspoon of baking soda for 2 teaspoons of baking powder.
- We tried to **substitute** a new toy for our dog's dirty old toy, but he noticed the change and got depressed.

Substitute means . . .
a. to improve something
b. to use something different
c. to be creative

WORDS AND DEFINITIONS

Read each definition and write the word it defines on the line.

1. _____ easily noticed or understood

2. _____ to use something new or different instead of something else

3. _____ a group of people who have been given the official job of finding out about something or controlling something

4. _____ to get something that you want or need

5. _____ felt or done by two or more people toward one another; shared by two or more people

6. _____ to do something to make something stronger or to support it

7. _____ a system of organization in which people have higher and lower ranks

8. _____ to join in the life or customs of a group or society or to help someone do so

9. _____ completely different or opposite

10. _____ something that is possible or likely to happen in the future or the possibility itself

COMPREHENSION CHECK

Choose the best answer.

1. Who **obtains** an A in math class?
   a. a student who skipped many classes
   b. a successful student
   c. the teacher

2. For which group of people is it usually easiest to **integrate** into a new culture?
   a. the elderly
   b. children
   c. people who do not speak the language

3. What is **contrary** to peace?
   a. love
   b. humor
   c. war

4. Who is at the top of the **hierarchy** of the U.S. government?
   a. the Supreme Court justices
   b. the president
   c. the secretary of defense

5. If you find yourself in a sudden rainstorm, what can you **substitute** for an umbrella?
   a. a newspaper
   b. sandals
   c. $10.00

6. If the boss says, "Mike's intelligence is **evident**," he means,
   a. "Clearly, Mike is intelligent."
   b. "Mike's intelligence is questionable."
   c. "Mike is stupid."

7. If you want to **reinforce** your message in an essay, you might
   a. give facts that support your argument.
   b. mention your idea only once.
   c. write about topics that are unrelated to your message.

8. If you and your mother have **mutual** interests, you and your mother
   a. sometimes enjoy the same activities and sometimes do not.
   b. have the same interests.
   c. often disagree about what is interesting.

9. A city's water **commission**
   a. produces water.
   b. inspects water.
   c. drinks water.

10. The **prospect** of going to college makes high school students
    a. skip class.
    b. study.
    c. exercise.

WORD FAMILIES

Now that you have studied the ten key words and their basic definitions, you are ready to learn words that belong to the same family as some of the key words. A word family includes words that look alike but have different functions (noun, verb, adjective, or adverb). Their meanings are related but different.

A. *Look at each model phrase and decide whether the word in **bold** is used as a noun, verb, adjective, or adverb. Put a check (✓) in the correct column.*

	NOUN	VERB	ADJECTIVE	ADVERB
1. **evident**				
• **evident** innocence				
• **evidently** wrong				
• look at the **evidence**				
2. **integrate**				
• **integrate** well				
• the **integration** of student				
3. **mutual**				
• **mutual** respect				
• a **mutually** beneficial plan				
4. **prospect**				
• an interesting **prospect**				
• **prospective** students				
5. **reinforce**				
• should **reinforce**				
• the soldiers need **reinforcement**				
6. **substitute**				
• you can **substitute** a $\frac{1}{2}$ cup of applesauce for 1 egg				
• a **substitute** for butter				

B. *Match each of the following sentences with the definition of the word in* **bold***.*

_____ 1. The work the doctors did together was **mutually** rewarding.

_____ 2. I don't recognize any of the roads we've been driving on. **Evidently**, we're lost.

_____ 3. The professor from Vilnius University described Lithuania's **integration** into the EU.

_____ 4. Dan's mother told him that a cup of coffee is not an adequate **substitute** for breakfast.

_____ 5. Elise sent a resume to her **prospective** employer.

_____ 6. Steel beams provide **reinforcement** for the bridge.

_____ 7. It is possible that dolphins communicate with their own language, but more scientific **evidence** is needed to prove it.

a. likely to do or be a particular thing or to happen

b. the act of doing something to make something stronger or to support it

c. done, felt, or experienced by two or more people

d. someone or something different that takes the place of another person or thing

e. facts, objects, or signs that make you believe that something exists or is true

f. joining in the life and customs of another group or society or helping someone do so

g. easily noticed or understood

▌SAME WORD, DIFFERENT MEANING

Most words have more than one meaning. Study the additional meanings of ***commission, integrate,*** *and* ***substitute****. Then read each sentence and decide which meaning is used.*

a. **commission** *n.*	a group of people who have been given the official job of finding out about something or controlling something
b. **commission** *n.*	an amount of money paid to someone for selling something
c. **commission** *v.*	to ask someone, especially an artist or musician, to do a piece of work for you
d. **integration** *n.*	the joining in the life or customs of a group or society or helping someone do so
e. **integration** *n.*	the ending of the practice of separating people of different races in a place or institution
f. **substitute** *n.*	someone or something different that takes the place of another person or thing
g. **substitute** *n.*	someone who does someone else's job for a limited period of time

_____ 1. There is no **substitute** for love.

_____ 2. In the United States, the **integration** of black students into white schools brought wide social change in the 1960s.

_____ 3. The sales clerk was pressuring us to buy that sofa—he was probably working on **commission**.

_____ 4. Because our art teacher is having a baby, we're going to have a **substitute** for the next three months.

_____ 5. The king **commissioned** his favorite artist to paint his wife's portrait.

_____ 6. **Integration** into French society was relatively easy for Asha.

_____ 7. The Federal Trade **Commission** warns consumers about dishonest businesses.

WORDS IN SENTENCES

Complete each sentence with one of the words from the box.

commissioned	evidently	integration	obtain	reinforce
contrary	hierarchy	mutually	prospective	substitute

1. I am sure that this business deal will be _____ rewarding; both you and I will benefit from it.

2. There is no sugar in diet soda; the soda is sweetened with a sugar _____.

3. _____ to what people believed a thousand years ago, the Earth is not flat.

4. Pope Julius II della Rovere _____ Michelangelo to paint the ceiling of the Sistine Chapel in 1508.

5. Gloria considered her three _____ husbands; all three had asked her to marry them, and all were good men. Finally, she chose Ben because he was the only one who could make her laugh.

6. A teenager's _____ into a new school can be difficult.

7. How long would it take you to _____ a Ph.D.?

8. You've eaten four pieces of pizza. _____ you were hungry!

9. In some African tribes, women have the most powerful positions in the _____ of their community.

10. Before the hurricane comes, _____ your windows with wood.

WORDS IN COLLOCATIONS AND EXPRESSIONS

Following are common collocations and expressions with some of the key words. Read the definitions and then complete the conversations with the collocations and expressions. You may have to change word forms for correct grammar.

1. **contrary**		
	• **contrary to popular belief**	used to show that something is true, even though people may think the opposite
	• **on the contrary**	used to show that the opposite of what has just been said is actually true
2. **commission**		
	• **out of commission**	not working correctly; unable to be used
3. **evident**		
	• **it's evident that**	it's clear or obvious that
4. **mutual**		
	• **the feeling is mutual**	said when you have the same feeling about someone as she or he has toward you
5. **substitute**		
	• **substitute (sth/sb) for (sth/sb)**	to use one thing instead of another

1.   CAR RENTAL WORKER: I'm sorry, sir, but you can't take that car. It's _____.

      PROSPECTIVE CUSTOMER: How about one of the other cars?

      CAR RENTAL WORKER: Sorry, but none of the three other cars we have here today is working either.

      PROSPECTIVE CUSTOMER: This business is terrible!

      CAR RENTAL WORKER: _____, sir, we are very successful.

      PROSPECTIVE CUSTOMER: Well, that may be, but your service is terrible! I'm going somewhere else.

2.   COOKING STUDENT: Is it true that the seeds are the hottest part of a chile pepper?

      COOK: _____, the seeds are not the hottest part. In fact, the greatest heat comes from the oil in a chile pepper.

3.   DETECTIVE 1:   Detective Smith, your excellent reputation is well deserved. Your work is first rate.

      DETECTIVE 2:   Thank you. _____.

      DETECTIVE 1:   Thank you.

4.   MARINE BIOLOGIST: _____ dolphins are intelligent animals. They communicate with each other using their own language. We're trying to figure their language out, but we still don't know what they're saying.

AQUARIUM VISITOR:	They're really cute, too.

5. BROTHER: Yuck! These cookies are terrible.

SISTER: Oops. When I was baking them, I didn't have any vanilla, so I decided to experiment and _____ soy sauce_____ the vanilla. Are they really that bad?

BROTHER: I think you've poisoned me.

WORDS IN A READING

Read this article about sports. Complete it with words from the boxes.

commission	contrary	evident	hierarchy	mutual

THE BIRTH OF YAO MING

Excited whispers traveled through the corridors of Shanghai No. 6 Hospital on the evening of September 12, 1980. It was shortly after 7:00 P.M., and a patient in the maternity ward had just endured a very difficult labor to give birth to an abnormally large baby boy. The doctors and nurses on duty should have anticipated something out of the ordinary. The boy's parents, after all, were retired basketball stars whose marriage the year before had made them the tallest couple in China. It was _____ from the beginning that their child could grow up to be one of the world's top
                      1
basketball stars.

News of Yao Ming's birth was quickly relayed across town to leaders at the top of the _____ of the Shanghai Sports _____. They were not surprised. These men
              2   3
and women had been trying to cultivate a new generation of athletes who would embody the rising power of China. This baby boy represented, in many ways, the result of their plan. The dream had begun more than a quarter-century earlier, when Chairman Mao Zedong asked his followers to send the nation's most genetically gifted youngsters into the emerging communist sports machine. Two generations of Yao Ming's forebears had been singled out by authorities for their giant physiques, and his mother and father had both been drafted into the sports system. Their _____ talent
                                                                              4
for basketball was passed on to their son.

_____ to everyone's expectations, Yao Ming was not interested in basketball as a
       5
child. Born during China's economic resurgence, Yao was part of the first Chinese generation in forty years that could entertain personal ambition. As a child, he fantasized about being an explorer traveling into new worlds rather than his parents' old one. Nevertheless, when his parents told him that he would have to start basketball training, Yao—not yet nine—didn't protest. Yao hated basketball, but he attended practice "purely for my parents because I respect them so much."

integrate   obtain   prospective   reinforce   substitute

Yao's size and clumsiness made people laugh at him at first. But the teasing wasn't nearly as painful as the training. Yao often came home from practice wanting to quit. Then his father would _____ his basketball skills by taking him behind their building to shoot at the hoop
6
hanging above the bicycle garage. For every basket Yao made, his father promised to buy him a little gift. "My father bribed me into playing!"

At thirteen Yao, already two meters tall, moved out of his parents' apartment to live at the Shanghai Sports Technology Institute. The city sports authorities, noticing Yao's size and his continuing awkwardness on the court, felt he would _____ the necessary skills only with more
7
professional training. Over the next eight years, Shanghai's top coaches and scientists worked to turn the _____ star into a world famous talent—and his parents rarely saw him. Letting go
8
wasn't easy for his mother, who was very close to her son.

Despite their years apart, Yao's parents continued to be an important part of his life. When he was chosen by the Houston Rockets as the number one pick in the NBA draft in 2002, Yao's mother made the unusual decision to move to the United States to live with her twenty-one-year-old son. The arrangement, while strange for many United States sports fans, struck many Chinese and Chinese-Americans as an admirable affirmation of Asian values. Although it has been difficult for Yao's parents to _____ into American culture, they felt the move was necessary for their son.
9
Yao's parents have gradually given him more freedom. Now twenty-five, the world-famous NBA star still lives most of the basketball season with his parents in a house in a suburb of Houston, where, despite his suggestion that his mother hire a housekeeper, his mom insists on doing the laundry and cooking all the meals. But Yao has also rented an apartment in downtown Houston as a(n) _____ home for game days and nights, enabling him to avoid the nightmarish Texas
10
traffic—and to be independent. Yao's mother now more readily accepts her son's decision to occasionally live on his own, to take unchaperoned trips with his first and only girlfriend, 1.9-meter Chinese national team player Ye Li, and to spend his money as he pleases.

(Adapted from "The Creation of Yao Ming," Time Asia, November 7, 2005, itself adapted from Brook Larmer, Operation Yao Ming, ©2005 by Penguin Group (USA).)

WORDS IN DISCUSSION

Apply the key words to your own life. Read and discuss each question in small groups. Try to use the key words.

1. **mutual**

   A person with whom I have many mutual friends:_____

   A person whom it is mutually rewarding to talk with: _____

2. **hierarchy**

   Where I am in the hierarchy of my school or company: _____

   The person who is at the top of the hierarchy in my native country's government:

   _____

3. **substitute**

   If I don't have time for a good breakfast, something I'll eat as a substitute:

   _____

   Something for which I believe there is no substitute in the world: _____

4. **evident**

   Something that is evident about my personality by looking at my room:

   _____

   Where I can find evidence to support my ideas:_____

5. **obtain**

   When I will be able to obtain a new car: _____

   Something I won't be able to obtain this year: _____

6. **commission**

   How I would feel about being part of an environmental commission:

   _____

   How likely it is that someone will commission me to paint a picture:

   _____

7. **integrate**

   A person I've helped integrate into a new group or culture: _____

   How I feel about integrating into a new culture: _____

8. **contrary**

   A person whose beliefs are contrary to my own: _____

   An adjective that is contrary to my personality: _____

9. **prospect**

   A prospect I have that I am excited about:_____

   My prospective husband or wife should _____

10. **reinforce**

    How I reinforce what I learn: _____

    The person I'll talk to if I need to reinforce my confidence: _____

▌WORDS IN WRITING

Choose two topics and write a paragraph on each. Try to use the key words.

1. Do you feel that poor people should be **integrated** into rich towns so that communities have more diversity? Explain why you approve or disapprove of this **integration**.

2. Explain something you believe that is **contrary to popular belief**.

3. What person (a celebrity or someone you know) would it be **mutually** rewarding for you to work with? Explain how you would help this person and how this person would help you.

4. If you could **substitute** a pill for a meal, would you? The pill would have all the nutrition of a meal. Explain why you like or don't like this idea.

5. Think about a specific **hierarchy** that you know about. How do you think people at the top of the **hierarchy** should treat people lower in the **hierarchy**? Is it **evident** to you that this usually happens? Explain why or why not.

Key Words

access	context	impose	monitor	parameter
considerable	equate	manipulate	notion	rational

▌WORDS IN CONTEXT

*Use the sentences to guess what each key word means. Choose the meaning that is closest to that of the key word in **bold**.*

1. **access**
/ˈæksɛs/
-noun

- Greg is a security guard at Madison Square Garden, so he has **access** to the stadium and the basketball players.
- Do you have Internet **access**?

Access means. . .
  a. information about someone or something
  b. the right to enter a place, use something, or see someone
  c. advice about a place or person

2. **considerable**
/kənˈsɪdərəbəl/
-adjective

- Melanie was happy that a **considerable** number of people came to her violin concert.
- If you have saved a **considerable** amount of money, you might want to invest some of it.

Considerable means . . .
  a. large enough to be important or have an effect
  b. medium-sized
  c. small but interesting

3. **context**
/ˈkɑntɛkst/
-noun

- It's helpful to look closely at the **context** when trying to understand the meaning of a new word in English.
- To know what Cleopatra was really like, we have to understand the **context** in which she was living.

Context means . . .
  a. a specific year in history
  b. the situation, events, or information related to something
  c. something that happened before something else

4. **equate**
/ɪˈkweɪt/
-verb

- Daphne **equates** truth with beauty; to her they are the same thing.
- Do you **equate** time with money?

Equate means . . .
  a. to think that two ideas are similar
  b. to consider that two ideas are very different
  c. to consider that one thing is the same as something else

5. **impose**
/ɪmˈpouz/
-verb

- Anne was not happy when Jeff tried to **impose** his beliefs on her.
- Strict parents **impose** a 7:00 P.M. bedtime on a ten-year-old child.

Impose means . . .
  a. to suggest that people do something you want them to do
  b. to force someone to have the same beliefs you have or to follow your rules
  c. to try to convince people to agree with you and do as you want

6. manipulate
/məˈnɪpyəˌleɪt/
-verb

- Don't trust Jessica; she is selfish, and she **manipulates** her friends into doing whatever she wants.
- Sometimes children try to **manipulate** their parents by pretending to cry.

Manipulate means . . .

a. to play a game

b. to make someone irritated or angry

c. to make someone do what you want by deceiving him/her

7. monitor
/ˈmɑnətɚ/
-verb

- If your cat is taking a strong new medication, you should **monitor** your pet's behavior to make sure that the medication is not harmful.
- Traders on Wall Street **monitor** the stock market, watching to see which stocks are losing or gaining value.

Monitor means . . .

a. to occasionally look at something

b. to pay for something

c. to carefully watch something

8. notion
/ˈnoʊʃən/
-noun

- Bernice has a strange **notion** that eating chocolate makes women more beautiful; I don't know why she believes that!
- Don't listen to Grandma's silly **notions**; you will not dream about your future husband if you put rose petals under your pillow.

Notion means . . .

a. an idea that you agree with

b. an idea, especially one that you think is wrong

c. an idea that charms or delights you

9. parameter
/pəˈræmətɚ/
-noun

- The archeologist explained the **parameters** of the research project to the team: all work had to be done within the marked area, and only special tools could be used.
- What **parameters** would you set for your fourteen-year-old daughter's social life?

Parameter means . . .

a. an explanation

b. advice

c. a limit

10. rational
/ˈræʃənəl/
-adjective

- In choosing your career, you should follow your heart, but you also need to be **rational**.
- My father is a **rational** man; he uses facts and logic to make his decisions.

Rational means . . .

a. making decisions based on intelligent thinking

b. making decisions using strong emotion or feeling

c. making decisions because of your relationships

▌WORDS AND DEFINITIONS

Read each definition and write the word it defines on the line.

1. _____ a limit that controls the way something should be done

2. _____ the right to enter a place, use something, or see someone

3. _____ sensible and able to make decisions based on intelligent thinking rather than emotion

4. _____ to force someone to have the same ideas or beliefs you have, or to introduce a rule, tax, or punishment and force people to accept it

5. _____ the situation, events, or information that relate to something and help you understand it

6. _____ an idea, belief, or opinion about something, especially one you think is wrong

7. _____ to make someone do exactly what you want by deceiving or influencing him/her

8. _____ to carefully watch, listen to, or examine something over a period of time to check for any changes or developments

9. _____ to consider that one thing is the same as something else

10. _____ large enough to be important or to have an effect

▮ COMPREHENSION CHECK

Choose the best answer.

1. Why is a volcano **monitored**?
   a. because its colors are beautiful
   b. because there is a good view from the top
   c. because it might erupt

2. Which is a **considerable** amount of money to lose on the street?
   a. 25 cents
   b. $1
   c. $100

3. Which decision seems most **rational**?
   a. Hank plans to swim across the Pacific ocean.
   b. Sue plans to swim twenty laps in the pool.
   c. Carly plans to swim in Antarctica.

4. Who has **access** to your health record?
   a. your doctor
   b. your friends
   c. a stranger on the Internet

5. Which statement describes a **notion**?
   a. 4 + 4 = 8
   b. If you have a cold, you should drink hot beer.
   c. You should hurry because the subway stops running at midnight.

6. In which **context** is it appropriate to scream?
   a. while studying in the library
   b. when feeling irritated on the subway
   c. after scoring a winning goal in a sports stadium

7. In which statement is the speaker trying to **manipulate** someone?
   a. "No one likes you, so you're lucky to be my friend. Now brush my hair!"
   b. "I really appreciate your friendship."
   c. "Can I help you?"

8. Which of the following can you **equate** with 12:00 A.M.?
   a. noon
   b. 12:00 P.M.
   c. midnight

In a study conducted at University College London, pairs of volunteers were hooked up to a mechanical device that allowed each of them to exert pressure on the other volunteer's fingers. The researcher began the game by exerting a fixed amount of pressure on the first volunteer's finger. The first volunteer was then asked to exert precisely the same amount of pressure on the second volunteer's finger. The second volunteer was then asked to exert the same amount of pressure on the first volunteer's finger. And so on. The two volunteers took turns applying equal amounts of pressure to each other's fingers while the researchers _____ the actual amount of pressure they applied.
                                                                    6

The results were striking. Although volunteers tried to respond to each other's touches with equal force, volunteers typically responded with _____ more force than they had just
                                                                    7
experienced. Each time a volunteer was touched, he touched back about forty percent harder, which led the other volunteer to touch back even harder.

Each volunteer was convinced that he was responding with equal force and that for some reason the other volunteer was _____ the situation by applying more force. Neither realized
                                                    8
that they could not _____ the pressure they felt and the pressure they gave, that a
                                    9
natural byproduct of the brain causes the pain we receive to seem more painful than the pain we produce. This is why we usually give more pain than we have received.

Research teaches us that our reasons and our pains are more obvious and real than are the reasons and pains of others. This leads to the escalation of mutual harm, to the illusion that others are solely responsible for it, and to the belief that our actions are justifiable responses to theirs.

This explanation is not meant to deny the role that hatred plays in human conflict. It is simply to say that basic principles of human psychology are important ingredients in conflict. Until we learn that it is _____ to stop trusting everything our brains tell us about others—and to start
        10
trusting others themselves—there will continue to be tears and hitting in the backseat of the car.

(Adapted from "He Who Cast the First Stone Probably Didn't," The New York Times, July 24, 2006.)

▍WORDS IN DISCUSSION

Read the questions and choose the best answers. Then discuss your answers in small groups.

1. If your friend tried to **manipulate** you, what would you do?
   a. I don't like conflict, so I would keep peace with my friend.
   b. I would not let my friend manipulate me, but I would keep my friend.
   c. I would end the friendship.

2. Which do you **equate** with success?
   a. being a good person
   b. having a lot of money
   c. having a happy family

3. How often are your decisions **rational**?

    a. always

    b. usually

    c. rarely

4. In what **context** would you drive 90 miles per hour?

    a. a normal day

    b. I am late to a concert by my favorite music group.

    c. A tornado is behind my car.

5. Do you disagree with any of your parents' **notions**?

    a. Yes, I disagree with many of their notions.

    b. Yes, I disagree with a few small ideas.

    c. No, we think in the same way.

6. If you did a **considerable** amount of extra work at your job, would you ask your boss for more money?

    a. Yes, immediately.

    b. Yes, but I'd wait and ask when my boss was in a good mood.

    c. No, my boss would never give me a raise.

7. As a teenager, how often did you follow the rules your parents **imposed**?

    a. almost always or always

    b. rarely or never

    c. My parents gave me a lot of freedom. They didn't impose rules on me.

8. Can you explain the **parameters** of a typical soccer match?

    a. Yes, I know all the limits the players must respect.

    b. I can explain some of the parameters but not all.

    c. No. I don't know much about soccer.

9. How closely do you want your teacher to **monitor** your work?

    a. Very closely. I want a lot of feedback.

    b. I want my teacher to pay attention to me, but she or he doesn't have to be aware of everything I do.

    c. Not closely. I like to learn independently.

10. How important is it for you to have Internet **access** every day?

    a. It's extremely important.

    b. It's not very important, but I'd like Internet access at least once a week.

    c. It's not at all important. I rarely use the Internet.

▎WORDS IN WRITING

Choose two topics and write a paragraph on each. Try to use the key words.

1. Explain a disagreement you once had with an **irrational** person.

2. In what **context**, if any, do you feel that it is appropriate to break the law? (If you feel that it is not appropriate in any **context**, explain why.)

3. What places do you believe teenagers should not have **access** to? Explain.

4. Describe what you consider to be the best strategy for dealing with a **manipulative** person.

5. Your grandfather wants to **impose** his old-fashioned beliefs on you. Will you live your life following his rules if he gives you a **considerable** amount of money? Explain why or why not.

QUIZ 6

PART A

Choose the word that best completes each item and write it in the space provided.

1. The prime minister has appointed a _____ to investigate the matter.
   - a. notion
   - b. context
   - c. commission
   - d. monitor

2. The new school system plans to _____ students from various neighborhoods into one school.
   - a. integrate
   - b. manipulate
   - c. substitute
   - d. impose

3. The lecturer _____ his main idea by underlining it on the board.
   - a. conducted
   - b. invested
   - c. emphasized
   - d. undertook

4. Despite being an intelligent woman, Aunt Giselle has many odd _____ about life.
   - a. ranges
   - b. notions
   - c. monitors
   - d. contexts

5. The prisoner's pain and misery were _____ as he cried for help.
   - a. secure
   - b. evident
   - c. accessible
   - d. contrary

6. It is never a good idea to be friends with a _____ person.
   - a. manipulative
   - b. secure
   - c. rational
   - d. prospective

7. You can use honey as a(n) _____ for sugar in your tea.
   - a. investment
   - b. strategy
   - c. substitute
   - d. emphasis

8. To understand a historical event, it's important to understand the _____ in which it happened.
   - a. prospect
   - b. notion
   - c. integration
   - d. context

9. The dictator had total power, _____ his beliefs and rules on the people.
   - a. contacting
   - b. obtaining
   - c. equating
   - d. imposing

10. Bharat wants to have a(n) _____ job before he gets married.
    - a. evident
    - b. secure
    - c. contrary
    - d. considerable

PART B

*Read each statement and write **T** for true and **F** for false in the space provided.*

_____ 1. A **rational** person thinks logically.

_____ 2. Fifty cents is a **considerable** amount of money.

_____ 3. Most professional sports teams do not have **strategies**.

_____ 4. Literature students typically **conduct** experiments in a lab.

_____ 5. It is possible for a person to have a wide **range** of interests.

_____ 6. A television always has a **monitor**.

_____ 7. A driver's license can be **obtained** by a ten-year-old in every country.

_____ 8. People often **invest** money in the stock market.

_____ 9. Everyone is equal in a **hierarchy**.

_____10. The **prospect** of going to college can motivate a teenager to study a lot.

PART C

Match each sentence with the letter it describes.

_____ 1. Allen's opinion is **contrary** to everyone else's, so he says this.

_____ 2. If you have **access**, you can do this.

_____ 3. This person helped set the government's **policy** on cell phone taxes.

_____ 4. If you **equate** two things, you think they are this.

_____ 5. This person **contacts** you by phone to try to sell something.

_____ 6. Kristen thinks that we are **undertaking** a lot, so she says this.

_____ 7. If you **reinforce** a fence, you make it this.

_____ 8. This person can give you **input** on ring tones, text messaging, and voicemail.

_____ 9. Sam and Josie have a **mutual** interest in the project, so Josie tells Sam this.

_____10. A **parameter** is this.

a. equal

b. "If we work together, we can make this happen."

c. a telemarketer

d. a politician

e. stronger

f. cellular phone salesperson

g. "I disagree."

h. a limit

i. enter

j. "This project is going to be very challenging."

▌ WORDS IN CONTEXT

*Use the sentences to guess what each key word means. Choose the meaning that is closest to that of the key word in **bold**.*

1. chart
/tʃɑrt/
-noun

- The doctor consulted the medical **chart** to see if the patient was improving.
- Yoo used **charts** in his presentation to show the rate of population growth over the last century.

Chart means . . .   a. a list of words   b. information shown   c. a machine used
                                                       as a graph   in hospitals

2. comprise
/kəmˈpraɪz/
-verb

- The United States **comprises** fifty states.
- The admissions team **comprises** four professors and two students.

Comprise means . . .   a. to consist of   b. to be one part of   c. to pay for many
                                        particular parts   something bigger   people

3. definite
/ˈdɛfənɪt/
-adjective

- Now that our plans are **definite**, we need to buy our tickets.
- You can't tell me, "Maybe." I need a **definite** answer.

Definite means . . .   a. clear and certain   b. negative or   c. inexpensive and
                                                                    uncertain   flexible

4. encounter
/ɪnˈkaʊntɚ/
-noun

- Carly's first **encounter** with a snake was harmless.
- Will didn't want to talk about his **encounter** with the police.

Encounter means . . . a. something that you   b. meeting someone   c. a dream
                                        plan to do   without planning to

5. external
/ɪkˈstɚnl/
-adjective

- This medicine is for **external** use only, so you can put it on your lips, but not in your mouth.
- The company experienced **external** pressure to take the product off the market.

External means . . .   a. relating to the inside   b. relating to the   c. relating to all of
                                        of something   outside of something   something

WOR

Now that
that belor
but have

A. Look a
Put a c

1. c

2. d

3. e

4. p

5. r

6. factor
/ˈfæktɚ/
-noun

- Several **factors** contributed to my decision to study at MIT.
- Climate was a **factor** Danny considered when deciding to move to Miami.

Factor means . . .
a. everything in a situation
b. one of several things that influence or cause a situation
c. the most important part of a situation

7. instance
/ˈɪnstəns/
-noun

- Different kinds of teas are usually drunk at different times of the day. For **instance**, people often drink Darjeeling in the afternoon.
- I can think of only one **instance** of crime in this neighborhood.

Instance means . . .
a. something certain
b. something unusual
c. an example

8.

internal
/ɪnˈtɚnl/
-adjective

- A spy got into the company, found **internal** documents, and stole them for a competitor.
- The doctor was happy to report that Hank was recovering from his surgery without any **internal** bleeding.

Internal means . . .
a. inside something
b. in more than one place
c. outside something

9. predict
/prɪˈdɪkt/
-verb

- The fortune teller **predicted** that Caroline would have six children.
- When do you **predict** that you will finish studying English?

Predict means . . .
a. to know a fact about the future
b. to tell a story about the past
c. to say that something will happen before it happens

10. reveal
/rɪˈvil/
-verb

- The newspaper investigation **revealed** government bribery.
- After ten years of silence, Vlad **revealed** the reason he had left his wife.

Reveal means . . .
a. to write or speak about something important
b. to show something that was previously hidden
c. to hide a secret

B. Raj is

WORDS AND DEFINITIONS

Read each definition and write the word it defines on the line.

1. _____ to say that something will happen before it happens

2. _____ information that is shown in the form of a picture or graph or a piece of paper with this information on it

3. _____ relating to the outside of something

4. _____ to show something that was previously hidden

5. _____ an example of a particular fact, event, etc.

6

7

8

9

10

CO

Choose

1. W
   de

a.

b.

c.

2. W

a.

b.

c.

3. W

a.

b.

c.

4. W
   in

a.

b.

c.

5. W

a.

b.

c.

DOCTOR: Let's talk about your test results, Raj. I have _____ your performance on the fitness test today. Now look at your results from five years ago. The differences are _____. You were in pretty good shape five years ago, but now you have the lung capacity of a 55-year-old.

4

5

RAJ: No way!

DOCTOR: It's true. I'm sorry to give you this bad news. The good news is that if you stop smoking you can reverse most of the bad effects. I hope you've had a(n) _____ today, Raj.

6

RAJ: Yes, I have. I'm going to stop smoking right away.

SAME WORD, DIFFERENT MEANING

*Most words have more than one meaning. Study the additional meanings of **chart**, **encounter**, and **factor**. Then read each sentence and decide which meaning is used.*

a. **chart** *n.*	information that is shown in the form of a picture or graph or a piece of paper with this information on it
b. **the charts** (plural) *n.*	the official list, produced each week, of the most popular songs and records
c. **factor** *n.*	one of several things that influence or cause a situation
d. **factor** *n.*	(technical) a number that divides into another number exactly
e. **encounter** *v.*	to meet someone or see something without planning to
f. **encounter** *v.*	to experience something bad that you have to deal with

_____ 1. On the subway, I **encountered** my history professor.

_____ 2. I liked the **charts** in your PowerPoint presentation.

_____ 3. 4 is a **factor** of 20.

_____ 4. Every week, the radio station plays forty songs that are at the top of the **charts**.

_____ 5. When Ali **encountered** racism for the first time, he felt sad.

_____ 6. What **factors** influenced your decision to move here?

WORDS IN SENTENCES

Complete each sentence on page 193 with two of the words from the box.

charts	definitely	external	instance	prediction
comprise	encounter	factors	internal	revelation

1. The house was well built. It collapsed because of _____ _____: the tornado and the flood.

2. Each week, the Music Billboard _____ _____ the most popular songs in the country.

3. Lucas dreamed that he had a spiritual _____ with a wise man, and when he woke up he had a(n) _____ about the meaning of life.

4. The expert's _____ about who would win the race _____ influenced the betting.

5. In this _____, a(n) _____ battle disrupted the peace in the tribe.

WORDS IN COLLOCATIONS AND EXPRESSIONS

Following are common collocations and expressions with some of the key words. Read the definitions and then complete the conversation with the collocations and expressions. You may have to change word forms for correct grammar.

1. **definite**	
• **definitely not**	certainly not
2. **encounter**	
• **an encounter with (sb/sth)**	an occasion when you meet someone or see something
3. **factor**	
• **an important factor in (sth)**	an important thing that helped to cause something
4. **instance**	
• **for instance**	for example
5. **prediction**	
• **make a prediction**	say that something is going to happen
6. **reveal**	
• **reveal that**	show that

ACADEMIC ADVISOR: I am impressed by your experiment, Greg. It _____ [1] more research needs to be done in this area. Maybe you'd like to pursue this topic in graduate school.

GREG: I'm _____ [2] interested in graduate school. After I graduate in six months, there are a lot of things I'd rather do than study more.

ACADEMIC ADVISOR: _____ [3]?

GREG: Skiing. And traveling. And money is also _____ [4] this decision. I don't have money for graduate school.

ACADEMIC ADVISOR: Student loans can help you pay for school. It sounds as if you need a break now. Maybe it is a good idea to take a year or two away from school. However, I'd like to _____ : you will be returning for your master's or even your Ph.D. You are very intelligent and can contribute a lot to science.

₅

WORDS IN A READING

Read this article about health. Complete it with words from the boxes.

charts	comprises	encounter	internal	reveal

A NEW GENERATION OF STRONGER BODIES

Valentin Keller had lung disease and could barely walk. In 1877, he died at age forty-one of congestive heart failure. His thirty-nine-year-old wife, Otilia, died a month before him of what her death certificate said was "exhaustion."

People of Valentin Keller's era, like those before and after them, expected to _____ chronic diseases by their forties or fifties. Keller's descendants had lung problems, heart problems, and liver problems. They died in their fifties or sixties.

Now, though, life has changed. The family's baby boomers are reaching middle age and beyond and are doing fine. The Keller family illustrates what may prove to be one of the most striking shifts in human existence—a change from small, relatively weak and sickly people to a population that _____ people so big and strong, their ancestors seem almost unrecognizable.

New research from around the world has begun to _____ a picture of humans today that is so different from what it was in the past that scientists say they are completely surprised. Over the past 100 years, says one researcher, Robert W. Fogel, humans in the industrialized world have undergone "a form of evolution that is unique among the 7,000 or so generations of humans who have ever inhabited the earth."

The difference does not involve changes in genes, as far as is known, but changes in the human form. It shows up in several ways, from those that are well known, like greater heights and longer lives, to ones that are emerging only with comparisons of health _____.

The biggest surprise emerging from the new studies is that many chronic _____ illnesses like heart disease, lung disease, and arthritis are occurring an average of ten to twenty-five years later than they used to. There is also less disability among older people today, according to a federal study that directly measures it. And that is not just because of medical treatments. Human bodies are simply not breaking down the way they did before.

Even the human mind seems improved. For _____ , the average I.Q. has been
                                              6
increasing for decades, and at least one study found that a person's chances of having dementia in old
age appears to have fallen in recent years.

The proposed reasons are as unexpected as the changes themselves. Improved medical care is only
part of the explanation; studies suggest that the effects seem to have been set in motion by
_____early in life, even before birth, that show up in middle and old age.
         7

"What happens before the age of two has a permanent, lasting effect on your health, and that
includes aging," said Dr. David J. P. Barker, a professor of medicine at Oregon Health and Science
University in Portland.

The effects are not just in the United States. Large and careful studies in Finland, Britain, France,
Sweden, and the Netherlands all confirm a(n) _____ pattern: the same things have
                                                         8
happened there. The effects also are beginning to show up in the underdeveloped world. Of course,
there were people in previous generations who lived long and healthy lives, and there are people today
whose lives are cut short by disease or who suffer for years with chronic ailments. But on average, the
changes, researchers say, are huge.

The extent of the changes is truly remarkable. In 1900, thirteen percent of people who were sixty-
five could expect to see eighty-five. Now, nearly half of sixty-five-year-olds can expect to live that long.
The change is _____as well; people look different today. American men, for example, are
                      9
nearly three inches taller than they were 100 years ago and about fifty pounds heavier.

"We've been transformed," Dr. Fogel said.

What's next? scientists ask. Today's middle-aged people are the first generation to grow up with
childhood vaccines and antibiotics. Early life for them was much better than it was for their parents,
whose early life, in turn, was much better than it was for their parents.

And if good health and nutrition early in life are major factors in determining health in middle and
old age, that bodes well for middle-aged people today. Investigators _____ that they may
                                                                                10
live longer and with less pain and misery than any previous generation.

(Adapted from "The New Age: So Big and Healthy Grandpa Wouldn't Even Know You," The New York Times, July 30, 2006.)

▎WORDS IN DISCUSSION

Read the questions and choose the best answers. Then discuss your answers in small groups.

1. Which kind of **chart** would you most like to
   work with?
   a. The music charts. I love to sing.
   b. A medical chart. I'd like to work in a
      hospital.
   c. A business chart. I'd like to be a business
      professional.

2. What do you feel most **definite** about?
   a. who I love
   b. the career I want
   c. the place where I want to live

3. What would you do if your best friend **revealed** your most private secret at a party?

   a. I'd run away from the party and never speak to my friend again.

   b. I'd handle the situation gracefully and later ask my friend to apologize.

   c. I'd laugh and have a good time.

4. Which **factor** most influences your decisions?

   a. my family

   b. my religion

   c. my dreams

5. How important is it for your husband or wife to have **external** beauty?

   a. Not important. I care more about my partner's soul.

   b. Somewhat important. She or he should be attractive.

   c. Important. I cannot fall in love with someone who is not beautiful.

6. In your opinion, what does a family **comprise**?

   a. a mother, a father, and one or more children

   b. two or more people who are related

   c. any group of people who love each other and live together

7. What is your approach when you **encounter** an overly talkative person?

   a. I leave quickly.

   b. I am polite, but I try to remove myself from the conversation.

   c. I happily talk to the person! No one is more talkative than I am.

8. Which feature would you like to be part of the **internal** design of your next car?

   a. heated seats

   b. a surround sound stereo system

   c. a navigation system

9. In which **instance(s)** would you happily wear a bathing suit in public?

   a. at the beach

   b. in a beauty contest

   c. jumping off a sinking ship

10. Whom do you **predict** will be very successful in business?

   a. someone in my family

   b. one of my friends

   c. me

▌ WORDS IN WRITING

Choose two topics and write a paragraph on each. Try to use the key words.

1. **Predict** one thing about the future of your city. Explain the **factors** that led to your **prediction**.

2. Would it be easier for you to face an **internal** problem (for example, a mental or physical illness) or an **external** problem? Explain why.

3. Explain what your face **reveals** about your personality.

4. If you could be given a **definite** description of your life ten years from now, would you want it? Explain why or why not.

5. Which animal would you least like to **encounter** in your home tonight? Explain why.

Key Words

criteria	dimension	integral	reside	sole
derive	initiate	orientation	site	unique

WORDS IN CONTEXT

*Use the sentences to guess what each key word means. Choose the meaning that is closest to that of the key word in **bold**.*

1. criteria
/kraɪˈtɪriə/
-*noun* (plural)

- When deciding which employees to rehire, the boss's **criteria** include achievement and dedication.
- What are the **criteria** that we should use when choosing the new principal?

Criteria means . . .
  a. unnecessary information
  b. creative ideas that many people suggest
  c. facts or standards used to help in deciding something

2. derive
/dɪˈraɪv/
-*verb*

- The doctor **derives** a lot of satisfaction from helping patients get well.
- The small business **derived** many benefits from its partnership with the larger company.

Derive means . . .
  a. to get something such as happiness or strength from someone or something
  b. to give something to someone
  c. to have a good relationship with a business

3. dimension
/dɪˈmenʃən, daɪ/
-*noun*

- The film seemed quite simple, but it had a **dimension** of mystery that kept me interested.
- Let's consider the global **dimension** of this issue.

Dimension means . . .
  a. an entire situation
  b. a special part of a situation
  c. an unimportant part of a situation

4. initiate
/ɪˈnɪʃiˌeɪt/
-*verb*

- When war broke out, the religious leader tried to **initiate** peace talks.
- We were impressed when Kelsey **initiated** the plan to open a soup kitchen for the homeless.

Initiate means . . .
  a. to follow someone's directions
  b. to try to stop something
  c. to arrange for something important to start

5. integral
/ˈɪntəgrəl/
-*adjective*

- The hard drive is an **integral** part of the computer.
- Calcium is **integral** to healthy bones.

Integral means . . .
  a. necessary
  b. interesting
  c. unhelpful

6. orientation
/ˌɔriən'teɪʃən/
-noun

- Lucas changed his political **orientation** when he learned about the corruption in his political party.
- The town, with its strong **orientation** toward tourism, was devastated by the flood.

Orientation means . . .

a. differences in opinion

b. a small group of people with the same interests

c. beliefs or interests that a person or group has

7. reside
/rɪ'zaɪd/
-verb

- Hugh has **resided** in California for six years.
- Approximately how many people **reside** in your hometown?

Reside means . . .

a. to move to a place

b. to live in a place

c. to work in a place

8. site
/saɪt/
-noun

- Plymouth Rock is the **site** where the Pilgrims first arrived in America in 1620.
- Several trucks are parked at the construction **site**.

Site means . . .

a. a plan for a very long trip

b. a very old building that needs to be repaired

c. a place where something happened or where something is being built

9. sole
/soʊl/
-adjective

- Fishing is Ryan's **sole** interest; he has no other hobbies.
- A lack of exercise was not the **sole** reason Carol gained weight; she also ate a lot of ice cream.

Sole means . . .

a. several

b. two

c. only

10. unique
/yu'nik/
-adjective

- Each person in the world is **unique**.
- Gloria designs her own clothing because she doesn't want to look like anyone else; every dress she wears is **unique**.

Unique means . . .

a. being the only one of its kind

b. being a copy of something else

c. being a part of a small group

▌WORDS AND DEFINITIONS

Read each definition and write the word it defines on the line.

1. _____ to arrange for something important to start

2. _____ to live in a particular place

3. _____ facts or standards used to help in judging or deciding something

4. _____ a place where something important or interesting happened or where something is being built

5. _____ a part of a situation that affects the way you think about it

6. _____ being the only one of its kind

7. _____ forming a necessary part of something

8. _____ the beliefs, aims, or interests a person or group has

9. _____ to get something such as happiness, strength, or satisfaction from someone or something

10. _____ only

▌COMPREHENSION CHECK

Choose the best answer.

1. What is NOT **integral** to an airplane?
   a. an engine
   b. a kitchen
   c. two wings

2. Sara loves hot weather. Which city would she be most likely to **derive** pleasure from visiting?
   a. Helsinki
   b. Rome
   c. Dublin

3. Which **criteria** should be used when evaluating a new driver?
   a. beauty and height
   b. sense of humor and quality of jokes
   c. driving skill and knowledge of driving rules

4. Who makes **unique** art?
   a. Mike, who copies the *Mona Lisa*
   b. Stella, who uses the style of the Impressionists
   c. Daniel, who makes an original sculpture that surprises everyone

5. Which area would be a good camping **site**? (You could set up a tent there.)
   a. wet and muddy land
   b. a bumpy hill
   c. a flat field

6. If Dana wants to **initiate** change in her city, she aims to
   a. start change.
   b. help change.
   c. stop change.

7. If Greg is the **sole** person on the desert island, he is
   a. the leader of the group.
   b. special.
   c. alone.

8. Who **resides** on the moon?
   a. Neil Armstrong
   b. no one
   c. several astronauts

9. If Maria asks Oliver about his religious **orientation**, she wants to know
   a. where he lives.
   b. what he does for fun.
   c. his beliefs and opinions about religion.

10. What could add a new **dimension** to Carl's life?
    a. adopting a child
    b. working for the same company
    c. taking more tennis lessons

WORD FAMILIES

Now that you have studied the ten key words and their basic definitions, you are ready to learn words that belong to the same family as some of the key words. A word family includes words that look alike but have different functions (noun, verb, adjective, or adverb). Their meanings are related but different.

A. *Look at each model phrase and decide whether the word in **bold** is used as a noun, verb, adjective, or adverb. Put a check (✓) in the correct column.*

	NOUN	VERB	ADJECTIVE	ADVERB
1. **initiate**				
• **initiate** progress				
• a promising **initiative**				
2. **orientation**				
• political **orientation**				
• **orient** yourself with a city				
• a career-**oriented** student				
3. **reside**				
• **reside** in the city				
• permanent **residence**				
• a **resident** of China				
4. **sole**				
• the **sole** idea				
• **solely** responsible				

B. *Match each of the following sentences with the definition of the word in **bold**.*

_____ 1. The map helped us **orient** ourselves in Manhattan.

_____ 2. Number 10 Downing Street, London, is the **residence** of the British prime minister.

_____ 3. Jacques is **solely** interested in collecting stamps from Asia, so don't bother showing him the Canadian stamps.

_____ 4. Aldora is a lifelong **resident** of Athens; she has never lived anywhere else.

_____ 5. The governor explained her health care **initiative** to her staff.

_____ 6. The office would benefit from a detail-**oriented** receptionist.

a. giving attention to a particular type of person or thing

b. the place where you live

c. a plan that has been started to achieve or solve something

d. only

e. to make someone familiar with a place or situation

f. someone who lives in a particular place

SAME WORD, DIFFERENT MEANING

Most words have more than one meaning. Study the additional meanings of **dimension**, **initiative**, and **sole**. Then read each sentence and decide which meaning is used.

a. **dimension** *n.*	a part of a situation that affects the way you think about it
b. **dimension** *n.*	the measurement or size of something
c. **initiative** *n.*	a plan that has been started to achieve or solve something
d. **initiative** *n.*	the ability to make decisions and take action without waiting for someone to tell you what to do
e. **sole** *adj.*	only
f. **sole** *n.*	the bottom of your foot or shoe

_____ 1. Fiona considered the **dimensions** of her bedroom when buying new furniture.

_____ 2. Sergey showed real **initiative** when he suggested the new business idea.

_____ 3. Ruth believes that her **sole** problem is getting out of debt.

_____ 4. The nurses are discussing the government's new health **initiatives.**

_____ 5. Sam was surprised by the social **dimension** of working in his office; his coworkers were all good friends.

_____ 6. Bubble gum got stuck to my **sole**, so I had to stop walking to scrape it off.

WORDS IN SENTENCES

Complete each sentence with two of the words from the box.

criteria	dimensions	integral	residents	solely
derive	initiative	orient	site	unique

1. Erik showed _____ when he came to the university three days early to _____ himself to the campus.

2. I would _____ a lot of satisfaction from seeing the _____ where my favorite writer, Henry David Thoreau, built a cabin in the woods.

3. Allison won the art contest because she met the _____: her painting was bold and _____.

4. The _____ of a building are _____ to its design.

5. _____ the _____ of the town can vote in the town elections; residents of other towns cannot.

WORDS IN COLLOCATIONS AND EXPRESSIONS

Following are common collocations and expressions with some of the key words. Read the definitions and then complete the conversation with the collocations and expressions. You may have to change word forms for correct grammar.

1. **criteria**
   - **criteria for** — facts or standards used for judging or deciding something

2. **integral**
   - **an integral part of** — a necessary part of

3. **initiate**
   - **show initiative** — to show the ability to make decisions or take action without waiting for someone to tell you what to do
   - **take the initiative** — to be the first one to take action to achieve or solve something

4. **orientation**
   - **orientation day** — a day of training and preparation for a new job or school
   - **orient yourself** — to make yourself familiar with a place or situation

CHRISTINE: What are the _____ joining the Honor Society?
                                                    1

PROGRAM COORDINATOR: We are looking for students who have excellent grades and a wide range of interests. We also want students who are motivated and independent thinkers who can _____.
                                                                              2

CHRISTINE: My grades are excellent, but I don't really think of myself as independent or a leader. Are those qualities really so important?

PROGRAM COORDINATOR: Yes, they are _____ acceptance to the program.
                                                        3
However, I think you may have these qualities, even if you don't realize it. After all, it's only your _____, and you've already
                                                                            4
asked to talk to me about the Honor Society. In this way, you definitely

_____.
            5

CHRISTINE: Thank you. So when can I apply for the Honor Society?

PROGRAM COORDINATOR: I suggest that you take some time to _____ to
                                                                          6
college life. Later in the semester, if you're still interested, I'd be happy to look at your application.

WORDS IN A READING

Read this article about Africa. Complete it with words and expressions from the boxes.

criteria for	integral	orient yourself	sites	unique

THE STONE CIRCLES OF AFRICA

Imagine that you find yourself flying in an airplane above a long river. Below, you can see over ninety ancient stone circles. It may take a while for you to _____. Are you looking down at Stonehenge in England? At circles in some other part of Europe? The rain forest below changes your idea. The stone circles, you realize, are in Africa.

The United Nations cultural organization, UNESCO, has just added the stone circles of Africa to the World Heritage List of cultural and natural _____ of outstanding universal value. The sites on this list are considered _____ to the common heritage of humankind and must be protected by the international community.

Why are the circles so important to world history? They meet the _____ the World Heritage List in two ways. First, the finely worked individual stones display precise and skillful stone-working practices. Also, the stone circles are a(n) _____ example of construction and funeral practices that lasted from the third century B.C. to the sixteenth century A.D. They reflect a sophisticated and productive society.

derive	dimension	initiated	reside	solely

The Stone Circles complex extends from northern River Gambia to the River Saloum in Senegal. In December 2004, the National Council for Arts and Culture _____ a workshop which brought together Gambian and Senegalese heritage officials to develop a management plan for the circles.

Ancient stone circles can be found throughout the world in various shapes and sizes. They served diverse functions over a long period of human history. Some studies claim that there are links between the stone circle phenomena worldwide, but this remains _____ a theory, as no functional relationship has been scientifically established between these cultures, which are often separated by more than 5,000 kilometers.

Although the African stone circles are smaller in _____ than their counterparts at Stonehenge in the United Kingdom or Carnac in France, the presence of such a large number of stones in a limited space is found nowhere else in the world.

Chapter 20   203

Many questions continue to be asked about the significance of the circles, their purpose, and who built them. What is certain is that people did not _____ in them; they are burial grounds.
9
The burials are either single or multiple. Bracelets, spears, and pottery have been found inside the graves. The burials appear to be pre-Islamic in nature. From the stone circles, researchers can

_____ evidence of a highly sophisticated and organized society with an early knowledge
10
of ironworking and a belief in life after death.

(Adapted from "Stone Circles in UNESCO World Heritage List," Daily Observer News, July 14, 2006.)

▌WORDS IN DISCUSSION

Read the questions and choose the best answers. Then discuss your answers in small groups.

1. Imagine that you fall in love with your new neighbor. (Both of you are single and about the same age.) Would you take the **initiative** and ask your neighbor on a date?
   a. Yes, immediately. I would take the initiative if I fell in love.
   b. I might, after a few months.
   c. No, I wouldn't.

2. How career-**oriented** are you?
   a. Very. I think about work all the time.
   b. Somewhat. I think about work sometimes.
   c. Not at all. My job is not important to me.

3. If you had to become a **resident** of another country, which country would you choose?
   a. Argentina
   b. Scotland
   c. India

4. Which **criteria** are most important for you when you choose your friends?
   a. common interests
   b. loyalty and respect
   c. popularity and good looks

5. Which kind of movie would you **derive** the most pleasure from watching?
   a. an action movie
   b. a documentary
   c. a romantic comedy

6. Which **site** would you most like to spend an afternoon at?
   a. a historical site
   b. a construction site
   c. a camping site

7. In what way are you **unique**?
   a. I have a unique personality.
   b. I have a unique face.
   c. Other _____

8. How would you feel if you had **sole** responsibility for an important project?
   a. confident
   b. pretty good
   c. nervous

9. Which activity is **integral** to your daily life?
   a. running
   b. talking with friends
   c. other _____

10. How big are the **dimensions** of your ideal home?
    a. very big
    b. medium
    c. small

▎ WORDS IN WRITING

Choose two topics and write a paragraph on each. Try to use the key words.

1. Imagine that you could set the **criteria** that all universities use when selecting new students. Explain what the **criteria** would be.

2. Describe a **unique** person you know.

3. What did you **derive** happiness from today? Explain.

4. If you could **initiate** a change in your school or workplace, what would it be? Explain.

5. Explain why your friends' political **orientation** or religious **orientation** is or is not important to you.

▌WORDS IN CONTEXT

Use the sentences to guess what each key word means. Choose the meaning that is closest to that of the key word in **bold***.*

1. coordinate
/koʊˈɔrdnˌeɪt/
-verb

- Danielle will **coordinate** the volunteer groups.
- Could you **coordinate** the menu for the party?

Coordinate means . . .   a. to follow someone's directions   b. to think of a good idea   c. to organize people or things

2. enable
/ɪˈneɪbəl/
-verb

- My scholarship **enabled** me to go to college.
- Computers **enable** students to access information on the Internet.

Enable means . . .   a. to make someone able   b. to pay for something   c. to work together

3. framework
/ˈfreɪmwɚk/
-noun

- The school board gave teachers a **framework** for teaching reading.
- Using the **framework** suggested by the health team, we developed a workshop for pregnant women.

Framework means . . .   a. orders that people have been given   b. a set of rules or knowledge   c. a copy of someone else's idea

4. hypothesis
/haɪˈpɑθəsɪs/
-noun

- The physics professor liked Jin's **hypothesis**; he suggested that she run an experiment to see if she was right.
- Some health experts have a **hypothesis** that corn syrup causes obesity, but this idea has not been proven.

Hypothesis means . . .   a. an unusual or completely new idea   b. a fact   c. an idea that has not yet been proven to be true

5. layer
/ˈleɪɚ/
-noun

- My birthday cake had four **layers**: chocolate cake, raspberry filling, more chocolate cake, and chocolate frosting.
- Max covered the walls with a **layer** of blue paint.

Layer means . . .   a. something that is placed on or between other things   b. something that is used to decorate something   c. a person who works with the law

6. negate
/nɪˈgeɪt/
-verb

- Peter and I are going to vote for different candidates, so my vote will **negate** his.
- Taking this medication will **negate** any seasickness you might feel on the sailboat.

Negate means . . .   a. to be harmful   b. to prevent something c. to help something

7. prime
/praɪm/
-adjective

- The warm weather was our **prime** reason for moving to Florida.
- The police spent most of the day questioning the **prime** suspect in the investigation.

Prime means . . .   a. most beautiful   b. most interesting   c. most important

8. priority
/praɪˈɔrət̬i/
-noun

- Let's discuss our **priorities** for the meeting.
- Is education a **priority** for you this year?

Priority means . . .   a. the thing you think   b. the thing you enjoy   c. the thing you don't
                          is most important   the most   care about

9. resolve
/rɪˈzɑlv/
-verb

- Lucy **resolved** her problems with Val by agreeing to share the desk with her.
- My academic advisor helped me **resolve** my problems with my schedule.

Resolve means . . .   a. to create a problem   b. to find an answer to   c. to talk about
                                                     a problem   a problem

10. voluntary
/ˈvɑlənˌtɛri/
-adjective

- Micha's decision to work for the homeless shelter was **voluntary**.
- I can't believe that Ted is washing the dishes! Did his mom make him, or is it really **voluntary**?

Voluntary means . . . a. done for a small   b. done without being   c. done without
                            amount of money   forced or paid   happiness

▌WORDS AND DEFINITIONS

Read each definition and write the word it defines on the line.

1. _____ to prevent something from having any effect

2. _____ to organize people or things so that they work together well

3. _____ most important

4. _____ something that is placed on or between other things

5. _____ a set of rules, beliefs, knowledge, etc. used in making a decision or planning something

6. _____ done willingly and without being forced or paid

7. _____ to find an answer to a problem or a way of dealing with it

8. _____ to make someone or something able to do something

9. _____ the thing that you think is most important and that needs attention before anything else

10. _____ an idea that is suggested as an explanation of something but that has not yet been proven to be true

▌ COMPREHENSION CHECK

Choose the best answer.

1. Which action **resolved** the boys' fight?
   a. Chris hit Ed.
   b. Ed said he was sorry and invited Chris to lunch.
   c. Ed said Chris's clothes looked funny.

2. Which **priority** does a bus driver usually have while driving?
   a. fame
   b. entertainment
   c. safety

3. What is true about a **hypothesis**?
   a. It is definitely true.
   b. It may be true.
   c. It is definitely wrong.

4. Which action is **voluntary**?
   a. Marta is paid to hand out newspapers on the street.
   b. Zadie must go to school.
   c. Brad helps his grandfather because he wants to.

5. What could **negate** the sound of a loud rock band?
   a. a television
   b. a soundproof wall
   c. metal

6. What does NOT **enable** a car to move?
   a. the brakes
   b. the fuel
   c. the engine

7. What skills are required to **coordinate** a picnic?
   a. organization skills
   b. cooking skills
   c. athletic skills

8. If Anne's skirt has many **layers**, it
   a. is very simple.
   b. is light.
   c. has a lot of fabric.

9. A country's legal **framework** should be understood by
   a. firemen.
   b. builders.
   c. lawyers.

10. In England, the **prime** minister is the
    a. most important person in the government.
    b. most intelligent person in the government.
    c. person who has been in the government the longest.

WORD FAMILIES

Now that you have studied the ten key words and their basic definitions, you are ready to learn words that belong to the same family as some of the key words. A word family includes words that look alike but have different functions (noun, verb, adjective, or adverb). Their meanings are related but different.

A. *Look at each model phrase and decide whether the word in **bold** is used as a noun, verb, adjective, or adverb. Put a check (✓) in the correct column.*

	NOUN	VERB	ADJECTIVE	ADVERB
1. coordinate				
• **coordinate** a group				
• the **coordination** of the day's event				
• a well-**coordinated** meeting				
• the volunteer **coordinator**				
2. hypothesis				
• an interesting **hypothesis**				
• a **hypothetical** question				
• **hypothetically** possible				
3. priority				
• our main **priority**				
• **prioritize** the things that need to be done				
4. resolve				
• **resolve** a problem				
• conflict **resolution**				
5. voluntary				
• **voluntary** work				
• leave **voluntarily**				

B. *Read the first half of each sentence and match it with the appropriate ending.*

_____ 1. Patty will be the project

_____ 2. The problem you're talking about is only

_____ 3. We were impressed by the company's

_____ 4. Hannah felt relieved when she finally found a

_____ 5. Your idea is

_____ 6. The volunteer fair was well-

_____ 7. The criminal

_____ 8. Before we start working, let's

a. **coordination** of the conference.

b. **coordinated**.

c. **coordinator**.

d. **hypothetical**.

e. **hypothetically** possible, but I need proof before I'll believe it.

f. **prioritize** what we need to do.

g. **resolution** to her legal problems.

h. **voluntarily** walked into the police station.

SAME WORD, DIFFERENT MEANING

*Most words have more than one meaning. Study the additional meanings of **coordination**, **prime**, and **resolve**. Then read each sentence and decide which meaning is used.*

a. **coordination** *n.*	the organization of people or things so that they work well together
b. **coordination** *n.*	the way the parts of your body work together to do something
c. **prime** *adj.*	most important
d. **prime** *adj.*	of the very best quality or kind
e. **resolve** *v.*	to find an answer to a problem or a way of dealing with it
f. **resolve** *v.*	to make a definite decision to do something

_____ 1. *A Farewell to Arms*, by Ernest Hemingway, is a **prime** example of American literature.

_____ 2. The marriage counselor helped the couple **resolve** their problems.

_____ 3. Professional athletes have excellent **coordination**.

_____ 4. After gaining ten pounds, Al **resolved** to go to the gym every day.

_____ 5. The budget **coordination** committee will meet on Thursday.

_____ 6. Helen's shopping addiction is the **prime** cause of her debt.

WORDS IN SENTENCES

Complete each sentence with one of the words from the box.

| coordinated | framework | layer | prime | resolution |
| enable | hypothetical | negated | prioritize | voluntarily |

1. Our new house is in a(n) _____ location.

2. My flight schedule was poorly _____, so there wasn't enough time for me to catch the second flight.

3. My enthusiasm for working in Silicon Valley was _____ by my two-hour commute from San Francisco every morning.

4. There was a thick _____ of dust over everything in the attic.

5. Zach will never _____ quit his job; we are going to have to fire him.

6. Harriett made a New Year's _____ to stop smoking.

7. The students asked their English professor to give them a(n) _____ before they began their research.

8. Having an excellent vocabulary will _____ you to improve your writing.

9. Your question addresses a(n) _____ problem. Let's discuss problems that we know exist.

10. Laura was completely disorganized, so her boss suggested that she _____ her projects.

WORDS IN COLLOCATIONS AND EXPRESSIONS

Following are common collocations and expressions with some of the key words. Read the definitions and then complete the conversation with the collocations and expressions. You may have to change word forms for correct grammar.

1. **prime**
   - **be in (one's) prime** — to be at the time in your life when you are strongest and most active
   - **a prime number** — a number that can be divided by only itself and the number one

2. **priority**
   - **low priority** — something you think is not important
   - **high priority** — something you think is very important
   - **top priority** — the most important thing for you

3. **resolve**
   - **resolve to (do sth)** — to make a definite decision to do something

4. **voluntary**
   - **on a voluntary basis** — without being paid

RON: Thank you for meeting with me, Professor Lee. I want to talk to you about the test I failed.

PROFESSOR LEE: Honestly, I don't think you studied. You made some very basic mistakes with your math. In the first equation, you needed _____ and you wrote four. You know that four can be divided by two, so that[1] was obviously wrong.

RON: I'm sorry. It's been a long time since my last math course. I didn't have time to review before the test. I work all day, and there was no time to study before the night class.

PROFESSOR LEE: It sounds as if this class is not your _____[2]. I can understand that your job comes first.

RON: Maybe the class isn't my top priority, but it's a _____[3] for me. Three months ago, when I turned sixty-five, I _____[4] go back to school and get my bachelor's degree.

PROFESSOR LEE: If I were sixty-five years old, studying would be a _____[5] for me. I'd rather relax and take it easy. Are you sure you want to study at your age?

RON: Excuse me, Professor Lee, but my age is perfect for studying. I'm not too old to learn. I _____[6]!

PROFESSOR LEE: I didn't mean to insult you. Of course you can learn, and I'm happy that you are serious about the class. I suggest that you find some time and review before the next test. Why not visit the math center on campus? There are some students from the math club who work there _____. They'll help you with any questions that you might have.
  7

RON: Thank you, Professor Lee. I appreciate your advice, and I promise I'll do much better on the next test.

▌WORDS IN A READING

Read this article about education. Complete it with words from the boxes.

framework	hypothesis	layers	prime

WHO NEEDS HARVARD?

It's the summer before your senior year, and you're sweating. _____ of college
  1
brochures are spread across the table, along with SAT review books, downloaded copies of Web pages that let you chart the grades and scores of every kid from your high school who applied to a certain college in the past five years and whether they got in or not. As you prepare your applications for college, you're hunting for the perfect school. Whether you are fifth-generation Princeton or the first in your family to apply to college, it's still the most important decision you've ever made and the most confusing. Do you have what it takes to get into a famous school?

College counselors have good news for you. The _____ they offer for choosing a
  2
college may surprise you. Famous schools are not the only excellent colleges in the country. There are hundreds of honors colleges in public universities that offer an Ivy League education at a state-school price, hundreds of small liberal arts colleges that offer a _____ undergraduate experience
  3
in a way the big schools can't rival. And if you hope to go on to grad school? Getting good grades at a small school looks better than getting so-so grades at a famous one. Perhaps you've heard the
_____ that a famous school is essential for your business career? In fact, counselors
  4
advise that going to a famous college is not necessary for you to be successful in business.

enable	priorities	resolve	voluntarily

More students—sixty-two percent more—are going to college now than did in the 1960s. The math is simple: when so many more kids are applying, a smaller percentage get in. Being accepted at a famous school such as Harvard, Dartmouth, or Princeton is amazingly difficult. This problem is resolved by new attitudes about which colleges are best for students. High school teachers and guidance counselors and especially students themselves have a new spirit, almost a liberation, when it comes to thinking about college. While a student may not be able to get into Harvard, it also does not matter anymore. Just ask the kids who have chosen to follow a different road.

Some kids end up getting into Harvard and then _____ turn it down because of the $30,000 tuition or the lecture hall class sizes or because in the course of the hunt they conclude that they would fit better elsewhere. In making their choice, they get to make their own statement about what their _____ are in an education, and they even teach their parents some lessons.

For students aspiring to go to graduate school, the more personalized education offered at small colleges can often provide the best preparation. Students see a strategy: choose a small school where the personal attention can _____ you to learn and grow a lot and reach for the world-class research university for grad school.

College is supposed to be the best four years of your life and about the love of learning, not to mention pizza and football and long, caffeinated nights of debate and confusion and discovery. All families have to do to succeed is to _____ to let go of some old assumptions and allow themselves to be pleasantly surprised by how much has changed on campuses across the country in the past generation. That ability in the end may be the admissions test that matters most.

(Adapted from "Who Needs Harvard," Time Magazine, August 21, 2006.)

▌WORDS IN DISCUSSION

Read the questions and choose the best answers. Then discuss your answers in small groups.

1. Do you enjoy talking about a **hypothesis**?
   a. Yes, very much.
   b. Yes, if it is related to a subject that interests me.
   c. No. I like to talk about more practical things.

2. Are you good at **resolving** conflict?
   a. Yes. I often help people resolve their fights.
   b. Yes, once in a while.
   c. No. I often create conflict.

3. If you were going to add a new **layer** of paint to the walls of your bedroom, which color would you choose?
   a. white
   b. yellow
   c. blue

4. Would you like to do work on a **voluntary** basis?
   a. Yes.
   b. Yes, if I had free time and the work really helped people.
   c. No.

5. Which do you consider the **prime** time of day to study?
   a. morning
   b. afternoon
   c. night

6. In your opinion, what can best **negate** a bad mood?
   a. eating my favorite food
   b. exercising
   c. laughing with a friend

7. Which **framework** are you interested in learning about?

   a. the framework for starting a new business

   b. the framework for writing a research paper

   c. the framework for building a car

8. Which of the following has the highest **priority** for you?

   a. making a lot of money

   b. learning about the world

   c. having good relationships

9. Imagine that you are hired to **coordinate** the next research team at NASA (National Aeronautics and Space Administration). How do you feel?

   a. excited

   b. interested

   c. scared

10. What could **enable** you to get to school or work faster?

    a. a better body

    b. a new car

    c. a bus or subway pass

▌WORDS IN WRITING

Choose two topics and write a paragraph on each. Try to use the key words.

1. At what age do you think that a person is in his or her **prime**? Explain.

2. If you have a problem with someone, do you prefer to try to work out the problem with the person or have a third person **resolve** the problem for the two of you? Explain your choice.

3. Explain an interesting **hypothesis**. It can be a **hypothesis** you have created or a **hypothesis** you have heard or read about.

4. What is your top **priority** this year, and what could **enable** you to achieve it?

5. How much **coordination** do you have when you play sports? Give examples to show how **coordinated** you are.

QUIZ 7

PART A

Choose the word that best completes each item and write it in the space provided.

1. My grandmother waters the garden often to _____ the drying effect of the lake breeze.
   - a. coordinate
   - b. derive
   - c. negate
   - d. comprise

2. The construction workers arrived at the building _____ early in the morning.
   - a. framework
   - b. layer
   - c. instance
   - d. site

3. I was surprised when I learned about Ron's political _____; I hadn't realized that he was a Republican.
   - a. coordination
   - b. orientation
   - c. negation
   - d. resolution

4. When the museum curator opened the curtains, he _____ the newly restored painting.
   - a. revealed
   - b. enabled
   - c. charted
   - d. predicted

5. Wooden canoes can be expensive. For _____, Ben paid $2,000 for his.
   - a. priority
   - b. instance
   - c. dimension
   - d. site

6. When buying a new wall-to-wall carpet, you should know the exact _____ of the floor it will be laid on.
   - a. criteria
   - b. layers
   - c. charts
   - d. dimensions

7. Time is an important _____ in a race.
   - a. site
   - b. factor
   - c. encounter
   - d. hypothesis

8. Don't bother to tell me everything. Just tell me your _____ reason for being here.
   - a. voluntary
   - b. external
   - c. predictable
   - d. prime

9. Could you _____ the schedule for the conference?
   - a. negate
   - b. coordinate
   - c. reside
   - d. encounter

10. An onion has many _____.
    - a. orientations
    - b. factors
    - c. layers
    - d. instances

PART B

Read each statement and write **T** for true and **F** for false in the space provided.

_____ 1. Troublemakers **resolve** fights.

_____ 2. Cost, safety, and style are **criteria** often used by people who buy cars.

_____ 3. A **hypothesis** has been proven.

_____ 4. The United States **comprises** many states.

_____ 5. People usually **derive** happiness from vacation.

_____ 6. If you **initiate** a plan, you finish it.

_____ 7. January is the **sole** month.

_____ 8. When Jared takes **internal** medicine, he puts it on his skin.

_____ 9. Astronauts have **resided** on the moon.

_____ 10. A window **enables** me to see through a wall.

PART C

Match each sentence with the letter it describes.

_____ 1. This person sometimes **encounters** wild animals.

_____ 2. When Laura does not give a **definite** answer, she says this.

_____ 3. A **unique** song is not this.

_____ 4. This person writes information about a patient's health on a **chart**.

_____ 5. Education is a **priority** for Will, so he says this about funding schools.

_____ 6. This is what a person is paid for **voluntary** work.

_____ 7. Vivian is **predicting** something when she says this.

_____ 8. An **integral** part is this.

_____ 9. This person sets the **framework** we must follow for the science project.

_____ 10. Something that is **external** is this.

a. "It is going to happen in five years."

b. a biology teacher

c. nothing

d. "We need to do this."

e. a nurse

f. common

g. a park ranger

h. outside

i. "Maybe. I'm not sure."

j. necessary

WORDS IN CONTEXT

*Use the sentences to guess what each key word means. Choose the meaning that is closest to that of the key word in **bold**.*

1. complex
/kəmˈplɛks/
-adjective

- Nuclear physics is a **complex** subject.
- The problem is so **complex** that we will need at least a few hours to analyze it.

Complex means . . .
a. consisting of many parts or details
b. filled with problems or disadvantages
c. simple and easy to understand

2. convene
/kənˈvin/
-verb

- The state representatives **convened** to discuss health care reform.
- A large group of railway engineers will **convene** in St. Petersburg.

Convene means . . .
a. have a party
b. have a disagreement
c. come together

3. incorporate
/ɪnˈkɔrpəˌreɪt/
-verb

- The pastry chef wants to **incorporate** new baking techniques in his kitchen.
- The hotel will **incorporate** dancing as part of the nightly entertainment.

Incorporate means . . .
a. to change something completely
b. to include something
c. to sell something

4. maximize
/ˈmæksəˌmaɪz/
-verb

- Raul bought as many lottery tickets as he could to **maximize** his chance of winning.
- Using effective advertising will **maximize** the company's profits.

Maximize means . . .
a. to increase something as much as possible
b. to have luck
c. to make a good investment

5. parallel
/ˈpærəˌlɛl/
-noun

- I can see a **parallel** between my grandmother's life as a young woman and my own life now: both of us loved traveling.
- One writer wrote in nineteenth-century London, and the other in late twentieth-century New York, but **parallels** can be seen in the themes of their work.

Parallel means . . .
a. a strong difference between two things
b. a question about two things
c. a relationship or similarity between two things

6. sequence
/'sikwəns/
-noun

- The teacher explained the **sequence** of bad choices that led Jozef to drop out of school.
- The police reviewed the **sequence** of events that led to the crime.

Sequence means . . .
a. an unorganized series of events
b. a series of related events
c. a series of negative actions

7. status
/'steɪt̬əs/
-noun

- The book club discussed the **status** of women in different countries.
- Do doctors in your country have a high social **status**?

Status means . . .
a. the money that someone has
b. the appearance of a person or group
c. social or professional rank or position

8. structure
/'strʌktʃɚ/
-noun

- I'm curious about the **structure** of the Leaning Tower of Pisa.
- Mrs. Williams criticized the **structure** of Todd's essay.

Structure means . . .
a. the way the parts of something connect
b. the amount of time it took to make something
c. the appearance of something

9. version
/'vɚʒən/
-noun

- Andres downloaded the latest **version** of the software onto his laptop computer.
- Annika was surprised by her sister's **version** of the story.

Version means . . .
a. a slightly different copy or description of something
b. a dishonest copy or description of something
c. an exact copy or description of something

10. virtual
/'vɚtʃuəl/
-adjective

- Quinn would rather go to a **virtual** school on the Internet than to his high school.
- We went online and did **virtual** tours of the houses for sale in our town.

Virtual means . . .
a. made or done in the real world
b. better than the real world
c. made, done, or seen on a computer

▌WORDS AND DEFINITIONS

Read each definition and write the word it defines on the line.

1. _____ to increase something as much as possible

2. _____ a series of related events or actions that happen in a particular order and lead to a particular result

3. _____ consisting of many different parts or details that are closely related and make something difficult to understand or deal with

4. _____ made, done, seen, etc. on the Internet rather than in the real world

5. _____ a person's social or professional rank or position considered in relation to other people

6. _____ a relationship or similarity between two things

7. _____ come together for a formal meeting

8. _____ the way in which the parts of something connect and form a whole

9. _____ a copy or description of something that is slightly different from its other forms

10. _____ to include something as part of a group, system, etc.

▌COMPREHENSION CHECK

Choose the best answer.

1. Which thing is part of the internal **structure** of a house?
   a. a table
   b. a pipe
   c. money

2. Which is a **sequence**?
   a. Nate opened the box and poured himself a bowl of cereal. Then he opened the milk. He spilled the milk on the table as he was pouring it.
   b. A bird flew in the sky.
   c. Yesterday the dog dug a hole under the fence.

3. "Diana's writing is **complex**," Mike said. What does he mean?
   a. The writing is very simple.
   b. The writing is terrible.
   c. The writing is intelligent and cannot be understood easily.

4. If the doctors **convene**, they
   a. perform an operation.
   b. have a formal meeting.
   c. leave the hospital.

5. How can you **maximize** the speed of a bicycle?
   a. use the brakes
   b. use the correct gear
   c. bike uphill

6. If Carly sees a **parallel** between life in Boston and life in Seoul, she notices
   a. a similarity.
   b. something funny.
   c. a big difference.

7. If Bill belongs to a **virtual** community of friends, he can
   a. shake hands with his friends.
   b. play computer games with his friends.
   c. play soccer with his friends.

8. Who has the most important **status** in a courtroom?
   a. a reporter
   b. a witness
   c. the judge

9. What can there NOT be a new **version** of?
   a. a person
   b. a song
   c. a computer

10. What will happen if Irene **incorporates** singing in her wedding ceremony?
   a. Her wedding will not have music.
   b. Her wedding will be very quiet.
   c. There will be songs in her wedding.

WORD FAMILIES

Now that you have studied the ten key words and their basic definitions, you are ready to learn words that belong to the same family as some of the key words. A word family includes words that look alike but have different functions (noun, verb, adjective, or adverb). Their meanings are related but different.

A. *Look at each model phrase and decide whether the word in **bold** is used as a noun, verb, adjective, or adverb. Put a check (✓) in the correct column.*

	NOUN	VERB	ADJECTIVE	ADVERB
1. **complex**				
• a **complex** situation				
• the book's **complexity**				
2. **convene**				
• the group **convenes**				
• a writer's **convention**				
3. **incorporate**				
• **incorporate** an idea into the plan				
• the **incorporation** of nature into her art				
4. **maximize**				
• **maximize** growth				
• the **maximum** amount				
5. **parallel**				
• notice a **parallel**				
• **parallel** ideas				
6. **structure**				
• interesting **structure**				
• **structure** your presentation				

B. *Emma is talking with a department store manager about selling the hats she has designed. Complete the conversation with words from the box.*

complexity	convention	incorporation	maximum	parallel	structure

EMMA: Thank you for meeting me. I came to this fashion _____ just to get a
1
chance to talk to you. Do you think you could sell my hats in your store?

STORE MANAGER: Unfortunately, no. The _____ of hats in a woman's wardrobe is no longer
2
common in the United States. Hats don't sell here.

EMMA: Maybe hats don't sell here because we don't offer truly beautiful hats in stores.
Look at my handmade hats. They're not like the simple, machine-made hats you
often see. Notice the _____ of the different colors, fabrics, and design.
3
Hats like this sell for a lot of money in the United Kingdom.

STORE MANAGER: Your hats are lovely, but we cannot draw a _____ between the way
4
women in the United Kingdom and the United States shop. My customers don't
wear hats. Anyway, it's not in my budget to offer you a good price for them.

EMMA: Where do you think I could get the _____ price for my hats?
5

STORE MANAGER: For the most money, I suggest talking to smaller boutiques. Their customers may
be more interested in hats than customers in my store. If I were you, I'd
_____ my time at the convention carefully. If possible, schedule
6
meetings with several owners of small, expensive shops.

▌SAME WORD, DIFFERENT MEANING

*Most words have more than one meaning. Study the additional meanings of **complex**, **incorporate**, **parallel**, and **structure**. Then read each sentence and decide which meaning is used.*

a.	**complex** *adj.*	having a lot of different parts and difficult to understand or deal with
b.	**complex** *n.*	a group of buildings or groups of rooms in one large building used for particular purposes
c.	**incorporate** *v.*	to include something as part of a group, system, etc.
d.	**incorporate** *v.*	to legally form a corporation
e.	**parallel** *n.*	a relationship or similarity between two things
f.	**parallel** *adj.*	two lines that are parallel to each other are the same distance apart along their whole length
g.	**structure** *n.*	the way in which the parts of something connect
h.	**structure** *n.*	a building or something else that has been built

_____ 1. When the students **incorporated** their business, they added the abbreviation "Inc." to the end of its name.

_____ 2. There are some interesting **parallels** between the film and the actor's real life.

_____ 3. My brothers work in the same office **complex**.

_____ 4. The Eiffel Tower is a beautiful **structure**.

_____ 5. A train goes on two **parallel** tracks.

_____ 6. David will **incorporate** your ideas in the new plan.

_____ 7. The inspector worried about the **structure** of the new racecar.

_____ 8. Salvador Dali's paintings are **complex**.

WORDS IN SENTENCES

Complete each sentence with one of the words from the box.

complexity	incorporate	parallel	status	version
convention	maximize	sequence	structures	virtual

1. The Pantheon is one of the oldest _____ in Rome.

2. To _____ the plant's growth, water it with rainwater.

3. My sister didn't like the new _____ of *Charlie and the Chocolate Factory;* she thought the original film was better.

4. I'd expected the movie to be quite dull, so I was surprised by its _____.

5. Using a ruler, Gwen drew two _____ lines an inch apart.

6. When Sal got his college degree and a good job, his social and economic _____ improved.

7. Zara is out of the office this week because she's going to a sales _____ in Chicago.

8. A(n) _____ of events led to Rebecca's decision to drop out of school.

9. The lawyer suggested that we _____ our new company.

10. Yoshi demanded that his girlfriend stop using her computer because she was spending more time with her _____ friends than with him.

WORDS IN COLLOCATIONS AND EXPRESSIONS

Following are common collocations and expressions with some of the key words. Read the definitions and then complete the conversation with the collocations and expressions. You may have to change word forms for correct grammar.

1. **complex**
   - **to have a complex about (sth)**   to have an emotional problem in which someone is too anxious about something or thinks too much about something

2. **sequence**
   - **in sequence/out of sequence**   in the correct order/not in the correct order

3. **status**
   - **high status/low status**   high or low position
   - **legal status**   the legal position of a person, group, or country
   - **the status of (sth)**   what is happening at a particular time in a situation
   - **status symbol**   something that you own that suggests that you are rich or important

4. **virtual**
   - **virtually impossible**   almost completely impossible

JOURNALISM PROFESSOR: What is _____ your report?
1

HELEN: I've changed topics, but don't worry. I've finished researching and I've begun writing. Originally I wanted to write about the _____
2
of immigrant teenagers at American universities. Then I decided that I'd like to save that topic for my term project, so I decided to focus on sororities and fraternities for this first paper. Here's a first draft. Could you look at it with me now?

JOURNALISM PROFESSOR: Sure. (*Looks at the report*) This begins with page 3. The pages must be

_____.
3

HELEN: Sorry, you have the wrong draft. Here, look at this copy.

JOURNALISM PROFESSOR: Okay, thanks . . . So you explain that many students who join sororities or fraternities on campus want to have a _____ social
4
_____. They are worried that without membership in these exclusive clubs, they will have a _____ and
5
therefore will not be invited to parties or make friends. I see that you quote several studies. Why not offer some real-life examples, also?

HELEN: That would be easy. My roommate is obsessed with her sorority. She hardly has time to study anymore. She _____ being perfect, and
6
she thinks that if she has a lot of _____, like the best
7
clothes, laptop, and cell phone, everyone in the sorority will love her and she'll be a very important person. Of course it is _____ to be
8
perfect, so she stresses out about every sorority event.

JOURNALISM PROFESSOR: Hmm. I'm not sure your roommate would feel comfortable with you writing about her. It's probably a better idea to interview various members of the sororities and fraternities on campus.

▌WORDS IN A READING

Read this article about magicians. Complete it with words and expressions from the boxes.

complex	convene	high status	sequence	versions

THE WORLD CHAMPIONSHIP IN MAGIC

In Stockholm, Sweden, a German magician makes a table covered with a purple cloth float in the air, as fellow magicians carefully watch the _____ of his movements. It's impossible to
1
figure out how he does the _____ trick.
2

Here, you can see many different _____ of tables floating shoulder-high, cards
3
sailing through the air, and rabbits being pulled out of hats. Every old trick in the book and plenty of new ones are being conjured up as over 2,000 magicians from China to the Virgin Islands

_____ this week to take part in the World Championship in Magic.
4

The pressure is high for the 156 top magicians competing in the main event for best illusionist stage show and sleight-of-hand* routine: three top finishers are guaranteed contracts for
_____ shows in Las Vegas, Paris, and Monaco.
5

| incorporate | maximize | parallel | structure | virtually impossible |

One magician here sees a(n) _____ between the magic competition and the
6
Olympics. As in the Olympics, the winners will probably go on to have very successful careers and become millionaires.

The championship lasts from Monday to Saturday and is open only to magicians registered for the event, not to the public. It's held every three years in a different city; winners get a gold medal and a trophy but no cash prize.

Arthur Trace of Chicago is one of the hopefuls to become the next Lance Burton, the celebrated Las Vegas magician who won the event in 1982 when it was staged in Lausanne, Switzerland. Trace, twenty-six, said he worked four years to perfect the ten-minute routine he performed in the stage competition—a conceptual artist interacting with a painting while balls and cards keep appearing and disappearing in his hands.

For most magicians here, the gathering is just a fun way to share secrets and _____
7
their potential by learning new tricks they can _____ in their shows. They also come to
8
sell their magical tools. The vast majority are not competing in the main event.

In the _____ where the competition is held, dozens of professionals have set up
9
booths to display their skills and products. This part of the event is open to the public, and it gives people a chance to discover the secrets of famous magic tricks.

Although sellers and performers have come from all over the world, many of their tricks are
_____ _____ to tell apart. Magic, it turns out, is much the same anywhere
10
you go.

"It is all based on the same secret," said Dirk Losander, the German magician. "It is like there are only seven notes in music, but you can arrange them in different ways."

Or according to top Las Vegas magician Jeff McBride: "Magic is an international language . . . It transcends all the language and cultural barriers."

*sleight of hand: *quick, skillful movements with your hands when performing magic tricks*

(Adapted from "Magician Contest a Tricky Business," cnn.com, August 2, 2006.)

WORDS IN DISCUSSION

Apply the key words to your own life. Read and discuss each question in small groups. Try to use the key words.

1. **incorporate**

   An activity I'd like to incorporate in my daily life: _____

   The probability that I will incorporate a business at some time in my life:

   _____%

2. **status**

   How high my status is in my school or workplace: _____

   What status I would like to have in my future career: _____

3. **version**

   How interested I am in learning about the latest versions of computers:

   _____

   A movie I have seen two different versions of: _____

4. **complex**

   A topic that I think is too complex for me to understand: _____

   A complex topic I'd like to talk about: _____

5. **structure**

   A structure I saw every day in my hometown: _____

   My favorite famous structure is _____

6. **maximize**

   What I should do to maximize my improvement in English: _____

   What I can do to maximize my happiness: _____

7. **parallel**

   What is parallel to the door in the room I am in: _____

   A parallel I notice between my country and another country: _____

8. **virtual**

   How much time I spend chatting online in virtual communities: _____

   Something that would be virtually impossible for me to do: _____

9. **convene**

   One type of convention I would like to go to: _____

   How I would feel if I were sitting with my government leaders when they convened:

   _____

10. **sequence**

    After seeing a movie, how easily I can describe the sequence of events in it:

    _____

    The sequence of events that led me to be sitting in this chair today:

    _____

WORDS IN WRITING

Choose two topics and write a paragraph on each. Try to use the key words.

1. Explain your opinion about a **complex** issue that is now in the news.

2. Explain why you would or would not like to drive a car that is a **status symbol**.

3. Your friend invites you to try **virtual** reality, an environment produced by a computer that looks and seems real to the person experiencing it. Do you accept? Explain why or why not.

4. Describe the **parallels** you can see between your life and someone else's. (The person can be someone you know or someone famous.)

5. What famous **structure** would you most like to visit? Explain why.

CHAPTER 23

Key Words

abandon	cycle	infer	maintain	unify
compound	enforce	inhibit	principle	vision

WORDS IN CONTEXT

*Use the sentences to guess what each key word means. Choose the meaning that is closest to that of the key word in **bold**.*

1. **abandon**
/əˈbændən/
-verb

- When the nuns found the baby on the steps of the church, they realized that his mother had **abandoned** him.
- It's very sad to learn how many pets are **abandoned** each year by families who decide they don't want them anymore.

Abandon means . . .   a. to have no family   b. to leave a person or thing   c. to lose a person or thing

2. **compound**
/ˈkampaʊnd/
-noun

- The Hollywood actor built a **compound** that included three houses, a swimming pool, and a stable for his horses.
- Have you ever visited a prison **compound**?

Compound means . . .   a. a group of buildings   b. a very large building   c. an area that is open to the public

3. **cycle**
/ˈsaɪkəl/
-noun

- All the water on Earth goes through a **cycle**: it evaporates (dries up), falls back to the Earth as rain or snow, and collects in rivers, oceans, or lakes.
- If you watch the sky every night, you can see the moon change as it goes through its monthly **cycle**.

Cycle means . . .   a. a number of related events that happen again and again in the same order   b. a part of nature   c. something that happens only once

4. **enforce**
/ɪnˈfɔrs/
-verb

- The babysitter **enforced** the children's bedtime.
- I wish that the waitress would **enforce** the no smoking rule in this café; the smoke is making me sick!

Enforce means . . .   a. to not care about a rule   b. to make people obey a rule or law   c. to give people special permission

5. **infer**
/ɪnˈfɚ/
-verb

- The people on the jury **inferred** that the witness was lying.
- I could **infer** that Will was upset by the tone of his voice.

Infer means . . .   a. to form an opinion with the information you have   b. to talk about something in great detail   c. to make a guess based on no information

6. **inhibit**
/ɪnˈhɪbɪt/
-verb

- Drugs sometimes **inhibit** teenagers' brain development.
- High oil prices could **inhibit** global economic growth.

Inhibit means . . .   a. to have no effect on   b. to prevent something   c. to be the result of
                                                                           from growing   something

7. **maintain**
/meɪnˈteɪn/
-verb

- After moving to Sweden, Anna made an effort to **maintain** her friendships with her friends back in Moldova.
- This old house is beautiful, but it will be expensive to **maintain**.

Maintain means . . .   a. to make something   b. to forget about   c. to spend a lot of time
           continue   thinking about

8. **principle**
/ˈprɪnsəpəl/
-noun

- Lee believes in the **principle** that all people are equal, so he treats everyone fairly.
- I don't trust Jasper. It's obvious that he has no moral **principles**.

Principle means . . .   a. a theory or set of   b. a moral rule or set   c. an honest friend
          ideas intended to   of ideas about what
          explain something   is right and wrong

9. **unify**
/ˈyunəˌfaɪ/
-verb

- Six student groups **unified** to demand free parking at the university.
- The states **unified** to make one country.

Unify means . . .   a. to talk together   b. to refuse to join   c. to combine the parts
                                                                                            to make a single unit

10. **vision**
/ˈvɪʒən/
-noun

- A person who has perfect **vision** does not need glasses.
- When the old man lost his **vision**, he learned how to read using Braille.

Vision means . . .   a. the ability to read   b. the ability to see   c. eyes

WORDS AND DEFINITIONS

Read each definition and write the word it defines on the line.

1. _____ to make people obey a rule or law

2. _____ a moral rule or set of ideas about what is right and wrong that influence how you behave

3. _____ an area that contains a group of buildings and is surrounded by a fence or wall

4. _____ to prevent something from growing or developing in the usual or expected way

5. _____ the ability to see

6. _____ to leave a person or thing, especially one that you are responsible for

7. _____ to form an opinion that something is probably true because of information you have

8. _____ to combine the parts of a country, organization, etc. to make a single unit

9. _____ a number of related events that happen again and again in the same order

10. _____ to make something continues in the same way or at the same standard as before

COMPREHENSION CHECK

Choose the best answer.

1. Which thing can you NOT **abandon**?
   a. a cat
   b. a ship
   c. yourself

2. Who **enforces** the law?
   a. the police
   b. criminals
   c. actors

3. What is good for your **vision**?
   a. reading in the dark
   b. staring at a computer screen for several hours a day
   c. vitamins A, C, and E

4. If Tom wants to **maintain** peace in his high school, he wants to
   a. keep the peace.
   b. create peace.
   c. fight peace.

5. What CANNOT **inhibit** the growth of a tree?
   a. sunlight
   b. a lack of water
   c. insects

6. If three different soccer teams **unify**, they
   a. have a big competition.
   b. become one team.
   c. have several games.

7. Walking home to his house at night, Allen sees light coming from the kitchen window. What can he **infer**?
   a. This is his house.
   b. His wife is home.
   c. He needs to wash the windows.

8. Which statement is a **principle**?
   a. 2 + 2 = 4
   b. It is important to respect my parents.
   c. There is a great sale at the mall this week.

9. What is NOT part of a washing machine's **cycle**?
   a. spin
   b. wash
   c. jump

10. A **compound** is surrounded by
    a. a fence or wall.
    b. security officers.
    c. grass.

▌WORD FAMILIES

Now that you have studied the ten key words and their basic definitions, you are ready to learn words that belong to the same family as some of the key words. A word family includes words that look alike but have different functions (noun, verb, adjective, or adverb). Their meanings are related but different.

A. Look at each model phrase and decide whether the word in **bold** is used as a noun, verb, adjective, or adverb. Put a check (✓) in the correct column.

	NOUN	VERB	ADJECTIVE	ADVERB
1. **abandon**				
• **abandon** the project				
• an **abandoned** dog				
2. **enforce**				
• **enforce** the speed limit				
• the **enforcement** of the law				
3. **infer**				
• **infer** that he's lying				
• an intelligent **inference**				
4. **maintain**				
• **maintain** the property				
• building **maintenance**				
5. **principle**				
• important **principles**				
• a strongly **principled** man				
6. **unify**				
• **unify** armies				
• the **unification** of three countries				

B. Read the first half of each sentence and match it with the appropriate ending.

_____ 1. The children looked in the broken window of the

_____ 2. The business leaders met to discuss the possible

_____ 3. The lifeguard always

_____ 4. A successful reader understands challenging books because he or she makes

_____ 5. Elizabeth won't lie because she is highly

_____ 6. I sold my house because I was tired of worrying about the

a. **enforces** the rule about no running by the pool.

b. **principled**.

c. **inferences**.

d. **unification** of their companies.

e. **abandoned** house.

f. **maintenance**.

SAME WORD, DIFFERENT MEANING

Most words have more than one meaning. Study the additional meanings of **compound**, **maintain**, and **vision**. Then read each sentence and decide which meaning is used.

a. **compound** *n.*	an area that contains a group of buildings and is surrounded by a fence or wall
b. **compound** *v.*	to make a difficult situation worse by adding more problems
c. **maintain** *v.*	to make something continue in the same way or at the same standard
d. **maintain** *v.*	to strongly express an opinion or attitude
e. **vision** *n.*	the ability to see
f. **vision** *n.*	an idea of what you think something should be like

_____ 1. Carol **maintains** that sleep is the best medicine.

_____ 2. Laser eye surgery may improve your **vision**.

_____ 3. A electric fence surrounds the prison **compound**.

_____ 4. Vince is trying to **maintain** a good relationship with his boss.

_____ 5. Our problems with our old car were **compounded** by the pouring rain and bumpy dirt road.

_____ 6. Let me tell you about my **vision** for the new school.

WORDS IN SENTENCES

Complete each sentence with two of the words from the box.

abandoned	cycle	inference	maintain	unify
compounded	enforcement	inhibited	principles	vision

1. The teacher made a(n) _____ that the problems Lin had adjusting to her new high school were _____ by the problems she had adapting to a new country.

2. Mary's development was _____ because her parents _____ her when she was three years old.

3. The mayor congratulated the chief of police and announced that law _____ had ended the _____ of violence in the city.

4. The two volunteer groups share the same _____, so they have agreed to _____.

5. Matt's _____ of a happy marriage is that he will always be able to _____ love and respect for his wife.

WORDS IN COLLOCATIONS AND EXPRESSIONS

Following are common collocations and expressions with some of the key words. Read the definitions and then complete the conversation with the collocations and expressions. You may have to change word forms for correct grammar.

1. **compound**	
• **be compounded by**	be made worse by
• **a chemical compound**	a chemical substance that consists of two or more different substances
2. **infer**	
• **infer from**	form an opinion from the information you have
3. **inhibit**	
• **lose your inhibitions**	lose the worry or embarrassment that stops you from expressing how you really feel or doing what you really want to do
4. **principle**	
• **the principle that**	the moral rule that
• **the basic principles of (sth)**	the ideas that a plan or system is based on

PROFESSOR: Frankly, your presentation was not good. It was confusing, and you spoke very quietly. I noticed that your hand was shaking when you tried to write

_____ on the board. You wanted to write H_2O, but it
                    1

looked like HZO. Were you nervous because you were unprepared?

HEIDI: No, I prepared a lot. I'm sorry, Professor. I really do understand

_____ chemistry, but when I tried to explain them, I was
                    2

too nervous to remember anything. I don't like public speaking to begin with, and

my fears _____ my poor English.
                    3

PROFESSOR: Your English is very good!

HEIDI: I was worried that my American classmates wouldn't understand my German accent.

PROFESSOR: Well, I think that I can _____ this conversation that your
                                    4

problem is not with chemistry. It's with your confidence about English. If you

_____ about your accent, you will be able to give a clear
          5

presentation.

HEIDI: I hope you're right. I believe in _____ it is wrong to quit.
                                        6

If you'd give me the chance, I'd like to try the presentation again.

WORDS IN A READING

Read this article about an unusual art gallery. Complete it with words and expressions from the boxes.

abandoned	compounded by	cycle	enforce

COME SEE ART—BUT MISS THE TIDE, AND YOU'RE STUCK AT SEA

At one of the most unusual art galleries in the world, the opening times will be advertised simply as being at low tide. These days, the only visitors to the _____ World War II bunkers on
1
Cramond Island are usually birds and brave day-trippers. However, five artists are planning to change that by using the crumbling concrete buildings as a temporary art gallery.

The only problem is the rigid restrictions on the times when people can see the paintings and sculptures. When the ocean is low, people can walk to the island. But when the _____ of
2
the tide brings higher water, it is impossible to walk from the shore to the island. This means that visitors will have a maximum of four hours at a time to get from the shore to the island gallery and back—or their stay will end up being considerably longer than they planned.

The coast guard tries to _____ rules about the times when it is safe to walk to the
3
island, warning anyone thinking of making the trip to pay close attention to the signs that tell the times when it is safe to walk there. In June, a young mother almost died after getting caught waist-deep in the freezing waters after trying to cross the causeway a quarter of an hour after the last crossing time. Lifeboats are regularly used to rescue visitors finding themselves trapped by the tide.

The coast guard warns that if anyone gets stuck on the island, their problems will be
_____ an attempt to make it back to the mainland. "The water comes in very quickly,
4
and it is safer to raise the alarm from the island."

inferred	inhibits	maintain	principles	unified	vision

The "Bunker" art exhibition will feature the work of five artists from Scotland, Iceland, Canada, and Turkey. These artists are _____ in their _____ of the unusual gallery.
5   6
They _____ that the cold atmosphere in many regular galleries _____ art
7   8
lovers' experience of art. In their opinion, the island gallery is a wonderful change. Getting to the art is an adventure, and adventure is one of the _____ of art. Here, the artists' message can be
9
_____ not only from their art, but also from the gallery itself.
10
Edinburgh artist Mike Corbet-Reakes, one of the artists taking part, believes the remote location would add to the experience for art lovers visiting the exhibition.

"We were very keen to create something almost directly the opposite of white cube gallery spaces," he said. "It's a real chance for people to get away from the normal gallery environment."

(Adapted from "Come See Art . . . but Miss the Tide and You'll Be all at Sea," Edinburgh News, August 17, 2006.)

▌WORDS IN DISCUSSION

Read the questions and choose the best answers. Then discuss your answers in small groups.

1. Do you wish that the police would **enforce** more laws in your city?
   a. Yes, I do.
   b. No, I don't.
   c. No, I wish they would enforce fewer laws!

2. How would you feel if your country were **unified** with another country?
   a. I'd feel happy; my country would be more powerful if it joined another country.
   b. I'd feel unhappy; I want my country to be independent.
   c. It depends which country my country would unify with!

3. Is it (or was it) easy for you to **maintain** good grades in school?
   a. Yes. It is (or was) always easy.
   b. No. Sometimes I have excellent grades, sometimes I don't.
   c. No. I never have good grades.

4. Have you ever entered an **abandoned** building?
   a. Yes. I have many times.
   b. Yes. I did once.
   c. No. I've never done so.

5. Are your **principles** similar to your parents' **principles**?
   a. yes
   b. somewhat
   c. no

6. You are dancing in a nightclub when a spotlight shines on you and your dance partner. Is it easy for you to lose your **inhibitions** and dance freely?
   a. Yes, very easy.
   b. It's not easy, but I keep dancing.
   c. No. I stop dancing and run away from the dance floor.

7. Would you like to live in an expensive **compound** protected by a security guard?
   a. Yes. I want to have a luxurious lifestyle.
   b. Yes, if I had enough money to pay the bills.
   c. No. I am a normal person, and I want to live in a normal home.

8. Which animal's life **cycle** would you most like to learn about?
   a. a butterfly
   b. a tiger
   c. a salmon

9. What can people **infer** from your smile?
   a. I have a good sense of humor.
   b. I am sweet.
   c. I am secretive.

10. Which words best describe your **vision** of your dream car?
    a. small, environmentally friendly, and cheap
    b. big, tough, and powerful
    c. stylish and expensive

WORDS IN WRITING

Choose two topics and write a paragraph on each. Try to use the key words.

1. Do people often **abandon** dogs and cats in your native country? Explain why this does or does not happen.

2. Describe your **vision** of a perfect day.

3. Describe something that has **inhibited** your progress in English and offer a solution to the problem.

4. Explain your ideas about **maintaining** a good friendship.

5. What do people **infer** about you from the way you speak? Explain if their **inferences** are correct or incorrect.

WORDS IN CONTEXT

*Use the sentences to guess what each key word means. Choose the meaning that is closest to that of the key word in **bold**.*

1. adjust
/ə'dʒʌst/
-verb

- Max **adjusted** easily to his new high school.
- It took several months for Su to **adjust** to life in Los Angeles.

Adjust means . . .
a. to gradually get used to a new situation
b. to fail to become comfortable in a new situation
c. to suddenly succeed in a new situation

2. advocate
/'ædvə,keɪt/
-verb

- Because she is an environmentalist, Angela **advocates** recycling.
- Kindergarten teachers **advocate** parents reading with their children.

Advocate means . . .
a. to show a small interest in something
b. to strongly support something
c. to talk about something

3. cite
/saɪt/
-verb

- At the town meeting, residents **cited** many problems with the new road.
- Our teacher reminded us to **cite** the sources we used for our essays.

Cite means . . .
a. to mention something as an example or proof
b. to complain about
c. to type something on a computer

4. confine
/kən'faɪn/
-verb

- The firefighters were able to **confine** the fire to the kitchen, so the rest of the house was not damaged.
- The police **confined** the suspect to a jail cell.

Confine means . . .
a. to keep someone or something within the limits of something
b. to fight someone or something
c. to stop the negative effect of something

5. coincide
/,koʊɪn'saɪd/
-verb

- This year Guntur's birthday **coincides** with spring break, so he's going to have a birthday party on the beach.
- My trip to Uruguay will **coincide** with Rick's vacation there, so we're planning to meet each other.

Coincide means . . .
a. to happen in the same place
b. to happen at the same time
c. to happen in the same way

6. ignorant
/ˈɪɡnərənt/
-*adjective*

- Mom told me not to listen to the **ignorant** man's insults; he knew nothing about where we came from.
- Richard knows that he is **ignorant** about history, so he wants to take a history class.

Ignorant means . . .   a. not knowing facts or information that you should know   b. interested in a subject   c. violent and dangerous

7. incidence
/ˈɪnsədəns/
-*noun*

- This is a safe town to live in. There is a low **incidence** of crime here.
- There is a high **incidence** of health problems in the polluted area.

Incidence means . . .   a. the frequency of something or number of times it happens   b. how dangerous something is   c. the reason something happens

8. intervene
/ˌɪntɚˈvin/
-*verb*

- The supervisor **intervened** in the nurses' argument, telling them both to calm down and return to work.
- If your friends start fighting, will you **intervene**?

Intervene means . . .   a. to join an argument   b. to do something to try to stop an argument or problem   c. to agree with one person in a fight

9. tense
/tɛns/
-*adjective*

- Before taking the TOEFL, Amanda felt **tense**, so she listened to some calming music.
- Pete was so **tense** after his first day at work that his wife told him to take a bath to relax.

Tense means . . .   a. nervous and anxious   b. excited   c. depressed

10. violate
/ˈvaɪəˌleɪt/
-*verb*

- Many people suspect that the election officials **violated** the law.
- I can't believe you **violated** our agreement!

Violate means . . .   a. to change   b. to disobey or go against   c. to tell people about

WORDS AND DEFINITIONS

Read each definition and write the word it defines on the line.

1. _____ to keep someone or something within the limits of something

2. _____ nervous and anxious

3. _____ to strongly support a particular way of doing things

4. _____ not knowing facts or information that you should know

5. _____ to mention something as an example or proof

6. _____ to do something to try to stop an argument, problem, war, etc.

7. _____ to disobey or do something against a law, rule, agreement, etc.

8. _____ to gradually get used to a new situation

9. _____ the frequency of something or number of times it happens

10. _____ to happen at the same time as something else

▌COMPREHENSION CHECK

Choose the best answer.

1. What is impossible to **confine?**
   a. a frog
   b. a problem
   c. time

2. If the celebration **coincides** with the winter solstice,
   a. the celebration is not because of the winter solstice.
   b. the celebration is at the same time as the winter solstice.
   c. the winter solstice follows the celebration.

3. If Melissa has **adjusted** to living in a dorm, her new home feels
   a. strange and different.
   b. scary.
   c. familiar and comfortable.

4. Saul wants to know about the **incidence** of HIV infection in New York City. In other words, he wants to know
   a. why HIV infection is occurring.
   b. how frequently HIV infection is occurring.
   c. where HIV infection is occurring.

5. Why might a person **cite** a hole in an apartment's wall?
   a. because the hole is ugly
   b. to give an example of why the apartment is not fit to live in
   c. because he is angry

6. Who is **intervening?**
   a. "Stop, both of you!"
   b. "I'm not going to get involved."
   c. "I'll help you beat him up."

7. My grandfather **advocates** safe driving. This means that he
   a. is a dangerous driver.
   b. always respects the speed limit and tells me to respect it, too.
   c. laughs at good drivers.

8. Who is **violating** something?
   a. Eileen, who is telling everyone her sister's secret
   b. Maggie, who is waiting for the traffic signal to tell her that it's safe to cross the street
   c. Beth, who is paying her taxes

9. An **ignorant** person
   a. understands the world.
   b. should learn more.
   c. has an excellent education.

10. Who probably feels **tense?**
    a. Yoshi, who is skiing on his favorite mountain
    b. Amos, who is reading a good book
    c. Demetrius, who is waiting to hear if he got his dream job

WORD FAMILIES

Now that you have studied the ten key words and their basic definitions, you are ready to learn words that belong to the same family as some of the key words. A word family includes words that look alike but have different functions (noun, verb, adjective, or adverb). Their meanings are related but different.

A. *Look at each model phrase and decide whether the word in **bold** is used as a noun, verb, adjective, or adverb. Put a check (✓) in the correct column.*

	NOUN	VERB	ADJECTIVE	ADVERB
1. **adjust**				
• **adjust** to a change				
• slow **adjustment**				
2. **advocate**				
• /ˈædvəˌkeɪt/ **advocate** change				
• /ˈædvəkət/ an **advocate** for children's rights				
3. **confine**				
• **confine** your spending				
• home **confinement**				
4. **ignorant**				
• an **ignorant** person				
• total **ignorance**				
5. **incidence**				
• the **incidence** of abuse				
• an unusual **incident**				
6. **intervene**				
• **intervene** in a fight				
• military **intervention**				
7. **tense**				
• **tense** atmosphere				
• feel the **tension**				
8. **violate**				
• **violate** my trust				
• a clear **violation**				

B. *Match each word on pages 239 and 240 with its definition.*

_____ 1. an action that breaks a law, rule, agreement, etc.

_____ 2. lack of knowledge or information about something

_____ 3. someone who publicly supports someone or something

_____ 4. a nervous and anxious feeling

a. **adjustment**

b. **advocate**

c. **confinement**

d. **ignorance**

e. **incident**

_____ 5. a change in the way you behave or think

_____ 6. the act of intervening

_____ 7. the act of forcing someone to stay in a room, prison, etc., or the state of being there

_____ 8. something unusual, serious, or violent that happens

f. **intervention**

g. **tension**

h. **violation**

SAME WORD, DIFFERENT MEANING

*Most words have more than one meaning. Study the additional meanings of **adjust**, **cite**, and **tense**. Then read each sentence and decide which meaning is used.*

a. **adjust** *v.*	to gradually get used to a new situation
b. **adjust** *v.*	to make small changes to something, especially its position
c. **cite** *v.*	to mention something as an example or proof of something else
d. **cite** *v.*	to order someone to appear before a court of law because he or she has done something wrong
e. **tense** *adj.*	nervous and anxious
f. **tense** *n.*	in grammar, one of the forms of a verb that shows actions or states in the past, present, or future

_____ 1. The young man was **cited** for drinking and driving.

_____ 2. Karla was so **tense**, she needed a back massage.

_____ 3. The maid **adjusted** the picture on the hotel wall so that it was straight.

_____ 4. The reporter **cited** three people who had witnessed the fire.

_____ 5. The present perfect **tense** is often used to describe actions that happened at an unspecific time in the past.

_____ 6. Ethan was surprised at how quickly he **adjusted** to life in Hong Kong.

WORDS IN SENTENCES

Complete each sentence with one of the words from the box.

adjusting	cite	confinement	incidence	tension
advocate	coincide	ignorance	intervention	violate

1. In our global issues class, we listened to a lecture by a human rights _____.

2. Because the vet is worried that the dog's illness will spread to other animals, the dog is being kept in _____.

3. The children were relieved when their teacher's _____ ended the fight.

4. Before the debate, the room was filled with _____.

5. After the baby was born, Matilda had a hard time _____ to having a little sister.

6. This study describes the high _____ of soldiers' mental problems after returning from war.

7. I was really surprised and embarrassed by my cousin's _____; he should have known better.

8. Travel agents know that vacations to hot countries often _____ with the winter holidays.

9. I can _____ two examples to prove that our advertising policy is effective.

10. The lawyer would not give any personal details because she refused to _____ her client's privacy.

WORDS IN COLLOCATIONS AND EXPRESSIONS

Following are common collocations and expressions with some of the key words. Read the definitions and then complete the conversations with the collocations and expressions. You may have to change word forms for correct grammar.

1. **adjust**
   - **adjust to**   gradually become familiar with

2. **advocate**
   - **an advocate for**   someone who publicly supports someone or something

3. **coincide**
   - **coincide with**   to happen at the same time as
   - **what a coincidence**   what a surprise that these two things happened at the same time

4. **ignorant**
   - **ignorance is bliss**   used to say that if you do not know about a problem, you cannot worry about it

5. **tense**
   - **a tense situation**   a nervous and anxious situation

1. AMY: I was born on March 4.

   SUMA: _____! I was born on March 4, too.

2. YOUNGER BROTHER: I'm worried about leaving home and going to college.

   OLDER BROTHER: You'll be fine. Once you _____ college life, you'll love it.

3. REPORTER: Troops are moving toward your country's border. It is _____. What do you think should be done?

   POLITICAL LEADER: I am _____ peace. I don't think we can solve our problems by fighting, so I will keep working toward a peaceful solution.

4. SHOE STORE OWNER: When should we have our sale?

   SALES MANAGER: The sale should _____ the holiday weekend so that
people have free time to shop.

5.   KIONA: Life was easier when we were kids. We didn't know about all the problems in
the world.

    BOB: It's true. _____ .

▌WORDS IN A READING

Read this article about snakes on planes. Complete it with words from the boxes.

coincide	confined	ignorant	intervenes	tense

SNAKES ARE FREQUENT FLIERS TOO

In the horror movie *Snakes on a Plane,* hundreds of deadly snakes are set loose inside an airplane, where they proceed to attack the passengers. An action hero then _____ to stop the

1
problem. It's only a movie, of course, but snakes are regular airline travelers in real life, too, crisscrossing the skies as part of the growing trade in pet reptiles.

If this news makes you _____ and you wish you were still _____ of the

2   3
fact that snakes travel on planes, don't worry. You're not likely to face one in the seat next to you.
Snakes—at least those traveling legally—go strictly cargo and must be safely _____

4
inside strong crates.

"In my twenty-odd years, I've never heard of an incident where a snake escaped into the passenger
area," said Mike Osborn, a wildlife inspector with the U.S. Fish and Wildlife Service (FWS) at the Los
Angeles International Airport.

LA's airport is the busiest port for the importation of live animals into the United States, receiving
seven or eight shipments of reptiles every week from Southeast Asia, South America, and Africa. If you
are flying to LA from one of those locations, it is possible that your flight will _____ with

5
a shipment of snakes. A typical shipment of thirty crates may contain 200 to 300 pythons, 100 to 200
turtles and tortoises, and thousands of small lizards, Osborn says.

adjust	advocate	cite	incidents	violated

The FWS has adopted a set of voluntary guidelines for shipping animals of all types. According to
these guidelines, reptiles should travel in cloth bags and be placed in ventilated crates. Crates
containing poisonous snakes must be clearly labeled "venomous." Osborn can _____

6
about four or five _____ when animals have escaped inside the cargo area. Usually they

7
died in the storage area of the aircraft.

Snake wrangler Jules Sylvester, whose LA-based company Reptile Rentals supplied the snakes for the *Snakes on a Plane* movie, is a(n) _____ for snakes traveling. He says the cold-blooded

8

creatures actually make excellent travelers. They easily _____ to their crates on the

9

plane.

According to Marvin Cummings, a Delta Dash customer service representative in Atlanta, Georgia, transporting snakes, even venomous ones, is "a regular, everyday thing" for the airline. The process is strictly controlled.

One practice that is more difficult to control is illegal snake smuggling. Passengers have

_____the law by secretly taking snakes on planes.

10

"Most of the illegal smuggling of snakes [in and out of the country] takes place in the passenger arena," Osborn, the FWS official, said. "A person may try to bring the snakes onto the plane in their carry-on luggage or even tape them to their body."

One traveler, Osborn says, was caught at the L.A. airport with fifty-three baby snakes concealed underneath his clothes. "To be honest", Osborn said, "you never know what the person sitting next to you on the plane might be wearing or carrying."

(Adapted from "Snakes on Your Plane? Serpents Are Frequent Fliers Too," National Geographic News, August 14, 2006.)

▌WORDS IN DISCUSSION

Read the questions and choose the best answers. Then discuss your answers in small groups.

1. Do you **advocate** smoking in cafes?
   a. Yes. People should be able to smoke there.
   b. Yes, but in a special smoking section of the café.
   c. No. People should not be able to smoke any place where food is served.

2. Do you believe that **ignorance** is bliss?
   a. yes
   b. sometimes
   c. no

3. How often are you **tense?**
   a. rarely
   b. sometimes
   c. All the time—in fact, I am tense now!

4. How would you feel if your mother **intervened** in a problem you were having with your boss?
   a. I'd be happy; I'd thank my mom for her help.
   b. I'd feel OK but a bit irritated.
   c. I'd feel angry at my mother.

5. Which **adjustment** do you think would be most difficult for you?
   a. moving away from my parents' house
   b. living in a new country
   c. becoming a parent

6. Is there a high **incidence** of unemployment in your hometown?
   a. Yes. Over 30% of people are unemployed.
   b. Yes. Between 10% and 30% of people are unemployed.
   c. No. Under 10% of people are unemployed

7. Do you **cite** academic sources when you write a school paper?

   a. always

   b. sometimes

   c. never

8. Do you think that drug users should be **confined** to jail?

   a. Yes. I don't want them to spread the drug problem.

   b. No. I think they should get help instead.

   c. No. I think drug users should have freedom.

9. If a business partner **violated** an agreement you had with him, what would you do?

   a. I'd end the partnership and sue him in a court of law.

   b. I'd discuss the problem with him and create a new agreement.

   c. I'd accept the violation.

10. You are planning your wedding when you remember that your parents' wedding anniversary is the week when you wish to marry. Do you schedule your wedding so that it **coincides** with your parents' wedding anniversary?

    a. yes

    b. maybe

    c. no

▍WORDS IN WRITING

Choose two topics and write a paragraph on each. Try to use the key words.

1. How would you feel if you were **confined** to your home for the weekend? Explain.

2. Describe an interesting **coincidence** that happened in your life.

3. Imagine that you are invited to speak to the president of your country about solving problems. When you speak to him, what group of people would you like to be an **advocate** for? (For example, children, the homeless, etc.) Explain why.

4. Explain why you agree or disagree with this statement: "It is dangerous for people to be **ignorant**."

5. Describe a time when you had to **adjust** to a new place.

QUIZ 8

PART A

Choose the word that best completes each item and write it in the space provided.

1. Daniel's mother was angry when she learned he'd _____ his children.
   a. maintained   c. unified
   b. abandoned   d. advocated

2. The nature writer explained an eagle's life _____.
   a. version   c. inference
   b. cycle   d. ignorance

3. Rosa's moving to San Francisco for six months, but she's going to _____ her close relationship with her family in Peru by calling and writing often.
   a. infer   c. cite
   b. abandon   d. maintain

4. Eric has amazing ideas, but his writing is disorganized. It needs _____.
   a. vision   c. structure
   b. version   d. complexity

5. There isn't just one style; this magazine _____ many different fashions.
   a. inhibits   c. confines
   b. violates   d. incorporates

6. From the title, what can you _____ about the poem?
   a. infer   c. compound
   b. maximize   d. adjust

7. Smoking on an airplane is a(n) _____ of the law.
   a. incorporation   c. violation
   b. version   d. inhibition

8. I prefer the original movie to the new _____.
   a. vision   c. version
   b. adjustment   d. cycle

9. The newspaper explained the _____ of events that led to the strike.
   a. sequence   c. coincidence
   b. inference   d. maintenance

10. Doctors are worried about the high _____ of obesity in our country.
    a. enforcement   c. confinement
    b. incidence   d. principle

PART B

*Read each statement and write **T** for true and **F** for false in the space provided.*

_____ 1. An **ignorant** person knows a lot about the world.

_____ 2. Academic writers usually **cite** the sources from which they get their information.

_____ 3. If one road crosses another road, the two roads are **parallel.**

_____ 4. **Tense** people have no stress.

_____ 5. If two countries have different agendas, they are **unified.**

_____ 6. Physics is a **complex** subject.

_____ 7. A typical business aims to **maximize** profits.

_____ 8. Good parents teach their children **principles.**

_____ 9. An **advocate** has no opinion about an issue.

_____ 10. A life guard **enforces** the rules at the swimming pool.

PART C

Match each sentence with the letter it describes.

_____ 1. When Ruth **intervenes** in the fight, she says this.

_____ 2. In many countries, this is a high-**status** job.

_____ 3. The police officer said this when he **confined** the suspects.

_____ 4. When Nick wants the group to **convene,** he says this.

_____ 5. This person can help you if you have a problem with your **vision.**

_____ 6. **Virtual** reality happens here.

_____ 7. If a problem is **compounded,** it becomes this.

_____ 8. This person can help you **adjust** to a new school.

_____ 9. Jill's confidence was **inhibited** by this.

_____ 10. Some people believe that strange behavior **coincides** with this phenomenon.

a. a full moon

b. a counselor

c. worse

d. "You must stay here."

e. a judge

f. failure

g. "Stop!"

h. on a computer

i. "Let's get together."

j. an eye doctor

▌WORDS IN CONTEXT

*Use the sentences to guess what each key word means. Choose the meaning that is closest to that of the key word in **bold**.*

1. analogy
/əˈnælədʒi/
-noun

- The kindergarten teacher made an **analogy** between a child and a tree, explaining that both needed care to grow.
- My history professor drew an **analogy** between the gladiator shows in the ancient Roman Colosseum and daytime talk shows today.

Analogy means . . .   a. a creative story   b. a comparison of two situations   c. a picture of two things

2. bias
/ˈbaɪəs/
-noun

- In my broadcasting class, we discussed how **bias** in the media can lead reporters to tell only one side of a story.
- Phil warned us that our new boss has a **bias** against older workers.

Bias means . . .   a. a lack of interest in something   b. an open mind about all people and groups   c. an opinion that influences you

3. confirm
/kənˈfɚm/
-verb

- The photograph **confirmed** my suspicion: my employee was not sick—she was vacationing in Mexico.
- The DNA test **confirmed** that Grace had Native American ancestors.

Confirm means . . .   a. to suggest that something might be possible   b. to say or prove that something is definitely true   c. to test an idea

4. exploit
/ɪkˈsplɔɪt/
-verb

- The owners of the sweatshop **exploited** the children, making them work long hours in dangerous conditions.
- The nanny complained that the family she worked for **exploited** her, forcing her to clean and do laundry, although she was paid only to take care of the children.

Exploit means . . .   a. to request help with an undesirable task   b. to treat someone unfairly in order to gain what you want   c. to make a fair business decision

5. finite
/ˈfaɪnaɪt/
-adjective

- There is a **finite** amount of oil on Earth, so it will be necessary to use other energy sources at some point in the future.
- Although the amount of English vocabulary seems endless, there is a **finite** number of words in the language.

Finite means . . .   a. continuing forever   b. a large amount   c. having an end or a limit

6. **ideology**
/ˌaɪdiˈɑlədʒi, ˌɪdi-/
-noun

- Mark decided to invest in the company because of its **ideology**; it was environmentally friendly.
- Margaret decided not to join the group because she sensed that some of its members had a racist **ideology**.

Ideology means . . .
a. a set of beliefs or ideas
b. a club for business people
c. a plan for spending money

7. **interval**
/ˈɪntɚvəl/
-noun

- The subway stopped. After a short **interval**, it began to move again.
- Allison took a year off between high school and college. During the **interval**, she worked as a waitress in Colorado.

Interval means . . .
a. trip
b. a period of time
c. difficulty

8. **legislate**
/ˈlɛdʒəˌsleɪt/
-verb

- The union workers wanted the government to **legislate** a higher minimum wage.
- Should the governor **legislate** a seat-belt law for school buses?

Legislate means . . .
a. to make a law about something
b. to pay for something
c. to prevent something from happening

9. **stress**
/strɛs/
-noun

- Sun-hi's difficult classes gave her a lot of **stress**.
- Working for a demanding boss put Allen under a lot of **stress**.

Stress means . . .
a. continuous feelings of pressure or worry
b. a small problem
c. something that makes you work hard

10. **trigger**
/ˈtrɪgɚ/
-verb

- The hurricane **triggered** the power failure.
- Ron stopped taking the medication when he learned that it could **trigger** heart attacks.

Trigger means . . .
a. to be the result of something
b. to prevent a problem
c. to make something happen

❙ WORDS AND DEFINITIONS

Read each definition and write the word it defines on the line.

1. _____ to say or prove that something is definitely true

2. _____ to make something happen

3. _____ a comparison between two situations or processes that seem similar

4. _____ a period of time between two events

5. _____ having an end or a limit

6. _____ an opinion about whether someone or something is good or bad that influences you

7. _____ to make a law about something

8. _____ continuous feelings of pressure or worry caused by difficulties in your life that prevent you from relaxing

9. _____ to treat someone unfairly to gain what you want

10. _____ a set of beliefs or ideas, especially political beliefs

COMPREHENSION CHECK

Choose the best answer.

1. Which must be **finite?**
   a. an idea
   b. a living room
   c. love

2. If politicians **legislate** a new speed limit, they
   a. discuss a new speed limit.
   b. drive the speed limit.
   c. make a new law.

3. If Doug makes an **analogy** between his work and prison, he
   a. is satisfied with his job.
   b. is a prison guard.
   c. hates his job.

4. If Laura asks about the **ideology** of communism, she asks about
   a. the beliefs and ideas of communism.
   b. the end of communism.
   c. the places where communism exists.

5. Is it fair for a judge to have a **bias**?
   a. yes
   b. sometimes
   c. no

6. What could **trigger** a headache?
   a. not eating all day
   b. watching a funny movie
   c. dancing

7. What CANNOT be **confirmed**?
   a. a flight
   b. something that is not true
   c. a belief

8. Which **interval** is typical between breakfast and lunch?
   a. forty-five minutes
   b. four hours
   c. an hour and a half

9. Which thing is NOT a common cause of **stress?**
   a. work
   b. family problems
   c. a hobby

10. Which statement is spoken by someone who is **exploiting** someone else?
    a. "You're a great friend."
    b. "You have to wash my floor, even though I'm not going to pay you anything."
    c. "I will give you honest work."

WORD FAMILIES

Now that you have studied the ten key words and their basic definitions, you are ready to learn words that belong to the same family as some of the key words. A word family includes words that look alike but have different functions (noun, verb, adjective, or adverb). Their meanings are related but different.

A. *Look at each model phrase and decide whether the word in **bold** is used as a noun, verb, adjective, or adverb. Put a check (✓) in the correct column.*

	NOUN	VERB	ADJECTIVE	ADVERB
1. **bias**				
• unfair **bias**				
• **biased** reporting				
2. **confirm**				
• **confirm** that it works				
• necessary **confirmation**				
3. **exploit**				
• **exploit** a friend				
• cruel **exploitation**				
4. **finite**				
• **finite** amount of time				
• **infinite** possibilities				
5. **legislate**				
• plans to **legislate**				
• new **legislation**				
• powerful **legislators**				
6. **trigger**				
• **trigger** growth				
• the accident's **trigger**				

B. *Read the first half of each sentence and match it with the appropriate ending.*

_____ 1. The best-selling novel was the

_____ 2. In the universe, there is a(n)

_____ 3. Chris won't go to the circus. He thinks it is a(n)

_____ 4. The president did not agree with the new

_____ 5. I checked the back of the textbook for

_____ 6. A new law is created by

_____ 7. Sally shouldn't judge the debate; she is

a. **biased** against one team.

b. **legislators**.

c. **exploitation** of animals.

d. **confirmation** of the correct answer.

e. **trigger** for record publishing sales.

f. **legislation**, so he vetoed it.

g. **infinite** number of stars.

SAME WORD, DIFFERENT MEANING

Most words have more than one meaning. Study the additional meanings of **exploit**, **stress**, and **trigger**. Then read each sentence and decide which meaning is used.

a.	**exploit** v.	to treat someone unfairly to gain what you want
b.	**exploit** v.	to use something completely or get as much as you can out of a situation
c.	**stress** n.	continuous feelings of pressure or worry that prevent you from relaxing
e.	**stress** v.	to emphasize a statement, fact, or idea
f.	**trigger** v.	to make something happen
g.	**trigger** n.	the part of a gun that you press with your finger to fire it

_____ 1. When the actress wore the unusual jeans on the TV program, she **triggered** a fashion trend.

_____ 2. Constant **stress** can be bad for your health.

_____ 3. The farmer **exploited** the illegal workers, forcing them to work fifteen hours per day.

_____ 4. An accidental shooting can occur when a child finds a gun and pulls its **trigger**.

_____ 5. The video game designer **exploited** the weaknesses he found in his rival's product to design a better game.

_____ 6. My guitar teacher **stresses** the importance of learning many different styles of music.

WORDS IN SENTENCES

Complete each sentence with one of the words from the box.

analogy	confirmation	infinite	interval	stress
biased	exploitation	ideology	legislation	triggered

1. Our science teacher is _____ in favor of boys. He doesn't believe girls can do as well as boys in science.

2. The Democratic Party has a different _____ from the Republican Party.

3. We need to work harder to stop the _____ of children.

4. The baseball coach drew a(n) _____ between the loss of their star player to a rival team and a divorce.

5. When my son asked me how many numbers there are, I explained that numbers are _____.

6. The heavy rain _____ the flood.

7. The newspaper reported on new _____ passed by the Senate.

8. The airline sent me a written _____ that I'd bought the tickets.

9. Senior year is a time when a lot of high school students are under a lot of _____.

10. In the _____ between dinner and the movie, we took a walk in the park.

▌WORDS IN COLLOCATIONS AND EXPRESSIONS

Following are common collocations and expressions with some of the key words. Read the definitions and then complete the conversations with the collocations and expressions. You may have to change word forms for correct grammar.

1. **analogy**	
• **make/draw an analogy**	make a comparison between two things that seem similar
2. **bias**	
• **be biased against**	be influenced by a negative opinion
3. **confirm**	
• **confirm that**	say or prove it is definitely true that
4. **interval**	
• **at regular intervals**	with the same amount of time or distance between each thing or activity
5. **stress**	
• **be under a lot of stress**	to have or experience a lot of stress
• **be stressed out**	to feel very stressed

1.   BANKER: Would you like the money now, or would you rather be paid in installments _____ for the next twenty years?

    LOTTERY WINNER: I'd like the money now.

2.   WIFE: Why did you _____ between our marriage and climbing Mt. Everest?

     HUSBAND: Because both are difficult but wonderful.

3.   CASSANDRA: I'm pretty certain that I didn't get a bonus because my boss _____ women. Should I stay at the company?

     LUCY: No. You should look for another job.

4.   MOTHER: The newspaper says that a new research study _____ teenagers _____.

    TEENAGER: Who needs a research study? I could have told you that, Mom.

5.   ED: I have too much work to do. I can't sleep and all my hair is falling out. I _____!

     NANCY: Don't worry. I think you'll look handsome bald. Just kidding. Try to relax. Tell yourself you have all the time you need.

Read this article about personal finance. Complete it with words from the boxes.

confirms	infinite	interval	stressed	triggered

SINKING IN CREDIT CARD DEBT

Aug. 16, 2006—At the height of their debt, Delilah and Kevin Lewis, of Chattanooga, Tennessee, had filed for bankruptcy twice, owed nearly $50,000, and were still spending on more than twenty-five credit cards. Though their yearly incomes had once totaled more than $90,000, Delilah was laid off in 1996, the result of a downsizing effort by the local newspaper where she worked. After a short _____, she suffered a stroke—and was hit with $5,000 in medical fees. "By then, we were
1
just sinking," the fifty-three-year-old says. "I was working overtime to try to make back all this money, and I had a heart attack at age 45. I was a young, healthy woman, but I was so highly _____ that I just made myself ill."
2

The Lewises' case is extreme—but it's far from rare. Americans are spending with plastic at an alarming rate. Consumer credit-card debt has almost tripled over the last two decades—from $238 billion in 1989 to $800 billion in 2005, according to one consumer advocacy group. The average American family now owes more than $9,000 in credit debt, _____ Gail Cunningham of
3
the Consumer Credit Counseling Service (CCCS). And with credit companies mailing out a record six billion credit-card offers last year (according to Mail Monitor, a market research group), American families are averaging about seven cards.

Across America, there seems to be a(n) _____ number of stories of families falling into
4
credit card debt. The Lewis family is typical. They are the first to admit that their spending habits were, at times, out of control. But there were also circumstances that were beyond them: Delilah's job loss and medical problems, for example, that _____ their debt. Their case is not unlike that of
5
millions of other middle-class Americans who in the face of stagnant wages and rising health and energy costs are using some form of credit to fill the gap between household earnings and the cost of living.

analogy	bias	exploitation	ideology	legislation

A(n) _____ can be made between credit card debt and quicksand; both are very
6
difficult to escape from once you fall in. Cunningham breaks the situation into more manageable terms: take a family that is $9,000 in debt on a card that has an 18 percent interest rate. Say they cut up the card and never use the account again. Even if they pay the minimum payment of two percent of the balance each month, plus interest, it will take them forty-seven years—and close to $33,000—to pay off that $9,000 debt.

James Scurlock, a finance expert and documentary filmmaker whose latest production, *Maxed Out*, won acclaim for its critical look at the lending industry, says his research has shown a vast

_____ of the young and poor by credit card companies. He says that those consumers
7

considered "risky" are in fact the ones that bring in the most profit, and he expressed concern over industry marketing tactics that often target young consumers. (According to a recent poll, one out of every ten teens is using credit cards today.) In the past, credit card companies had a(n)

_____ against people who might fall into debt. Now the opposite is true. "We're in a
8

totally different time now where we're deluged every day with offers of credit," says Scurlock. "College students are a really attractive market because they have parents who will bail them out, they love spending money, and they're not nearly as sophisticated as they think they are."

Senator Robert Menendez of New Jersey hopes to get _____ passed that will help
9

prevent consumers from being taken advantage of. With average households now paying more than $800 in penalty fees and interest payments each year—or $90 billion annually, according to the Center for American Progress, Menendez feels that it is time for a change in the _____ of the
10

credit card culture. His "Credit Card Bill of Rights" would establish public education programs aimed at financial literacy, set twenty-one as the minimum age to nonvoluntarily receive credit card solicitations, and create industry standards related to excessive fees and interest rates.

(Adapted from "Plastic Predicament," Newsweek, August 18, 2006.)

▌ WORDS IN DISCUSSION

Read the questions and choose the best answers. Then discuss your answers in small groups.

1. Imagine that someone makes this **analogy**: "You sing the same way my pet bird sings." How do you feel?

   a. happy

   b. amused

   c. insulted

2. Are you a **biased** person?

   a. yes

   b. occasionally

   c. absolutely not

3. You break up with your girlfriend or boyfriend. What **interval** should you wait before starting a new relationship?

   a. over a year

   b. a few months

   c. a day

4. If your doctor **stressed** that you should never eat sweets, would you follow his or her advice?

   a. yes

   b. No, but I would eat them only occasionally.

   c. no

5. You are offered a high-paying job at a famous sneaker company when you learn that it **exploits** its workers who make the sneakers in China. Do you accept the job?

   a. Yes. No company is perfect.

   b. Yes, if I really need a job.

   c. No. I couldn't work for a company like that.

6. When buying a new TV, would you rather have a **finite** or infinite number of choices?

    a. Finite. I get confused by too many options.

    b. Finite, but I'd like at least seven choices.

    c. Infinite. You can never have too any choices.

7. What is most likely to **trigger** your anger?

    a. traffic

    b. rude people

    c. a large bill

8. Have you ever signed a petition for new **legislation?**

    a. Yes. I have often done this on the street.

    b. Yes. once or twice.

    c. No. I've never done this.

9. If you want to **confirm** that your spelling of a word is correct, where do you look?

    a. in a dictionary

    b. on the Internet

    c. Nowhere. I am very careless about my spelling.

10. Does your political **ideology** match that of one political party?

    a. yes

    b. no

    c. I am not interested in politics, so I don't have an ideology.

❙ WORDS IN WRITING

Choose two topics and write a paragraph on each. Try to use the key words.

1. Describe a **bias** that you have encountered.

2. Explain three things that **trigger stress** in your daily life.

3. Could you marry a person whose political **ideology** was very different from your own? Explain why or why not.

4. Make an **analogy** between the way you do something and the way an animal does something. Explain the **analogy** logically.

5. Tell a story that you have heard about a person who was **exploited**.

CHAPTER

26

Key Words

adapt	differentiate	liberal	revenue	sector
appreciate	implement	mode	rigid	phenomenon

WORDS IN CONTEXT

Use the sentences to guess what each key word means. Choose the meaning that is closest to that of the key word in **bold**.

1. **adapt**
/əˈdæpt/
-verb

   • When Peng joined the military, he had to **adapt** to the strict rules.
   • When the budget was cut in half, we had to **adapt** our plans for the party.

   Adapt means . . .
   a. to make something smaller
   b. to stop doing something
   c. to change to fit a new situation

2. **appreciate**
/əˈpriʃiˌeɪt/
-verb

   • Without you, I never could have succeeded. I really **appreciate** your help.
   • Visiting my father's factory made me **appreciate** how hard he worked.

   Appreciate means . . .
   a. to be grateful for something
   b. to pay money for something
   c. to change your opinion

3. **differentiate**
/ˌdɪfəˈrɛnʃiˌeɪt/
-verb

   • I cannot **differentiate** between the taste of Coke and Pepsi.
   • It is difficult to **differentiate** between the two dialects unless you have a very sensitive ear.

   Differentiate means . . .
   a. to compare things
   b. to test two things or people
   c. to recognize a difference

4. **implement**
/ˈɪmpləˌmɛnt/
-verb

   • After receiving funding, the team **implemented** plans to build a new hospital.
   • The police are going to **implement** a new safety program in our neighborhood.

   Implement means . . .
   a. to begin to make a plan happen
   b. to plan something
   c. to build

5. **liberal**
/ˈlɪbrəl, -bərəl/
-adjective

   • San Francisco is a **liberal** city: people with very different lifestyles are accepted there.
   • Abby's traditional father thinks she is too **liberal**.

   Liberal means . . .
   a. entertaining and exciting
   b. willing to respect different ideas
   c. following many rules that control behavior

6. **mode**
/moʊd/
-noun

- The train is a very efficient **mode** of transportation.
- At the sound of the alarm, the firefighters stopped playing cards and went into rescue **mode**.

Mode means . . .   a. a group activity   b. a particular way of doing something   c. an attempt to do something

7. **revenue**
/ˈrɛvəˌnu/
-noun

- The candle company did very well last year, with a twenty percent rise in **revenue**.
- Our boss called a special meeting to discuss why **revenue** was down this month.

Revenue means . . .   a. money that is earned by a company   b. visitors to a store   c. new products that a company sells

8. **rigid**
/ˈrɪdʒɪd/
-adjective

- Dennis begged his father to let him go to the party, but his father refused to bend his **rigid** rules.
- The university refused to relax the **rigid** policy about having no alcohol on campus.

Rigid means . . .   a. very old   b. unwilling to change   c. intelligent and logical

9. **sector**
/ˈsɛktɚ/
-noun

- After working for the government for several years, Carl decided that he'd prefer to work in the private **sector**.
- Growth in the manufacturing **sector** strengthened the country's economy.

Sector means . . .   a. a part of an area of activity, especially of business   b. an important building   c. a company that does business privately

10. **phenomenon**
/fɪˈnamənən, -ˌnan/
-noun

- The photographer was fascinated by the **phenomenon** of snow in August.
- The northern lights, aurora borealis, are a natural **phenomenon** that lights up the night sky in Alaska.

Phenomenon means . . .   a. a common part of the natural world   b. something beautiful that is a part of society or nature   c. something that is unusual or difficult to understand

WORDS AND DEFINITIONS

Read each definition and write the word it defines on the line.

1. _____ money that is earned by a company

2. _____ to change your behavior or ideas to fit a new situation

3. _____ a part of an area of activity, especially of business

4. _____ a particular way or style of behaving, living, or doing something

5. _____ very strict and difficult or unwilling to change

6. _____ to be grateful for something and understand its value

7. _____ willing to understand or respect the different behavior and ideas of other people

8. _____ something that happens or exists in society, science, or nature that is unusual, remarkable, or difficult to understand

9. _____ to recognize, express, or make a difference between things or people

10. _____ to begin to make a plan happen

▌COMPREHENSION CHECK

Choose the best answer.

1. If Fang works in the private **sector**, he works
   a. at home.
   b. for a company.
   c. for the government.

2. Who **appreciates** the modern oil painting?
   a. Henry, who admires the artist's use of color and symbolism
   b. Dan, who thinks his four-year-old son could have painted a similar painting
   c. Rebecca, who wonders why the painting looks like a giant tomato

3. When **implementing** a plan, you
   a. talk.
   b. take action.
   c. stop everything.

4. A **liberal** person
   a. worries if his neighbor wears strange clothing.
   b. thinks that everyone should follow strict rules.
   c. believes that other people should have the freedom to live differently.

5. Pierre cannot **differentiate** between yellow and blue. He
   a. loves both colors.
   b. is color blind.
   c. prefers yellow.

6. Why does Annie go into panic **mode**?
   a. She feels like shopping.
   b. Her history final is in an hour, and she hasn't studied.
   c. Dancing is good exercise.

7. Which of the following is **revenue**?
   a. an award
   b. a good job
   c. sales totaling $1,600

8. A **phenomenon** is
   a. surprising.
   b. ordinary.
   c. harmful.

9. Hikers **adapt** to the air of high mountains. This means that
   a. mountain air is the same as air on flat ground.
   b. hikers can't breathe well on a high mountain.
   c. hikers are able to get used to the change in air.

10. If Audrey has **rigid** ideas about education, she
    a. probably will never change her opinion.
    b. is flexible.
    c. is correct.

WORD FAMILIES

Now that you have studied the ten key words and their basic definitions, you are ready to learn words that belong to the same family as some of the key words. A word family includes words that look alike but have different functions (noun, verb, adjective, or adverb). Their meanings are related but different.

A. *Look at each model phrase and decide whether the word in **bold** is used as a noun, verb, adjective, or adverb. Put a check (✓) in the correct column.*

	NOUN	VERB	ADJECTIVE	ADVERB
1. adapt				
• **adapt** to the situation				
• **adaptable** child				
• **adaptation** of the design				
2. appreciate				
• **appreciate** your help				
• **appreciative** friend				
3. implement				
• **implement** an idea				
• immediate **implementation**				
4. rigid				
• **rigid** mentality				
• **rigidly** control				
5. phenomenon				
• a new **phenomenon**				
• **phenomenal** view				

B. *Read the first half of each sentence and match it with the appropriate ending.*

_____ 1. The strict professor will not allow you to bend the rules; he

_____ 2. The ideal candidate will be able to change and be successful in the new office;

_____ 3. The business leaders met to plan the

_____ 4. The audience gave the opera singer a standing ovation to show how

_____ 5. Eva Hoffman's biography, *Lost in Translation,* describes her emigration from Poland and

_____ 6. The first movie we saw was great. The second movie was also

a. **implementation** of the project.

b. **phenomenal**.

c. **appreciative** they were of his voice.

d. **rigidly** enforces them.

e. he or she must be **adaptable**.

f. **adaption** to life in a new country.

SAME WORD, DIFFERENT MEANING

*Most words have more than one meaning. Study the additional meanings of **implement**, **liberal**, and **revenue**. Then read each sentence and decide which meaning is used.*

a.	**implement** *v.*	to begin to make a plan happen
b.	**implement** *n.*	a tool
c.	**liberal** *adj.*	willing to understand or respect the different behavior and ideas of other people
d.	**liberal** *adj.*	supporting political ideas that include more involvement by the government in business and in people's lives and more freedom in people's private lives
e.	**liberal** *adj.* (formal)	given in large amounts
f.	**revenue** *n.*	money that is earned by a company
g.	**revenue** *n.*	money that the government receives from taxes

_____ 1. **Liberal** voters tend to support programs that benefit children, the poor, and the homeless.

_____ 2. A drop in **revenue** forced the business to lay off forty employees.

_____ 3. Mark is **liberal** with his teenage children. He respects their opinions even when they are different from his own.

_____ 4. A rake is an **implement** that is used to remove leaves from the ground.

_____ 5. By April 15, Americans must send their tax returns to the Internal **Revenue** Service.

_____ 6. How can I **implement** my idea?

_____ 7. Ted's **liberal** spending worried his family; they wished that he would save some of his money.

WORDS IN SENTENCES

Complete each sentence with one of the words from the box.

adaptation	differentiate	liberal	revenue	sector
appreciative	implementation	mode	rigidly	phenomenal

1. In the political system of the United States, Republicans tend to be conservative and Democrats are _____.

2. The German government reported an increase in tax _____.

3. How can we _____ our product from our competitor's?

4. The actor immediately became famous because the movie was a(n) _____ success.

5. Luke was really _____ of the care his sister gave his dogs while he was on vacation.

6. After the hurricane, hundreds of volunteers went into rescue _____.

7. Our plan was brilliant, but the _____ of it was more difficult than we'd expected.

8. Aziz's quick _____ to life in a new country impressed us all.

9. Have you ever considered working in the health _____?

10. The academic honesty policy is _____ enforced by all instructors.

WORDS IN COLLOCATIONS AND EXPRESSIONS

Following are common collocations and expressions with some of the key words. Read the definitions and then complete the conversations with the collocations and expressions. You may have to change word forms for correct grammar.

1. **adapt**
   - **adapt to** — change to fit a new situation
   - **an adaptation of (a book)** — a play, film, or television program that is based on a book or play

2. **appreciate**
   - **(I'd) appreciate it if** — (I'd) be thankful if

3. **differentiate**
   - **differentiate between** — to recognize a difference between

4. **phenomenon**
   - **a new phenomenon** — a new occurrence that is remarkable
   - **a phenomenal success** — a great success

1. TIM: Why can't you _____ my brother and me?

    TEACHER: Because you're twins.

2. LIZ: I just saw _____ *The Lion, the Witch and the Wardrobe.* Now I want to read the book.

    LIBRARIAN: Good decision. The book is better than the movie! We'd _____ you would return this book on time. It's very popular, and other readers are waiting to borrow it.

3. ACTRESS: How are the reviews for the play?

    DIRECTOR: Opening night was _____. As a result, tickets are sold out for the next three weeks.

4. PHILIP: I want to work in China because I'm interested in the culture, the language, and the people.

    EMPLOYER: From your attitude I can tell that you will _____ Chinese life easily. You're hired.

5. SAM: Did you know that Google is building a digital library of millions of books on the Internet? Digital books are _____.

    DAD: Well, I'm sure they are useful for research purposes, but I prefer to read real books.

Read this article about Dubai. Complete it with words from the boxes.

| appreciated | differentiate | liberally | mode | phenomenon |

WELCOME TO DUBAI

Down the silvery escalators they glided, eyes afire and credit cards within easy reach. On a warm Tuesday night in the Persian Gulf, a multicultural pageant of shoppers, diners, and drinkers _____ Dubai's nightlife. They fanned out into the majestic, wintry-cool shopping mall

₁ beneath the Middle East's tallest building, the 1,163-foot Emirates Office Tower in Dubai.

Indian women in colorful saris and Middle Eastern women in black veils strolled through the pristine, white marble corridors, pausing to window shop at luxury stores. White-robed Middle Eastern businessmen, fat gold watches glittering at the edges of their sleeves, talked into green-glowing cellphones. Three Arab men in baggy jeans, who were in social _____, chatted warmly

with three young European-looking women. Just behind them, noisy British expatriates in business suits tried to push into an overpacked bar.

Outside, night-shift taxis and BMWs streamed down crowded highways, cruising near the soaring, sail-shaped Burj Al Arab, which bills itself as the world's tallest hotel—and snaking around the rising foundation for the world's tallest building (the Burj Dubai, which at more than 2,300 feet, will surpass the current one, the 1,667-foot Taipei 101, when it opens in 2008). The cars pass the construction sites for two competing retail projects, the bigger of which is impossible to _____ at this

point, as each insists it will be the largest shopping mall in the world.

Bigger, taller, grander, richer: these words describe the _____ that is Dubai. One of

the seven city-states of the United Arab Emirates, Dubai has already been through an extreme makeover, in less than a decade, that would awe the most ambitious builder. And as it continues trying to write its own chapter in the record books, travelers from all over the globe are coming to luxuriate at the five-star hotels, romp in the surf at fine white beaches (bikinis allowed), dance to tunes spun by international DJs in myriad nightclubs, and spend _____ at dozens of malls and the gold

souk, the largest gold market in the world. Many Dubai vacationers also bring children, who play at the beach and hurtle down water slides at the Wild Wadi Water Park.

| adapted | implementing | revenue | rigid | sector |

Some 5.45 million travelers passed through the gates of this Middle Eastern paradise in 2004, a nine percent jump over the year before and a nearly twentyfold increase from a mere decade earlier, according to the Government of Dubai Department of Tourism and Commerce Marketing. Two-thirds came on business, but more and more, Dubai is a tourist destination.

Joining the pleasure seekers and international executives are the fortune seekers, rich and poor, who fly in from India, Pakistan, Iran, Lebanon, the Philippines, Europe, Australia, and South Africa. There is no _____ limit on immigration. In fact, only a fifth of Dubai's resident
6
population of 1.2 million is made up of citizens. The other eighty percent are expatriates, including an underclass of foreign workers in construction and menial jobs. Although Arabic is the official language, English, the language of commerce, holds this global mix together. Only a third of Dubai's residents are female.

Concerned that Dubai is running out of beachfront, its crown prince, Sheik Mohammed bin Rashid al-Maktoum, is _____ a plan to have three palm-tree-shaped islands created on
7
sand being dredged from the gulf and held in place by enormous plastic membranes. The hope is that this move will further strengthen the tourist _____ of Dubai's economy.
8

Petroleum has financed Dubai's boom. But its reserves will be depleted within a decade, and the UAE's rulers have _____ by diversifying the economy. Oil now accounts for just eight
9
percent of the city-state's income. Tourism brings in seventeen percent of the _____, and
10
could bring in much more in the future.

(Adapted from "The Oz of the Middle East," The New York Times, May 8, 2005.)

▌ WORDS IN DISCUSSION

Apply the key words to your own life. Read and discuss each question in small groups. Try to use the key words.

1. **adapt**

   How long it took me to adapt to my current school or job: _____

   A person I know who is adaptable: _____

2. **mode**

   The last person I saw who was in rescue mode: _____

   The first thing I'll do if I'm lost in the woods and in survival mode: _____

3. **phenomenon**

   A natural phenomenon I would like to learn more about: _____

   The probability that I will be a phenomenal success in business: _____%

4. **differentiate**

   Two people's voices that are difficult for me to differentiate: _____

   Two English words I often have trouble differentiating: _____

5. **revenue**

   If I started a business, the revenue I'd hope to make in the first year:

   $_____

   How much revenue the federal government got from my taxes last year:

   $_____

6. **rigid**

   A person I know who is rigid about his or her daily routine: _____

   A rule or law I feel is too rigid: _____

7. **implement**

   A change that is being implemented in my city:_____

   A plan I once implemented but never finished:_____

8. **sector**

   The possibility that I'll work for the government in the public

   sector:_____%

   The possibility that I'll work in the health care sector: _____%

9. **liberal**

   How liberal I am:_____

   Something that I'd like to distribute liberally to my friends:_____

10. **appreciate**

    Someone who should be more appreciative:_____

    Something I really appreciate:_____

▌WORDS IN WRITING

Choose two topics and write a paragraph on each. Try to use the key words.

1. Describe a person whom you really **appreciate.** Explain why you are so **appreciative** of this person.

2. How **liberal** do you plan to be in allowing your children to have their own beliefs about life? Explain.

3. Describe an interesting natural **phenomenon** from your country.

4. Describe the most difficult situation you have had to **adapt** to.

5. Suggest a plan that you would like to **implement** to improve the quality of life in the town where you live.

WORDS IN CONTEXT

*Use the sentences to guess what each key word means. Choose the meaning that is closest to that of the key word in **bold**.*

1. **comprehensive**
/ˌkɑmprɪˈhɛnsɪv/
-adjective

- Instead of giving several tests, the teacher designed one **comprehensive** test that would cover all the material.
- My **comprehensive** guide to travel in Europe included information on accommodations, transportation, and the most popular tourist sites.

Comprehensive means . . .
a. long and complicated
b. including everything
c. easy to use

2. **consent**
/kənˈsɛnt/
-noun

- Children need their parents' **consent** before they can go on the school trip to the zoo.
- When the prisoner asked to get out of jail, the judge denied her **consent**.

Consent means . . .
a. permission
b. an answer
c. help

3. **domestic**
/dəˈmɛstɪk/
-adjective

- The airline provides only **domestic** flights, so you need to a different airline to fly to another country.
- Todd knows a lot about **domestic** news but very little about what is happening in the rest of the world.

Domestic means . . .
a. happening within one country
b. important for one city
c. occurring in one region of a country

4. **entity**
/ˈɛntəti/
-noun

- We considered combining the debate club and the speech club but decided to keep them as two separate **entities**.
- A large portion of the population of Quebec would like their region to leave Canada and form a new political **entity**.

Entity means . . .
a. a single and complete unit
b. something that is very small
c. something that is part of something larger

5. **ethics**
/ˈɛθɪks/
-noun,(plural)

- Leaders from different religions met to discuss their common **ethics**.
- The two scientists argued about the **ethics** of cloning a sheep from its DNA; one thought it was acceptable, but the other thought it was wrong.

Ethics means . . .
a. concerns about society
b. moral rules
c. ways to make money

6. **implicate**
/'ɪmplɪ,keɪt/
-verb

- Wang **implicated** three students in cheating on the final test.
- The witness **implicated** the man who had robbed the convenience store.

Implicate means . . .
a. to show that someone is involved in something wrong
b. to be involved in an investigation
c. to commit a crime

7. **persist**
/pɚ'sɪst/
-verb

- I **persisted** in my run despite the heavy snow.
- The doctor said, "If your back pain **persists**, come back on Monday."

Persist means . . .
a. to be painful
b. to continue
c. to delay

8. **pose**
/pouz/
-verb

- The author listened carefully as his fan **posed** a question about the meaning of his novel.
- The violent wind **posed** a threat to the campers.

Pose means . . .
a. to present
b. to think about
c. to end suddenly

9. **straightforward**
/,streɪt'fɔrwɚd/
-adjective

- Ben's mother gave him a confusing explanation when he asked how boys are different from girls, but his grandfather gave him a **straightforward** answer.
- Yumiko can think of **straightforward** solutions to even the most complicated problems.

Straightforward means . . .
a. long and detailed
b. funny
c. simple

10. **underlying**
/'ʌndɚ,laɪ-ɪŋ/
-adjective

- Anne went to a psychologist to try to find the **underlying** cause of her nightmares.
- The **underlying** reason that the company failed was its poor relationship between employees and management.

Underlying means . . .
a. important but not easy to see
b. clear
c. very dishonest

WORDS AND DEFINITIONS

Read each definition and write the word it defines on the line.

1. _____ something that exists as a single and complete unit

2. _____ simple or easy to understand

3. _____ including everything that is necessary

4. _____ to continue to happen or continue to do something even though it is difficult or other people do not like it

5. _____ to show that someone is involved in something wrong

6. _____ permission to do something

7. _____ most important but not easy to discover

8. _____ happening within one country and not involving any other countries

9. _____ moral rules or principles of behavior for deciding what is right and wrong

10. _____ to present a problem or a serious question

COMPREHENSION CHECK

Choose the best answer.

1. In which class are you most likely to talk about **ethics**?
   a. algebra
   b. French
   c. philosophy

2. If dry weather **persists** in Texas, there is
   a. suddenly a lot of rain.
   b. no rain.
   c. a mix of rain and sun every day.

3. **Comprehensive** medical insurance covers
   a. some hospital visits.
   b. no medication.
   c. everything.

4. Which thing or person is an **entity**?
   a. a country
   b. a basketball player
   c. a wall

5. If your brother uses your bike without your **consent**, you
   a. told him he could use your bike.
   b. suggested that he take your bike.
   c. did not give him permission to ride your bike.

6. Which speaker is **posing** a question?
   a. "What inspired you to write this song?"
   b. "I'll answer the question with a story."
   c. "Someone already asked that question."

7. An **underlying** reason is
   a. obvious.
   b. hidden.
   c. not very important

8. Mr. Jones asks, "Who drew the rude pictures on the board?" Which answer is **straightforward**?
   a. "Well, that's difficult to say."
   b. "Um, nobody, really."
   c. "I'll be honest with you. I did."

9. What can **implicate** the athlete in taking performance-enhancing drugs?
   a. lab tests
   b. an award
   c. his bicycle

10. Which is a **domestic** sports event?
    a. Italy battles Brazil in the World Cup.
    b. The Boston Red Sox play the New York Yankees.
    c. Runners from many countries race each other in the Olympics.

WORD FAMILIES

Now that you have studied the ten key words and their basic definitions, you are ready to learn words that belong to the same family as some of the key words. A word family includes words that look alike but have different functions (noun, verb, adjective, or adverb). Their meanings are related but different.

A. *Look at each model phrase and decide whether the word in **bold** is used as a noun, verb, adjective, or adverb. Put a check (✓) in the correct column.*

	NOUN	VERB	ADJECTIVE	ADVERB
1. **consent**				
• give **consent**				
• **consent** to the plan				
2. **ethics**				
• a question of **ethics**				
• **ethical** problem				
• clearly **unethical**				
3. **implicate**				
• **implicate** involvement				
• the **implication** of the criminal				
4. **persist**				
• **persist** in studying				
• a **persistent** person				
• admire your **persistence**				
5. **underlying**				
• **underlying** cause				
• the problem that **underlies** the situation				

B. *Read the first half of each sentence and match it with the appropriate ending.*

_____ 1. It's important to teach a child to make

_____ 2. I was shocked by the

_____ 3. Jack said he didn't want any more cake, but Grandma was

_____ 4. Sa Ra's boss

_____ 5. A pacifist believes that violence is always

_____ 6. A lack of trust

_____ 7. Success is often the result of

a. **consented** to her request for vacation time.

b. **ethical** choices.

c. **implication** of my neighbor in the crime.

d. **persistent**; she asked him three more times if he'd have more.

e. **persistence**.

f. **underlies** Lars' relationship with his father.

g. **unethical**.

SAME WORD, DIFFERENT MEANING

Most words have more than one meaning. Study the additional meanings of **domestic**, **implication**, and **pose**. Then read each sentence and decide which meaning is used.

a. **domestic** *adj.*	happening within one country and not involving any other countries
b. **domestic** *adj.*	relating to family relationships and life at home
c. **implication** *n.*	the act of making a statement that suggests that someone has done something wrong or illegal
d. **implication** *n.*	a possible effect or result of a plan, action, etc.
e. **implication** *n.*	something you do not say directly but that you want people to understand
f. **pose** *v.*	to present a problem or a serious question
g. **pose** *v.*	to sit or stand in a particular position to be photographed or painted

_____ 1. When her son said he wanted to quit his job, Emma urged him to consider the **implications.**

_____ 2. The model **posed** for the camera.

_____ 3. The **implication** that the teacher was involved in bribery led the principal to fire her.

_____ 4. Jane was a victim of **domestic** violence, so she got a divorce.

_____ 5. The new tax laws might **pose** some problems for Don's company.

_____ 6. Jansen didn't say it directly, but his **implication** was that he was looking for a new job.

_____ 7. American movie theaters show far more **domestic** films than international films.

WORDS IN SENTENCES

Complete each sentence with one of the words from the box.

| comprehensive | domestic | ethics | persistence | straightforward |
| consent | entity | implication | pose | underlies |

1. Becoming good at anything requires _____; you may fail many times before finally succeeding.

2. Your idea solves part of the problem, but we need a _____ solution.

3. The company's _____ were in question when it was reported that its executives had spied on some of its employees.

4. I asked a simple question, but our history teacher confused me with a twenty-minute explanation. I wish she had given me a(n) _____ answer!

5. The police came to the house after neighbors called to complain about the _____ dispute.

6. Drugs _____ a threat to peace and safety in the neighborhood.

7. After being ruled by Portugal for several centuries, Cape Verde became an independent political _____ in 1975.

8. Even though she's over ninety and no longer able to take care of herself, Audra will not _____ to leaving her home.

9. Victor was insulted by your _____ that he is not a good father.

10. A need for financial security _____ her decision to continue working at the bank.

▌WORDS IN COLLOCATIONS AND EXPRESSIONS

Following are common collocations and expressions with some of the key words. Read the definitions and then complete the conversations with the collocations and expressions. You may have to change word forms for correct grammar.

1. **consent**	
• **without my consent**	without my permission
2. **domestic**	
• **domestic animal**	an animal that lives in someone's house or on a farm
3. **pose**	
• **pose a question**	to ask a question that needs to be thought about carefully
• **pose as (sb)**	to pretend to be someone else in order to deceive people
4. **ethics**	
• **an ethical dilemma**	a situation in which you have to make a very difficult moral decision
5. **straightforward**	
• **a straightforward answer**	a direct or honest answer
6. **underlying**	
• **underlying reason**	the reason that is most important but not easy to discover

1.   CHILD: Why can't I adopt a wolf?

        DAD: Because a wolf is not a _____.

2. ROCK CLIMBER 1:   Do you think there's a(n) _____ that explains our love of rock climbing?

  ROCK CLIMBER 2:   Yes, I think we're bored with our desk jobs.

3.   GENETICIST: I hope that my talk has helped you understand DNA. Any questions?

STUDENT: Yes, I'd like to _____ about the future of DNA research. What developments do you expect to see in the next ten years?

4. DOCTOR 1: I have _____. My elderly patient asked me how long he has left to live. Should I tell him the truth, that he only has a month to live? Or would it be kinder to tell him that everything is okay?

DOCTOR 2: I think you should give him _____. He should know the truth.

5. JULIE: You took my cheerleading jacket _____!

JULIE'S COUSIN: Sorry. I tried to _____ a cheerleader to impress a boy. It didn't work.

▍WORDS IN A READING

Read this article about Google. Complete it with words and expressions from the boxes.

| comprehensive | persisting | posed | a straightforward answer | underlying |

GOOGLE COFOUNDER COMES TO CLASS AT BERKELEY

Sergey Brin, cofounder of Google, showed up for class at Berkeley this week, a surprise guest speaker in the Search Engines: Technology, Society, and Business classroom Monday afternoon. Casual and relaxed, Brin talked about how Google came to be, answered students' questions, and showed that someone worth $11 billion (give or take a billion) still can be comfortable in an old pair of blue jeans.

Indistinguishable in dress, age, and demeanor from many of the students in the class, Brin covered a lot of ground in his remarks, but his _____ message was this: To those with focus and
                                                                        1
passion, all things are possible.

In his remarks to the class, Brin, thirty, stressed simplicity. Simple ideas sometimes can change the world, he said. Google started out with the simplest of ideas, with a global audience in mind. In the mid-1990s, Brin and Larry Page were Stanford students pursuing doctorates in computer science. Brin recalled that at that time, there were some five major Internet search engines, and the importance of search was being deemphasized. Brin and Page felt they could offer more useful and _____ results than
                                                                                                     2
the search engines that existed at that time.

"We believed we could build a better search. We had a simple idea, that not all pages are created equal. Some are more important," related Brin. In this way, Google could rank pages more effectively than other search engines. The system Google uses to rank pages has evolved over the years, Brin said, but the concept that not all pages are equal remains the key to Google's success. By _____
                                                                                                            3
with this simple idea, Google grew to be a worldwide success.

Both during the class and for about forty-five minutes after, students _____ questions
                                                                                          4
to Brin, including several about how Google will react to competition from Microsoft and others. Brin gave _____; He responded that it was a waste of time to worry about other companies.
          5

Instead, he suggested, think about your ambitions and your hopes. Google is a(n)

_____ that focuses on the opportunities and possibilities made possible by the
    6

company's vast computing resources and its army of talented employees. And, said Brin, Google will

continue to bring new and better computing tools to the public.

Google is successful in not only the _____ market; it provides search services in over
                                                7

a hundred countries. Brin said he was particularly proud of the honors Google has won for its

language translation technology. Many students asked about the _____ that Google was
                                                                              8

cooperating with the Chinese government, _____ to the censorship of online
                                                        9

information.

Brin said Google complies with the laws of the countries in which it operates, including laws in the

United States and Germany that the company "does not necessarily support." He denied that Google

itself was censoring information in China, and he said that Google does good in China by making it

possible for the Chinese people to have broad access to information.

Google has a philanthropic arm, and company cofounders Brin and Page spell out their hopes for

it at Google.org. The site, still under development, explains their _____ by bearing this
                                                                                  10

simple message from the Google cofounders: "We hope that someday this institution will eclipse

Google itself in overall world impact by ambitiously applying innovation and significant resources to

the largest of the world's problems."

(Adapted from "Google Cofounder Sergey Brin Comes to Class at Berkeley," UC Berkeley News, October 4, 2005.)

▌WORDS IN DISCUSSION

Read the questions and choose the best answers. Then discuss your answers in small groups.

1. You win a free round-trip airplane ticket to anywhere in the world. Do you choose a **domestic** ticket or an international ticket?

   a. a domestic ticket

   b. an international ticket

   c. I don't accept the ticket. I don't like to fly!

2. Do you think it is **ethical** for a man to steal bread to feed his children?

   a. Yes. It is ethical.

   b. It is unethical, but it is necessary.

   c. No. It is never ethical to break the law.

3. Imagine that you are given $1 million. What **implications** will this gift have for your life?

   a. I'll probably change where I live and/or what I do.

   b. I'll become more popular and will have many opportunities when dating.

   c. Nothing will change.

4. An attractive tourist stops you on the street and asks you to **pose** for a photograph with him or her. Do you agree?

   a. Yes. Why not?

   b. Yes, and I invite the tourist out to lunch.

   c. No. I'm uncomfortable posing for a photo with a stranger.

5. If your twelve-year-old daughter wanted to wear lipstick, would you give your **consent**?

    a. yes

    b. yes, but only for a party

    c. absolutely not

6. Are you **straightforward** when someone asks you a question about your private life?

    a. Yes. I have nothing to hide.

    b. It depends on the question and how well I know the person.

    c. No. I'm not comfortable talking about my private life with anyone.

7. You are a drama major and dream about becoming an actor. One of your professors tells you that you have no talent and should change your major. Will you take his advice or **persist** in your dreams?

    a. I'll listen to my professor and change my major.

    b. I'll be so depressed that I'll drop out of college.

    c. I'll persist. One bad opinion can't stop my dreams.

8. Would you rather have a **comprehensive** education covering many different fields or study one subject intensely?

    a. A comprehensive education. I want to understand a lot of things.

    b. One subject. It's more interesting to focus my attention on my favorite field.

    c. Neither. I don't want to study.

9. Do you think your country is better off being its own **entity** or belonging to a union of other countries?

    a. I want it to be its own entity so that its culture won't change.

    b. I want it to be its own entity because I don't trust other countries.

    c. I want it to belong to a union. It will be economically stronger that way.

10. A doctor tells you that the **underlying** cause of your occasional but strong headaches is television. What do you do?

    a. I stop watching TV.

    b. I watch only two hours of TV per week.

    c. I keep watching TV.

▌WORDS IN WRITING

Choose two topics and write a paragraph on each. Try to use the key words.

1. Are people **straightforward** in your native country? Give examples to explain why or why not.

2. Describe something you have **persisted** in doing despite the challenges you have faced.

3. Are you more interested in **domestic** or international news? Explain.

4. Describe an **ethical** dilemma and give your opinion about it.

5. A famous magazine is doing a story on your town. You are asked to **pose** alone for the magazine's cover. Do you **consent**? Explain why or why not.

QUIZ 9

PART A

Choose the word that best completes each item and write it in the space provided.

1. A(n) _____ neighborhood accepts people with different lifestyles and beliefs.
   - a. rigid
   - b. liberal
   - c. stressful
   - d. underlying

2. The Earth has a(n) _____ amount of natural resources.
   - a. infinite
   - b. straightforward
   - c. finite
   - d. biased

3. Raj enjoyed working for the government, but now he'll work in the private _____.
   - a. phenomenon
   - b. ideology
   - c. analogy
   - d. sector

4. When I took a break from writing my report, I put my computer in sleep _____.
   - a. implement
   - b. mode
   - c. trigger
   - d. consent

5. Mark Twain made a(n) _____ between the age of the Earth and the height of the Eiffel Tower.
   - a. interval
   - b. confirmation
   - c. analogy
   - d. entity

6. Our grammar teacher _____ the importance of memorizing verb forms.
   - a. consented
   - b. stressed
   - c. legislated
   - d. implicated

7. When a month contains two full moons, the second full moon is a(n) _____ called "a blue moon."
   - a. exploit
   - b. phenomenon
   - c. pose
   - d. sector

8. The jury left the courtroom for a(n) _____ of thirty minutes.
   - a. implication
   - b. interval
   - c. adaptation
   - d. entity

9. Josie is flexible, so it was easy for her to _____ to her new school.
   - a. adapt
   - b. pose
   - c. trigger
   - d. implement

10. In my philosophy class, we discuss _____: what is morally right and wrong.
    - a. revenue
    - b. ethics
    - c. intervals
    - d. persistence

PART B

*Read each statement and write **T** for true and **F** for false in the space provided.*

____ 1. A **straightforward** answer is difficult to understand.

____ 2. A **biased** judge is unfair.

____ 3. If Jeff explains his political beliefs, he describes his political **ideology**.

____ 4. A **rigid** rule can be easily changed.

____ 5. Good bosses **exploit** their workers.

____ 6. It is impossible to **differentiate** an American accent from a British accent.

____ 7. A **comprehensive** program does not include all the necessary parts.

____ 8. Criminals **legislate** laws.

____ 9. Strong winds can **trigger** a loss of power.

____10. When the team **implements** the plan, they begin to make it happen.

PART C

Match each sentence with the letter it describes.

____ 1. Kim says this when he wants his wife to **persist** in doing something.

____ 2. The doctor said this when he **confirmed** Lucy's condition.

____ 3. This person does **domestic** work.

____ 4. The **underlying** reason is this.

____ 5. This person **appreciates** high-quality canvas, paint, and brushes.

____ 6. Andrea's older sister says this when she gives her **consent.**

____ 7. If Ted **implicates** Henry, Ted shows that Henry is this.

____ 8. An **entity** is this.

____ 9. This person **poses** for a painting.

____10. The manager feels this when the company generates a lot of **revenue.**

a. "OK, you can do it."

b. a model

c. single and complete

d. "You can't give up. You have to try until you succeed."

e. a maid

f. guilty

g. important but hidden

h. "Yes. You are definitely pregnant."

i. satisfied

j. an artist

▌WORDS IN CONTEXT

*Use the sentences to guess what each key word means. Choose the meaning that is closest to that of the key word in **bold**.*

1. **conceive**
/kənˈsiv/
-*verb*

- It's difficult to **conceive** how the dog escaped over the six-foot fence.
- For the competition, the children had to **conceive** of, build, and race small cars.

Conceive means . . .   a. to imagine   b. to talk about   c. to follow a plan

2. **contract**
/ˈkɑntrækt/
-*noun*

- The writer has a three-book **contract** with the publisher.
- When the Raymonds bought their home, they signed a **contract** with the previous owners.

Contract means . . .   a. a payment   b. a legal written agreement   c. a letter

3. **enormous**
/ɪˈnɔrməs/
-*adjective*

- The gym's new swimming pool is **enormous!** It's twice the size of the old pool.
- Buckingham Palace is so **enormous** that it has seventy-eight bathrooms.

Enormous
means . . .   a. expensive   b. extremely large   c. excellent

4. **erode**
/ɪˈroʊd/
-*verb*

- Because the ocean has **eroded** the shore, the coastline is different from the way it was five hundred years ago.
- The historical society worries that acid rain will **erode** important buildings and historical monuments.

Erode means . . .   a. to destroy something gradually   b. to change suddenly   c. to touch

5. **explicit**
/ɪkˈsplɪsɪt/
-*adjective*

- The construction manager gave the workers **explicit** directions, explaining each step in detail.
- Fred's opinion was **explicit**; I knew exactly how he felt.

Explicit means . . .   a. intelligent   b. expressed in a way that is very clear   c. stubborn and difficult

6. **nevertheless**
/ˌnɛvɚðəˈlɛs/
-adverb

- It was cold and rainy. **Nevertheless**, we jumped into the lake.
- Reviews of the movie were terrible; **nevertheless**, tickets for it sold out.

Nevertheless means . . .   a. and; in addition   b. because of this   c. in spite of what has just been mentioned

7. **offset**
/ˌɔfˈsɛt/
-verb

- My A on the final test **offset** two Ds I got on quizzes.
- The actor's donation of a large sum of money to the homeless shelter will help to **offset** the bad publicity that he got last week.

Offset means . . .   a. to change a situation for the better   b. to balance; to have the opposite effect   c. to put an end to an undesirable situation

8. **ongoing**
/ˈɔnˌgoʊɪŋ/
-adjective

- The professor has been involved in **ongoing** research since 1992.
- The company's search for a new CEO is **ongoing**; several people have been considered, but no one has been chosen.

Ongoing means . . .   a. continuing   b. future   c. long

9. **regime**
/reɪˈʒim/
-noun

- Millions of people were killed during Stalin's **regime**.
- In a debate about politics over dinner, Allen's brother criticized the Cuban **regime**, but Allen defended it.

Regime means . . .   a. a person who gains power through violence   b. a country where there is no peace   c. a system of government, especially one you disapprove of

10. **restrain**
/rɪˈstreɪn/
-verb

- The police officer grabbed the drunk man and **restrained** him from jumping off the bridge.
- Mandy came up with a monthly budget to **restrain** her spending.

Restrain means . . .   a. to physically control or prevent   b. to be presented with a serious problem   c. to help something happen in any way you can

▌WORDS AND DEFINITIONS

Read each definition and write the word it defines on the line.

1. _____ expressed in a way that is very clear

2. _____ to imagine a situation or what something is like

3. _____ a system of government, especially one that you disapprove of

4. _____ to destroy something gradually by the action of wind, rain, or acid, or to gradually destroy someone's power

5. _____ extremely large in size or amount

6. _____ to physically control or prevent someone from doing something

7. _____ to balance a situation by having the opposite effect as something else

8. _____ continuing

9. _____ a legal written agreement between two people or companies

10. _____ in spite of what has just been mentioned

COMPREHENSION CHECK

Choose the best answer.

1. Jim says, "It's difficult to **conceive** of living anywhere else." This means that
   a. he dreams of moving to a different place.
   b. he doesn't have enough money to move.
   c. he can't imagine living anyplace else.

2. What can **offset** the high cost of airline tickets for your vacation?
   a. staying in a cheap hotel
   b. going out to the city's best restaurants
   c. buying expensive souvenirs

3. If a difficult school year **eroded** Nathan's confidence, Nathan
   a. immediately lost his confidence at the start of the year.
   b. still has his confidence.
   c. slowly lost his confidence over the year.

4. If a writer describes her country's **regime**, she writes about its
   a. culture.
   b. government.
   c. people.

5. Which statement is **explicit**?
   a. "I want to buy a beautiful hardcover edition of *To Kill a Mockingbird,* by Harper Lee."
   b. "I want to buy a good book."
   c. "I'm looking for something to read."

6. Amy asks for a **contract** before she starts her new job. This means that
   a. she wants to talk with her boss.
   b. she wants a written agreement.
   c. she wants more money.

7. Pawel is allergic to cats. **Nevertheless**, he
   a. avoids cats.
   b. sneezes when he meets a cat.
   c. loves cats.

8. An **ongoing** investigation
   a. will start soon.
   b. is continuing.
   c. is conducted by many people.

9. At the birthday party, who asks for an **enormous** piece of cake?
   a. a hungry thirteen-year-old boy
   b. a man who is on a diet
   c. a woman who has a stomachache

10. A sign in the park says, "Please **restrain** your dog." It means that you should
    a. use a leash to prevent your dog from running free.
    b. give your dog a lot of exercise.
    c. not bring your dog to the park.

Now that you have studied the ten key words and their basic definitions, you are ready to learn words that belong to the same family as some of the key words. A word family includes words that look alike but have different functions (noun, verb, adjective, or adverb). Their meanings are related but different.

A. *Look at each model phrase and decide whether the word in **bold** is used as a noun, verb, adjective, or adverb. Put a check (✓) in the correct column.*

	NOUN	VERB	ADJECTIVE	ADVERB
1. **conceive**				
• **conceive** of the idea				
• a **conceivable** plan				
• **inconceivable** crimes				
2. **enormous**				
• an **enormous** mountain				
• **enormously** successful				
3. **erode**				
• slowly **erode**				
• the **erosion** of the land				
4. **explicit**				
• **explicit** instructions				
• **explicitly** stated				
5. **restrain**				
• **restrain** the toddler				
• a serious **restraint**				

B. *Darren is talking with a park ranger about swimming in a protected lake. Complete the conversation with words from the box.*

conceivable	erosion	explicity	inconceivable	restraint

PARK RANGER: Hey, get out of the water! Can't you read? The sign _____ says NO SWIMMING.
                                                                        1

DARREN: Oh, hello, Ranger! Sorry, I saw the sign but it was _____ to me
                                                                      2
that swimming could be banned at such a beautiful and natural-looking lake. Don't worry. I'm an excellent swimmer.

PARK RANGER: I'm not worried about you, I'm worried about the environment! No swimmers are allowed this summer because tourists have done damage to the shoreline.

DARREN: Oh. Well, it's _____ that tourists are a problem because they
                            3
might leave trash behind, but I'm not littering. I'm just going for a swim!

PARK RANGER: Trash is only one part of the problem. Heavy foot traffic on the shore has added to shoreline _____.
                                                          4

DARREN: Erosion? That explains the fence.

PARK RANGER: Yes. It's a(n) _____ to keep people off the shoreline.
                                              5

DARREN: Sorry about that. Now that I understand the environmental concerns, I'll get out
                        of the water.

SAME WORD, DIFFERENT MEANING

*Most words have more than one meaning. Study the additional meanings of **conceive**, **contract**, and **explicit**.*
Then read each sentence and decide which meaning is used.

a.	**conceive** *v.*	to imagine a situation or what something is like
b.	**conceive** *v.*	to think of a new idea
c.	**conceive** *v.*	to become pregnant
d.	**contract** *n.*	a legal written agreement between two people or companies
e.	**contract** *v.*	/kən'trækt/, to get an illness
f.	**explicit** *adj.*	expressed in a way that is very clear
g.	**explicit** *adj.*	language or pictures that are explicit show a lot of sex or violence

_____ 1. It's difficult to **conceive** of all the different languages being spoken at this instant all over the
world.

_____ 2. Movies that are rated R are too **explicit** for children.

_____ 3. The musician hopes to sign a **contract** with a major recording studio.

_____ 4. Miranda and her husband wanted a baby very much, so they were very happy when she
conceived.

_____ 5. My brother **contracted** the flu by sharing a desk with a sick student.

_____ 6. Tessa gave **explicit** orders on how she wanted the room decorated.

WORDS IN SENTENCES

Complete each sentence with one of the words from the box.

conceived	enormous	explicitly	offset	regime
contract	erosion	nevertheless	ongoing	restraints

1. It is impossible to _____ AIDS by shaking hands with someone.

2. My teenage son has such a(n) _____ appetite that it's difficult to keep food in the
house.

3. I am on a diet; _____, I'll have some strawberry ice cream.

4. The bonus Sheila got from work _____ her large heating bill.

5. Once a baby is _____, it grows inside the mother for nine months.

6. _____ caused the beach to slowly disappear.

7. The rebels were unhappy with their government; they wanted a new _____.

8. The professor _____ described the research process so that everyone would know her expectations.

9. The town hoped the new speed bumps and traffic light would act as _____ on speeding drivers.

10. Richard and Cho are having _____ talks about starting a company together.

▌WORDS IN COLLOCATIONS AND EXPRESSIONS

Following are common collocations and expressions with some of the key words. Read the definitions and then complete the conversations with the collocations and expressions. You may have to change word forms for correct grammar.

1. **conceive**	
• **conceive of (sth)**	imagine what something is like
• **it is conceivable that**	it is believable that
2. **explicit**	
• **explicit instructions**	very clear instructions
3. **contract**	
• **contract to (do sth)**	a written legal agreement to do something
4. **restrain**	
• **restrain (sb) from (doing sth)**	prevent someone from doing something
• **show restraint**	have calm and controlled behavior

1. JOHN: How long will you have your job with the Army?

   JOHN'S ROOMMATE: I have a _____ work for the Army for three years.

2. HANK: I read that you can buy anything in the world on the Web site eBay.

   ZOE: _____ that you can buy almost anything on eBay, but I'm sure there are certain things you can't find there.

3. MOTHER: Why are the kids watching TV at 11:00 P.M.? I gave you _____ that their bedtime is at 9:00.

   BABYSITTER: They were scared of the dark, so I let them stay up.

4. TIMMY: That guy insulted me. I am going to punch him!

   HAL: Hey, calm down. _____ some _____!

TIMMY: I can't calm down. I'm going to hit him.

HAL: (grabs Timmy) Sorry, Timmy, but I have to _____ you _____ starting a fight.

5.   FAN: Thank you for your work. I can _____ many ways in which your inventions will improve people's lives.

INVENTOR: You're welcome. That's what I hope for.

▍WORDS IN A READING

Read this article about a famous author. Complete it with words from the boxes.

conceiving	contract	enormous	offset	ongoing

GABRIEL GARCÍA MÁRQUEZ AGREES TO HOLLYWOOD MOVIE

Unswerving defender of Fidel Castro and Latin American literary patriarch he may be, but Gabriel García Márquez appears to have finally succumbed to Hollywood's call, signing a _____ that gives away the film rights to *Love in the Time of Cholera.*
₁

The Los Angeles production company Stone Village Pictures is reportedly paying the Colombian Nobel laureate between $1 million and $3 million to make a movie of what producer Scot Steindorff recently termed "the best love story ever told, next to *Romeo and Juliet.*"

Despite his _____ success selling millions of books around the globe, the seventy-six-year-old novelist, who is fighting a(n) _____ battle with cancer, is said to be worried about the financial future of his lifetime partner, Mercedes, and their two sons, Gonzalo and Rodrigo. The fortune García Márquez made from his novels was _____ by the substantial sums he reportedly sank into a newsmagazine called *Cambio.* He started the magazine in Colombia before launching a version in Mexico, where he has lived most of the time since 1961.

Born in Colombia in 1928, García Márquez spent years as a struggling journalist before making his name _____ fantastic tales told with breathtaking naturalness, often inspired by the lives of his own family and the turbulent history of his native country and continent.

erode	explicitly	nevertheless	regimes	restrained

García Márquez rose to international literary fame with his 1967 novel *One Hundred Years of Solitude,* loosely based on the experiences of his own grandparents. In his recent autobiography, Bill Clinton _____ praised the book, calling it "the greatest novel in any language since William Faulkner died."

Love in the Time of Cholera, published in 1985, follows the struggles of Florentino Ariza to win the heart of Fermina Daza. She resists the hero for fifty-one years, nine months, and four days. _____, he wins her in the end.

7

The Colombian newspaper *El Espectador* quoted a triumphant Steindorff as saying it took him two years of persisting to _____ the novelist's resistance to a film. Finally, García Márquez

8

agreed to sell the rights. "Like the main character in the book I persevered and never lost hope until I achieved my goal," said Steindorff.

The project is an apparent about-turn for García Márquez, a veteran defender of Latin American independence under pressure from successive U.S. _____ intent on imposing their

9

political priorities and cultural trends on the whole hemisphere.

The novelist's fierce loyalty to Fidel Castro has not been _____, even after many

10

others on the left distanced themselves from the Cuban leader because of his harsh treatment of dissidents and political use of the death penalty. Last year this issue drew García Márquez into a bitter debate with Susan Sontag, who publicly argued with the author for not criticizing his old friend.

Up to now García Márquez has always resisted the temptation to allow high-budget English language films of his work. Of *Love in the Time of Cholera,* producer Steindorff says, "We are going to work very hard to make the most beautiful film Hollywood has ever made."

(Adapted from "Author Green Lights Cholera Film," The Guardian, August 9, 2004.)

WORDS IN DISCUSSION

Apply the key words to your own life. Read and discuss each question in small groups. Try to use the key words.

1. **contract**

   A contract I have signed: _____

   How I can avoid contracting an illness: _____

2. **enormous**

   An enormous building in my city: _____

   The person I call when I have an enormous problem: _____

3. **nevertheless**

   I haven't achieved all my dreams. Nevertheless, _____

   I've been studying English for a while now. Nevertheless, _____

4. **conceive**

   An invention conceived of by someone in my country: _____

   Something that seems inconceivable to me: _____

5. **restrain**

   When something upsets me, I show restraint: _____% of the time

   Something you could never restrain me from doing: _____

6. **explicit**

   My opinion of explicit violence in movies:_____

   The last person I gave explicit instructions to:_____

7. **offset**

   If something depresses me, the thing that can offset my bad mood: _____

   When I feel hungry but don't have any food, I offset my hunger by _____

8. **regime**

   One political regime from history that I know about: _____

   How much I know about the regimes of different countries: _____

9. **erode**

   How concerned I am about acid rain causing erosion of buildings in my city:

   _____

   Something I hope will never erode: _____

10. **ongoing**

    A topic about which there are ongoing discussions in my school or workplace:

    _____

    My study of the English language will be ongoing until the year _____

▌WORDS IN WRITING

Choose two topics and write a paragraph on each. Try to use the key words.

1. Up until what age do you think women should **conceive** children? Explain why.

2. You have worked very hard for three years at a job you like. **Nevertheless**, your low salary has not increased, even though you've asked for a raise. Does your enjoyment of your job **offset** your low pay? Explain why you will stay at the job or why you will leave it.

3. Should a public library have books or magazines with **explicit** pictures? Explain why or why not.

4. Describe someone or something that you have had to **restrain**.

5. Imagine that you will sign a **contract** tomorrow. Explain what kind of **contract** you want it to be (for example, a contract for an apartment, a job, or a deal with a record company).

WORDS IN CONTEXT

*Use the sentences to guess what each key word means. Choose the meaning that is closest to that of the key word in **bold**.*

1. **allocate**
/ˈæləˌkeɪt/
-verb

- The artist **allocates** three days a week to painting.
- My mother **allocates** half her salary to paying the rent.

Allocate means . . .
   a. to spend time doing something important
   b. to pay
   c. to decide money or time should be used for a particular purpose

2. **amend**
/əˈmɛnd/
-verb

- The couple asked the priest if they could **amend** their marriage vows by changing a few words.
- The majority of voters wanted the law to be **amended**.

Amend means . . .
   a. to make small changes or improvements
   b. to stop a legal ceremony
   c. to change entirely

3. **civil**
/ˈsɪvəl/
-adjective

- Our teacher told us how African-Americans fought for **civil** rights in the 1960s.
- When Aaron called the police, he was not reporting a crime; he was making a **civil** complaint about the trash in his neighbor's yard.

Civil means . . .
   a. related to violence and crime
   b. related to laws concerning private affairs of citizens
   c. related to the work of the police

4. **clause**
/klɔz/
-noun

- Before signing her business contract, Annette asked for a **clause** to be added that would allow her to break the contract if her employer treated her unfairly.
- The Supreme Court ruled to remove the controversial **clause** from the law.

Clause means . . .
   a. a part of a written law or legal document
   b. a winter holiday
   c. a large amount of money paid to lawyers

5. discriminate
/dɪˈskrɪməˌneɪt/
-verb

- In giving the best seats to the children from the richest neighborhood, the teacher **discriminated** against the poorer students.
- Has someone ever **discriminated** against you because of the country you come from?

Discriminate means . . .

a. to like a person or group of people

b. to test people separately

c. to treat one person or group differently

6. dispose
/dɪˈspoʊz/
-verb

- After chewing her gum, Jenny **disposed** of it in the wastebasket.
- The criminal **disposed** of the evidence by throwing it into the ocean.

Dispose means . . .

a. to get rid of

b. to keep for a short time

c. to hide

7. hence
/hɛns/
-adverb

- The symphony was composed of world-famous musicians; **hence**, the concert was amazing.
- White truffles, a kind of mushroom you can eat, are rare and **hence** expensive.

Hence means . . .

a. not very

b. for this reason

c. despite this

8. invoke
/ɪnˈvoʊk/
-verb

- When Professor Rivera explained that he would not tolerate any cheating in his class, he **invoked** the university's academic honesty policy.
- To strengthen his call for greater immigration rights in the United States, the politician **invoked** the immigrant roots of all Americans.

Invoke means . . .

a. to tell a story to entertain a group of people

b. to ask a question

c. to use a law, principle, etc. to support your opinions and actions

9. margin
/ˈmɑrdʒɪn/
-noun

- Sometimes I write notes in the **margins** of my Spanish textbook.
- Mrs. Huntsworth asks her students to leave a one-inch **margin** on the sides of their papers.

Margin means . . .

a. the back of a printed page

b. the empty space at the side of a printed page

c. the first page of a book or essay

10. suspend
/səˈspɛnd/
-verb

- The principal **suspended** Avery from coming to school for one week.
- After Jessie was stopped for driving ninety miles per hour, her driver's license was **suspended**.

Suspend means . . .

a. to officially stop someone from doing something for a fixed period because he or she broken the rules

b. to stop someone from ever doing something again

c. to make someone pay a lot of money because he or she did something has dangerous

WORDS AND DEFINITIONS

Read each definition and write the word it defines on the line.

1. _____ related to the laws concerning the private affairs of citizens, such as laws about business or property, rather than laws about crime

2. _____ to get rid of

3. _____ to use a law, principle, etc. to support your opinions or actions

4. _____ to treat one person or group differently from another in an unfair way

5. _____ a part of a written law or legal document

6. _____ to decide that a particular amount of money, time, etc. should be used for a particular purpose

7. _____ for this reason

8. _____ the empty space at the side of a printed page

9. _____ to officially stop someone from doing something for a fixed period because he or she has broken the rules

10. _____ to make small changes or improvements, especially in the words of a law

COMPREHENSION CHECK

Choose the best answer.

1. If the **margins** of a library book are filled with writing, there is writing
   a. on the cover.
   b. everywhere.
   c. on the sides of the pages.

2. Where is there NOT a **clause**?
   a. in a law
   b. in a film
   c. in a contract

3. Which thing CANNOT be **allocated**?
   a. three hours
   b. $100
   c. hope

4. There was a big snowstorm yesterday; **hence**,
   a. the children are out building a snowman.
   b. it's hot today.
   c. cars are driving fast on the highway.

5. If the president wants to **amend** a law, he intends to
   a. follow it.
   b. change it.
   c. destroy it.

6. If the principal **suspends** Yao-Ting from coming to school for three days, Yao-Ting probably

   a. did something bad.

   b. did great work.

   c. gave the principal a nice gift.

7. Where should you **dispose** of junk?

   a. in your closet

   b. at the dump

   c. in the middle of the street

8. If Hannah has a **civil** duty, she must do something because she is

   a. in the military.

   b. religious.

   c. a citizen of a country.

9. Which of the following is spoken by someone who is **discriminating** against someone else?

   a. "You are not educated enough to be my friend."

   b. "Why did you copy my answers?"

   c. "You're so funny."

10. Why does Jill **invoke** her constitutional rights?

   a. She disagrees with the Constitution.

   b. She wants to support what she is doing with what is in the Constitution.

   c. She feels that the Constitution does not give her enough rights.

▌WORD FAMILIES

Now that you have studied the ten key words and their basic definitions, you are ready to learn words that belong to the same family as some of the key words. A word family includes words that look alike but have different functions (noun, verb, adjective, or adverb). Their meanings are related but different.

A. *Look at each model phrase and decide whether the word in **bold** is used as a noun, verb, adjective, or adverb. Put a check (✓) in the correct column.*

	NOUN	VERB	ADJECTIVE	ADVERB
1. **allocate**				
• **allocate** funds				
• the **allocation** of three hours				
2. **amend**				
• **amend** an agreement				
• an **amendment** to the law				
3. **civil**				
• **civil** problem				
• an ordinary **civilian**				
4. **discriminate**				
• don't **discriminate**				
• illegal **discrimination**				
5. **suspend**				
• **suspend** him from driving				
• a one-week **suspension**				

B. *Read the first half of each sentence and match it with the appropriate ending.*

_____ 1. I'm not a police officer or a soldier; I'm just a

_____ 2. The fight led to Brad's

_____ 3. The finance officer provided a report detailing the

_____ 4. Preventing her from joining the club because of where her family comes from is

_____ 5. If there is a problem with the law, a(n)

a. **amendment** should be made.

b. **suspension** from the soccer team.

c. **discrimination**.

d. **allocation** of the company's money.

e. **civilian**.

SAME WORD, DIFFERENT MEANING

*Most words have more than one meaning. Study the additional meanings of **civil**, **margin**, and **suspend**. Then read each sentence and decide which meaning is used.*

a. **civil** *adj.*	relating to laws concerning the private affairs of citizens, such as laws about business or property, rather than laws about crime
b. **civil** *adj.*	polite but not really very friendly
c. **margin** *n.*	the empty space at the side of a printed page
d. **margin** *n.*	the difference in the number of votes, points, etc. that exists between the winners and the losers of an election or competition
e. **suspend** *v.*	to officially stop someone from doing something for a fixed period because he or she has broken the rules
f. **suspend** *v.*	to officially stop something, usually for a short time

_____ 1. The rival presidential candidates were **civil** to each other when they met on the street.

_____ 2. Flights are **suspended** from leaving the airport until a thunderstorm passes.

_____ 3. To become a citizen, Selena learned about her **civil** rights and responsibilities.

_____ 4. My professor wrote comments in the **margin** of my test.

_____ 5. The student who threatened to set a fire was **suspended** from school.

_____ 6. Greg won the competition by a **margin** of ten votes.

WORDS IN SENTENCES

Complete each sentence with one of the words from the box.

allocate	civil	discrimination	hence	margin
amendment	clause	dispose	invoked	suspended

1. I know you don't like the postman, but please try to be _____ to him.

2. When the police asked Max where he'd been on the night of the murder, he _____ his right to remain silent about the case.

3. Mustafa didn't agree with his manager's _____ to the contract.

4. It could be a mistake to _____ so much of our time to the least important project.

5. Grayson won the race by a(n) _____ of seven seconds.

6. The world would be a better place if there were no _____.

7. It's time to _____ of these dusty old magazines.

8. August was born in the eighth month of the year, _____ his name.

9. Stella was scared to tell her parents that she'd been _____ from school.

10. The movie star insisted that a(n) _____ be added to the prenuptial agreement that said she would receive all of her husband's money if he was unfaithful to her.

WORDS IN COLLOCATIONS AND EXPRESSIONS

Following are common collocations and expressions with some of the key words. Read the definitions and then complete the conversations with the collocations and expressions. You may have to change word forms for correct grammar.

1. allocate	
• **allocate (sth) to**	decide that a particular amount of something should be used for a particular purpose
2. civil	
• **civil unrest**	fighting between different groups of people in the same country
• **civil ceremony**	a marriage ceremony that is legal but not related to a religious organization
3. discriminate	
• **discriminate against**	to treat a person or group of people unfairly
4. dispose	
• **dispose of (sth)**	get rid of something
5. margin	
• **margin of error**	the degree to which a calculation can be wrong without affecting the final results

1. **New Tenant:** Where can I _____ my garbage?

   Landlord: In the big dumpster behind the apartment building.

2. **Juan:** What do you think about the results of my survey?

   Professor: I don't think it worked. You write that your _____ is seven percent. That's too high.

3. **Aunt:** How do you plan to spend your time this summer?

   Nephew: I'm going to _____ most of my time _____ studying, some time to volunteer work at the hospital, and the rest of my time to having fun.

4. **Michael:** Why is there _____ in your country?

   Daniel: One group _____ another group, which has caused a lot of fighting.

5. **Amy:** Did you have a religious wedding ceremony?

   Gretchen: No. We are not religious, so we had a(n) _____.

WORDS IN A READING

Read this article about casinos. Complete it with words from the boxes.

allocating	amend	clause	hence	invokes

CASINO ADS TARGET VOTERS

Harrah's Entertainment must overcome a fundamental challenge before building a casino in Rhode Island: historically, voters don't like gambling.

The industry's largest gaming company is _____ more than $650,000 to advertising
1
in the next two months to persuade residents in the nation's smallest state to vote in favor of the casino, according to television station records. Public opinion counts because Rhode Islanders will vote in November on whether to _____ the state constitution so that Harrah's and the
2
Narragansett Indian tribe can build a casino in West Warwick.

Harrah's, a Fortune 500 firm, reported $236.4 million in earnings last year. _____,
3
paying for advertising isn't an obstacle for the company.

Political analysts say that Harrah's is following a strategy used by gambling companies in other states. It's downplaying its own involvement in the casino while highlighting a local partner. And it's offering voters a trade-off in return for a casino, in this case, property tax relief.

National polls show that voters are typically not in support of gambling, according to Robert Blendon, a professor at Harvard University's Kennedy School of Government, and that remains true in Puritan-influenced New England, he said. Casino backers are hoping a(n)_____ in the
4

amendment promising property tax relief will be attractive to voters. The ballot question promises that taxes on casino revenue will be dedicated to reducing property taxes.

The ballot question's language _____ 5 the Narragansett Indian tribe but not Harrah's. Narragansett Chief Sachem Matthew Thomas never uses Harrah's name during a radio advertisement funded by the company. The ad emphasizes that casino profits could alleviate Indian poverty. But tax breaks are a more effective advertising tool than social justice arguments, Blendon said. More voters pay taxes than follow centuries-old history, tragic or not.

| civil | discrimination | dispose | margin | suspend |

An April survey of 364 people by Rhode Island College showed how property tax promises could swing the vote. Participants were about evenly split when asked whether the constitution should be amended for Harrah's and the Narragansetts. However, when told casino revenue would be earmarked for property tax relief, fifty-five percent said they favored the proposal and thirty-three percent were opposed. The _____ 6 of error was five percentage points.

Public opinion may have shifted since then. A June poll conducted by Brown University found that voters are almost evenly split on whether the proposed casino will lower taxes. Neither poll asked whether the constitution should be amended to aid the Narragansetts for past injustices.

Colonial wars devastated the Narragansetts, who lost much of their land during the following centuries. _____ 7 against the Native Americans continued for hundreds of years. Rhode Island authorities even detribalized the Narragansetts after a suspect land deal in the 1880s.

Casino critics are hitting back publicly. A group called Save Our State is pressuring the Narragansetts not only to _____ 8 their deal with Harrah's, but ultimately to _____ 9 of the plan. Governor Don Carcieri maintains a(n) _____ 10 tone when questioned about Harrah's, but he clearly expresses that he hates the idea of amending the state constitution for the casino, saying, "This is not going to be a casino owned or operated by the Narragansetts. They're going to get a small piece of this."

(Adapted from "Casino Ads Geared to Sway R.I. Voters in Favor of Amendment," Boston Globe, July 20, 2006.)

3. What is the longest amount of time that you have been **suspended** from school?

   a. three or more days

   b. one or two days

   c. I've never been suspended.

4. How much of your time do you **allocate** to improving your English?

   a. not much

   b. a lot

   c. all the time I possibly can

5. How do you feel about having a **civil** wedding ceremony?

   a. I feel good about it.

   b. Unhappy. I want a religious wedding ceremony.

   c. Nervous. I'm not ready to get married in any kind of ceremony!

6. You made dinner. **Hence**, the meal is

   a. delicious.

   b. OK.

   c. so bad it is inedible.

7. A man is standing on a busy street corner in New York City, saying crazy things in a loud voice. When the police try to stop him, he **invokes** his constitutional right, under American laws, to freedom of speech. Do you think the man has a right to speak?

   a. Yes, he does.

   b. Yes, as long as he is not dangerous to other people.

   c. No, he doesn't.

8. You break up with your girlfriend or boyfriend. When do you **dispose** of her or his pictures?

   a. that day

   b. when I fall in love with someone new

   c. never

9. Have you ever been **discriminated** against?

   a. yes, many times

   b. yes, once or twice

   c. no

10. You are given the opportunity to **amend** one policy in your school or workplace. Which do you choose?

    a. I amend the number of hours that I am supposed to be there.

    b. I amend the requirements about the clothing I am supposed to wear.

    c. I amend the rules about not bringing pets there.

▌WORDS IN WRITING

Choose two topics and write a paragraph on each. Try to use the key words.

1. What is something that you will never **dispose** of? Explain why.

2. Describe an experience in which you witnessed **discrimination**.

3. Tell a story about a time when you or one of your friends was **suspended** from school.

4. You are given $1 million to improve the quality of life in your city. How do you **allocate** the money?

5. Describe a time of **civil unrest** in your country.

CHAPTER
30

Key Words

abstract	component	fluctuate	induce	refine
accumulate	exceed	grant	intrinsic	restore

WORDS IN CONTEXT

*Use the sentences to guess what each key word means. Choose the meaning that is closest to that of the key word in **bold**.*

1. abstract
/əbˈstrækt/
-adjective

- Rather than write about events in her life, Jill writes in her journal about **abstract** feelings like hope and trust.
- Beauty is not something you can touch; it is an **abstract** concept.

Abstract means . . .   a. related to something that you can take a picture of   b. existing only as an idea or quality   c. related to an important part of life

2. accumulate
/əˈkyumyəˌleɪt/
-verb

- During the night, two inches of snow **accumulated** on the ground.
- If I continue to add $10.00 to my savings account each month, my savings will **accumulate**.

Accumulate means . . .   a. to slowly disappear   b. to increase in quantity or size   c. to freeze at a particular level

3. component
/kəmˈpoʊnənt/
-noun

- Education is a key **component** of the fight against crime.
- To improve its sound, Randell bought several new **components** for his stereo.

Component means . . .   a. source of power   b. one of several parts   c. instruction guide for a machine or system

4. exceed
/ɪkˈsid/
-verb

- You can get a speeding ticket if you **exceed** the speed limit.
- I was happily surprised when the results **exceeded** what I'd hoped for.

Exceed means . . .   a. to be more or go over   b. to be equal to   c. to be less than

5. fluctuate
/ˈflʌktʃuˌeit/
-verb

- Della is a freelance artist, so her income **fluctuates** from month to month; in some months she makes a lot of money, in others, very little.
- Terry's weight **fluctuates** from 140 pounds to 160 pounds during a typical year

Fluctuate means . . .   a. to change very often from a high level to a low one and back again   b. to increase slowly   c. to have serious problems during a period of time

6. grant
/grænt/
-noun

- Isaac is getting paid for his research through a **grant** from the National Science Foundation.
- Hoping for funding for his video art project, James applied for a **grant** from the Boston Arts Council.

Grant means . . .
a. instructions for an important project
b. an amount of money given by an organization
c. an unpaid job that you do for a large organization

7. induce
/ɪnˈdus/
-verb

- My love of nature **induced** me to buy a house on an island.
- What **induced** you to move to Nepal?

Induce means . . .
a. to pay for something unusual
b. to help someone do something
c. to make someone decide to do

8. intrinsic
/ɪnˈtrɪnzɪk,-sɪk/
-adjective

- The philosopher said, "Each life has **intrinsic** value."
- The way Ellie played the piano so naturally and beautifully led us to understand her **intrinsic** talent.

Intrinsic means . . .
a. part of the basic nature or character of someone or something
b. added to someone or something
c. learned and important

9. refine
/rɪˈfaɪn/
-verb

- The architect **refined** the design by adding more steps to the porch.
- This schedule is good, but it should be **refined** before we print it.

Refine means . . .
a. to ask for more money for something
b. to improve with small changes
c. to destroy something and start again

10. restore
/rɪˈstɔr/
-verb

- After the biking accident, Heidi's dad took her on short and easy bike rides to **restore** her confidence.
- The army **restored** order to the dangerous city, making it a peaceful place again.

Restore means . . .
a. to make something exist again
b. to create something for the first time
c. to fight a problem

▌WORDS AND DEFINITIONS

Read each definition and write the word it defines on the line.

1. _____ to gradually increase in quantity or size

2. _____ to make someone decide to do something

3. _____ existing only as an idea or quality rather than as something real that you can see or touch

4. _____ to make something exist again or return something to its former condition

5. _____ to improve a method, plan, system, etc. by amending it

6. _____ an amount of money given to someone by an organization for a particular purpose

7. _____ part of the basic nature or character of someone or something

8. _____ to be more than an amount or go over a limit

9. _____ one of several parts that make up a whole machine or system

10. _____ to change very often from a high level to a low one and back again

▌COMPREHENSION CHECK

Choose the best answer.

1. Why does Paula want a **grant**?
   a. She needs money to pay for her research.
   b. She wants $1,000.
   c. She needs a break from work.

2. What CANNOT be **restored**?
   a. an old house
   b. trust
   c. a dead tree

3. Which thing is a **component** of a radio?
   a. a speaker
   b. a screen
   c. education

4. If Gareth **refines** the concept, he
   a. uses it twice.
   b. improves it with small changes.
   c. destroys it.

5. Nagihan spends all her extra money shopping. Does she **accumulate** savings?
   a. yes, a lot
   b. yes, a small amount
   c. no

6. Which thing is **abstract**?
   a. happiness
   b. a mug of tea
   c. a sneaker

7. If Barak's mood **fluctuates** throughout the day,
   a. he is always depressed.
   b. his emotions change from hour to hour.
   c. his feelings rarely change.

8. What could **induce** a person to move to another country?
   a. hearing that the country is dangerous
   b. a bad job offer
   c. acceptance at a good university

9. The speed limit is 30 miles per hour. Alexi **exceeds** it. How fast does he drive?
   a. 30 miles per hour
   b. 27 miles per hour
   c. 35 miles per hour

10. Something **intrinsic**
    a. cannot be removed.
    b. is additional.
    c. is not very important.

WORD FAMILIES

Now that you have studied the ten key words and their basic definitions, you are ready to learn words that belong to the same family as some of the key words. A word family includes words that look alike but have different functions (noun, verb, adjective, or adverb). Their meanings are related but different.

A. *Look at each model phrase and decide whether the word in **bold** is used as a noun, verb, adjective, or adverb. Put a check (✓) in the correct column.*

	NOUN	VERB	ADJECTIVE	ADVERB
1. **accumulate**				
• rainwater **accumulates**				
• the **accumulation** of evidence				
2. **exceed**				
• to **exceed** at your job				
• an **excess** of information				
• **excessive** homework				
3. **fluctuate**				
• numbers **fluctuate**				
• daily **fluctuation**				
4. **intrinsic**				
• an **intrinsic** part				
• **intrinsically** good				
5. **refine**				
• **refine** the way				
• the **refinement** of the idea				
6. **restore**				
• **restore** peace				
• slow **restoration**				

B. *Read the first half of each sentence and match it with the appropriate ending.*

_____ 1. Alice went to her doctor because she was concerned about the

_____ 2. It's unreasonable to expect us to pay the

_____ 3. Although it was snowing, it was too warm for there to be any

_____ 4. We were disappointed by the governor's

_____ 5. Barbara was born to be an artist; she is

_____ 6. The plan is good but needs

_____ 7. The grant of $5,000 will pay for the

a. **accumulation** of snow on the ground.

b. **fluctuation** of her weight.

c. **intrinsically** creative.

d. **refinement**.

e. **excess** spending.

f. **excessive** student fees

g. **restoration** of the old ship.

SAME WORD, DIFFERENT MEANING

Most words have more than one meaning. Study the additional meanings of **grant**, **induce**, and **refine**. Then read each sentence and decide which meaning is used.

a. **grant** *n.*	an amount of money given to someone by an organization for a particular purpose
b. **grant** *v.*	(formal) to give someone something that he or she has asked for or earned, especially official permission to do something
c. **induce** *v.*	to make someone decide to do something
d. **induce** *v.*	to cause a particular physical condition
e. **refine** *v.*	to improve a method, plan, system, etc. by making small changes to it
f. **refine** *v.*	to make a substance more pure using an industrial process

_____ 1. The Italian embassy **granted** Marina a tourist visa.

_____ 2. Boredom **induced** me to watch too much TV.

_____ 3. White sugar is **refined**.

_____ 4. The drug **induced** depression in elderly patients, so the doctor stopped prescribing it.

_____ 5. The investor gave the technology group a $500,000 **grant**.

_____ 6. The team needs more time to **refine** its plan.

WORDS IN SENTENCES

Complete each sentence with one of the words from the box.

| abstract | components | fluctuate | induce | refined |
| accumulation | exceed | grant | intrinsic | restoration |

1. Bill Clinton refused to _____ the reporter an interview.

2. It is impossible to _____ the time limit when taking the TOEFL test.

3. If you can't convince me that this project has some _____ value, we are going to stop it immediately.

4. The _____ of papers on Rioji's desk made it difficult to find the report we needed.

5. Desert temperatures _____ dramatically, sometimes as much as forty degrees over a twenty-four-hour period.

6. The Statue of Liberty was closed until its _____ was complete.

7. _____ oils and sugars have gone through an industrial process that makes them more pure.

8. The ballet will not tell a story; instead, the dancing will symbolize _____ feelings and ideas.

9. The doctor warned the patient that the medication might _____ an allergic reaction.

10. The machine was old, but Han Lin was able to repair it by replacing a few crucial _____.

WORDS IN COLLOCATIONS AND EXPRESSIONS

Following are common collocations and expressions with some of the key words. Read the definitions and then complete the conversations with the collocations and expressions. You may have to change word forms for correct grammar.

1. **abstract**	
• **abstract art**	art that is made of shapes and patterns that do not look like real things or people
2. **grant**	
• **take (it) for granted (that)**	to believe that something is true without making sure
• **take (sb) for granted**	to expect that someone will always be there when you need him or her, and never thank him or her
3. **induce**	
• **induce (sb) to (do sth)**	make someone decide to do something
4. **refine**	
• **a refined person (or lady/gentleman)**	a polite and well-educated person who is interested in high-quality books, music, and food

1. RACHEL: Your grandmother is so graceful and intelligent!

   CHRIS: I know. She is the most _____ in my family.

2. HENRIETTA: I wash my son's clothing, cook him three meals a day, drive him to school and band practice, and help him with his homework. He never says thank you.

   GLORIA: That's terrible. It sounds like he _____ you _____.

3. ART LOVER: What _____ you _____ paint in this style?

   SALVADOR DALI: _____ fascinates me. Its possibilities are endless.

4. STUDENT 1: I'm not sure when the quiz is. It's probably on Friday.

   STUDENT 2: We can't _____ that it's on Friday. If it's earlier, we'll be in trouble. I'll call John to see if he knows when it is.

Read this article about talent. Complete it with words from the boxes.

abstract	accumulated	component	induced	refined

THE SOCCER BIRTH MONTH RIDDLE

If you were to examine the birth certificates of every soccer player in the World Cup tournament, you would most likely find a noteworthy quirk: elite soccer players are more likely to have been born in the earlier months of the year than in the later months. If you then _____ your search by

₁

looking at the European national youth teams that feed the World Cup and professional ranks, you would find this quirk to be even more noticeable. On recent English teams, for instance, half of the elite teenage soccer players were born in January, February, or March, with the other half spread out over the remaining nine months. In Germany, fifty-two elite youth players were born in the first three months of the year, with just four players born in the last three. This suggests that the month in which a person is born may be a(n) _____ in whether or not he becomes a soccer star.

₂

What causes this pattern? Could there be a relationship between certain _____

₃

astrological signs and superior soccer skills? Anders Ericsson, a psychology professor at Florida State University, does not think so. Ericsson is the leader of what might be called the Expert Performance Movement, a group of scholars trying to answer the question: When someone is very good at a given thing, what is it that actually makes him or her good? Ericsson's interest in skill _____

₄

him to try to solve the soccer birth month riddle.

Ericsson has _____ research results showing that memory itself is not genetically

₅

determined, leading him to conclude that the act of memorizing is more a cognitive exercise than an intuitive one. In other words, more important than the differences two people may exhibit in their abilities to memorize is how well each person "encodes" the information. And the best way to learn how to encode information meaningfully, Ericsson determined, was a process known as deliberate practice.

fluctuates	grant	intrinsic	restore

In Ericsson's opinion, the trait we commonly call talent is highly overrated. Expert performers—whether in surgery, ballet, or computer programming—are nearly always made, not born. Practice makes perfect.

Ericsson's research suggests that when it comes to choosing a life path, you should do what you love—because if you don't love it, you are unlikely to work hard enough to get very good. Most people

are naturally reluctant to do things they aren't "good" at. So their effort _____, then
6
lessens, and they eventually give up, telling themselves that they simply don't possess the
_____talent for math or skiing or the violin. But what they really lack is the desire to be
7
good and to undertake the practice that would _____their confidence and make them
8
better at the activity.

This insight explains the riddle of why so many elite soccer players are born early in the year. Since youth sports are organized by age group, teams inevitably have a cutoff birth date. In the European youth soccer leagues, the cutoff date is December 31. So when a coach is assessing two players in the same age group, one who happens to have been born in January and the other in December, the player born in January is likely to be bigger, stronger, more mature. Guess which player the coach is more likely to _____ the spot on the team to? He may be mistaking maturity for ability, but he
9
is making his selection nonetheless. And once chosen, those January-born players are the ones who, year after year, receive the training, the deliberate practice, feedback, and confidence that will turn them into elites.

(Adapted from "A Star Is Made," The New York Times, May 7, 2006.)

▌WORDS IN DISCUSSION

Apply the key words to your own life. Read and discuss each question in small groups. Try to use the key words.

1. **fluctuate**

   How much the temperature has fluctuated in the last twenty-four hours:

   _____

   Something that often fluctuates in price in my country:_____

2. **intrinsic**

   An intrinsic quality I have: _____

   Someone who has intrinsic talent:_____

3. **accumulate**

   The most snow that has ever accumulated in my city: _____

   How much money will accumulate in my savings account by the year 2015:

   $_____

4. **refine**

   How much I care about refining the details of a plan before I begin:

   _____

   The amount of refined sugar I eat in a typical day: _____

5. **induce**

   What induced me to improve my English: _____

   What could induce me to run for seven miles: _____

6. **abstract**

My opinion of abstract art: _____

How I feel about discussing abstract ideas rather than events: _____

7. **exceed**

How I often exceed my budget and spend too much money: _____

How many cookies I think is excessive to eat: _____

8. **grant**

A country that granted citizenship to one of my relatives: _____

A famous person whom I'd like to grant me an interview: _____

9. **component**

An important component of friendship: _____

A crucial component of a good government: _____

10. **restore**

A place in the world where I wish peace could be restored: _____

Something I would like to restore or see restored to its original condition:

_____

▌WORDS IN WRITING

Choose two topics and write a paragraph on each. Try to use the key words.

1. Imagine that you are given a **grant** to **restore** a building in your hometown. Which building do you restore, and why?

2. After you perfect your English, what could **induce** you to learn another language? Explain.

3. What things do teenagers often **take for granted**? Give examples.

4. Do you believe an artist needs genuine talent or skill to produce **abstract** art? Explain why or why not.

5. Describe a movie or television program that **exceeded** your expectations and was much better than you'd originally thought it would be.

QUIZ 10

PART A

Choose the word that best completes each item and write it in the space provided.

1. Love is _____. You can't touch it or see it.
   - a. enormous
   - b. abstract
   - c. offset
   - d. explicit

2. I was exhausted. _____, I went to the party.
   - a. Discriminating
   - b. Hence
   - c. Accumulating
   - d. Nevertheless

3. Before starting the job, it's necessary to sign a _____.
   - a. component
   - b. regime
   - c. contract
   - d. restraint

4. The good news _____ Dan's bad mood.
   - a. offset
   - b. allocated
   - c. induced
   - d. accumulated

5. The library is _____ $6,000 for the purchase of new books this year.
   - a. allocating
   - b. fluctuating
   - c. eroding
   - d. refining

6. The sculpture is gorgeous and, _____, expensive.
   - a. intrinsically
   - b. hence
   - c. nevertheless
   - d. abstractly

7. We celebrated when we _____ our target by an extra $1,000.
   - a. restrained
   - b. conceived
   - c. exceeded
   - d. invoked

8. After she was caught smoking in the gym, Hilda was _____ from school.
   - a. disposed
   - b. suspended
   - c. discriminated
   - d. granted

9. Part of Ella's skill came from practice, but the rest came from _____ talent.
   - a. intrinsic
   - b. inconceivable
   - c. explicit
   - d. civil

10. The actress added a _____ to the prenuptial agreement to protect her money.
    - a. clause
    - b. grant
    - c. margin
    - d. regime

PART B

*Read each statement and write **T** for true and **F** for false in the space provided.*

_____ 1. **Explicit** instructions should be given in preparation for a dangerous task.

_____ 2. Women usually want to **dispose** of jewels.

_____ 3. A **civil** war involves two countries.

_____ 4. An **ongoing** conflict has not begun yet.

_____ 5. Snow **accumulates** on the ground during a typical snow storm.

_____ 6. When prices **fluctuate**, the cost remains the same.

_____ 7. The Pacific Ocean is **enormous**.

_____ 8. The **margin** is in the center of a page.

_____ 9. A man can **invoke** a law to show that his actions were legal.

_____ 10. With only your hands, it's easy to **restrain** a bear from attacking you.

PART C

Match each sentence with the letter it describes.

_____ 1. A clever person can easily **conceive** of this.

_____ 2. Oil is **refined** to make this.

_____ 3. This person **discriminates** against immigrants.

_____ 4. A reporter says this about **erosion**.

_____ 5. This person **amends** the immigration law.

_____ 6. Once this is broken between friends, it is difficult to **restore**.

_____ 7. This person controls a **regime**.

_____ 8. Eliza knows what **induced** the negative advertisement, so she says this.

_____ 9. If an artist receives a **grant** to paint a portrait, she gets this.

_____ 10. When Bart describes a **component** of success, he says this.

a. a dictator

b. money

c. a legislator

d. "Practice is a necessary part of the plan."

e. a good idea

f. a prejudiced person

g. "The desert wind is slowly destroying the ancient buildings of Timbuktu."

h. gasoline

i. trust

j. "The company has lost a lot of money, so it is attacking its rival."

APPENDIX: Word Builders

WORD BUILDER 1: Synonyms and Similar Words

A. Academic Synonyms

Match the key words which have the same meaning.

_____	1. assess	a. adequate
_____	2. sufficient	b. infer
_____	3. deduce	c. evaluate

B. Academic and Casual Synonyms

Match the academic key words with their less formal synonyms. Remember that the key words are better choices for academic speech and writing, while the less formal words are more appropriate for casual conversation.

_____	1. cease	a. keep
_____	2. inconceivable	b. create
_____	3. convene	c. notice
_____	4. generate	d. use
_____	5. perceive	e. stop
_____	6. retain	f. unbelievable
_____	7. utilize	g. meet

C. Similar Academic Words, Different Uses

Perfect your word use by understanding how similar key words are used differently. Match each word with its definition and then use both words in each sentence. You may need to alter word forms for correct grammar.

1. **attain** and **obtain**

   Note: Both words are much more formal than the word **get**. *They are most often used in academic speech and writing.*

_____	attain	a. to achieve something
_____	obtain	b. to get something that you want

   - Hans needs to _____ information about immigration. He is determined to _____ his goal of becoming a citizen.
   - Philosophers say that it is not necessary to _____ many possessions in order to _____ happiness.

2. **eliminate** and **terminate**

_____	eliminate	a. to end
_____	terminate	b. to get rid of something completely

- The computer programmer will _____ his work on the code after he has _____ the bugs from it.

- Unless we can _____ the problems from this plan, we will have to _____ it.

3. **apparent** and **coherent**

Note: The word **coherent** *often relates to ideas, logic, speech, and writing. The word* **apparent** *often relates to emotions, sights, and facts.*

_____ apparent   a. clear and easy to understand

_____ coherent   b. easily seen or understood

- Michael's essay was _____. It was _____ to me why the professor gave him an "A".

- Karen gave me a(n) _____ explanation about why she was getting married, but it wasn't necessary. The love on her face was _____.

4. **demonstrate** and **illustrate**

_____ demonstrate   a. to show or explain how to do something; to prove something clearly

_____ illustrate   b. to explain or make clear by giving examples; to draw or paint pictures for a book

- The art teacher will _____ how to draw a cartoon similar to those often used to _____ magazines.

- The results _____ that more research is needed; I will also tell a story from real life to _____ the need for change.

5. **bond** and **link**

_____ bond   a. a shared feeling or interest that unites people

_____ link   b. a relationship or connection between events, people, ideas, etc

- There is a _____ between Lance's interest in photography and the photography lessons his dad gave him. Love of photography is a _____ that the father and son share.

- Professor Smith suggested that there is a _____ between modern relationships and ancient ones by explaining how mothers and their babies have always had close _____.

WORD BUILDER 2: Antonyms

A. *Antonyms are words with opposite meanings. Match the key words below and on page 307 with their antonyms.*

_____ 1. internal   a. terminate

_____ 2. unique   b. immature

_____ 3. initiate   c. preceding

_____ 4. maximize   d. release

_____ 5. initial   e. rigid

_____ 6. restrain   f. external

_____ 7. flexible   g. normal

B. *Complete each sentence using the antonym of the word in* **bold**. *Use correct word forms. Do the exercise without looking at exercise A. When you have finished, check your answers using exercise A.*

1. Brandon is **mature** enough to work in the lab, but don't hire Josh. He is really _____.

2. When the police officer realized that he was **restraining** the wrong person, he _____ the innocent man.

3. Having been dissatisfied with the **initial** house plan, the architect worked on several drafts before presenting her clients with the _____ design.

4. Don't give me a(n) _____ answer; please be **straightforward**.

5. The _____ damage to the building was much worse than the **internal** damage.

6. The committee plans to _____ the old program and **initiate** a new one.

7. Humans often act as if there were an **infinite** number of natural resources on the planet, but in fact these recourses are _____.

8. The program at Jim's school is **flexible**. He and his parents think it's better than his old school where the rules were very _____.

9. The boss wants to _____ our profits and **minimize** our debts.

10. In the **preceding** rehearsal, the actors were assigned their roles. Today they read through the script for the first time, and in _____ rehearsals they will act out their scenes without using the script.

11. Helena did not want to wear a **normal** wedding dress; she wanted her dress to be _____.

KEY WORD INDEX

Here you can find the words that are taught in this book and the chapters in which they are introduced. Each key word is in bold and is sometimes followed by words from the same word family. Every key word comes from the Academic Word List (AWL).

A

abandon 23

abstract 30

access 18

accompany 2

accumulate 30

accumulation

accumulates

acknowledge 7

acknowledgement

adapt 26

adaptable

adaptation

adequate 5

adjust 24

adjustment

advocate 24

allocate 29

allocation

alter 13

ambiguous 1

amend 29

amendment

analogy 25

annual 9

annually

anticipate 11

anticipation

apparent 7

apparently

appreciate 26

appreciative

appropriate 10

inappropriate

aspect 8

assess 4

assessment

assure 6

assurance

attain 3

attainable

attribute 15

aware 14

awareness

unaware

B

bias 25

biased

bond 9

C

capable 11

cease 4

chart 19

circumstances 15

circumstantial

cite 24

civil 29

civilian

clarify 5

clarification

clause 29

coherent 3

coherence

coherently

incoherent

coincide 24

coincidence

collapse 10

commission 17

commit 8

commitment

committed

compatible 6

compatibility

compensate 12

compensation

complex 22

complexity

component 30

compound 23

compounded

comprehensive 27

comprise 19

conceive 28

conceivable

inconceivable

conduct 16

confer 10

conference

confine 24

confinement

confirm 25

confirmation

conform 7

conformity

consent 27

consequently 13

consequence

considerable 18

considerably

constrain 15

constraints

contact 16

contemporary 4

context 18